To Mark
Thanks for
your reaction
& advice -

Mary

PLACES OF REDEMPTION

Places of Redemption

Theology for a Worldly Church

MARY McCLINTOCK FULKERSON

OXFORD
UNIVERSITY PRESS

OXFORD

UNIVERSITY PRESS

Great Clarendon Street, Oxford OX2 6DP

Oxford University Press is a department of the University of Oxford.
It furthers the University's objective of excellence in research, scholarship,
and education by publishing worldwide in

Oxford New York

Auckland Cape Town Dar es Salaam Hong Kong Karachi
Kuala Lumpur Madrid Melbourne Mexico City Nairobi
New Delhi Shanghai Taipei Toronto

With offices in

Argentina Austria Brazil Chile Czech Republic France Greece
Guatemala Hungary Italy Japan Poland Portugal Singapore
South Korea Switzerland Thailand Turkey Ukraine Vietnam

Oxford is a registered trade mark of Oxford University Press
in the UK and in certain other countries

Published in the United States
by Oxford University Press Inc., New York

© Mary McClintock Fulkerson 2007

The moral rights of the author have been asserted
Database right Oxford University Press (maker)

First published 2007

British Library Cataloguing in Publication Data

Data available

Library of Congress Cataloging in Publication Data

Data available

Typeset by SPI Publisher Services Ltd, Pondicherry, India
Printed in Great Britain
on acid-free paper by
Biddles Ltd, King's Lynn, Norfolk

ISBN 978–0–19–929647–7

1 3 5 7 9 10 8 6 4 2

This book is dedicated to Hopie and Will

Contents

Acknowledgements

First and foremost I thank the people of Good Samaritan United Methodist Church for allowing me to participate in their community, for their seriousness and their humor, their openness to my questions, and all the ways they educated me. I am particularly grateful to the pastors and their wives, who were welcoming and honest. Thanks also go to the colleagues who were willing to read this project as it took shape over the years. Teresa Berger, Maurice Wallace, and Sharon Welch have been especially helpful with suggestions, along with Cheryl Kirk-Duggan, Rick Lischer, Bonnie Miller-McLemore, Doug Ottati, and Robin Lovin. Thanks to Emily Askew for putting me on to place theory and to Peter Hodgson and Ed Farley for their continued support. The Theology and Culture group listened to many versions of these chapters, beginning with our long ago first meeting in Chicago. Thanks to Margaret Adam and Natalie Cames for their help and Anne Weston for her marvelous editing. I thank Bill, Hopie, and Will for making my nonacademic life so rich and full.

Part I

Theology from a Place

1

Introduction

God calls us and places us here to intentionally take the Good
News of Jesus Christ to people of all races, nationalities, cultures, ages, backgrounds, and special needs.

God calls us and places us here to build a growing church and
to be a loving and nurturing community of faith that will educate
and assist people in need in our community and the world.

Good Samaritan United Methodist Church Mission Statement

You go sit on a bench and nobody else sits on that bench. I'd say
that's a very good clue.

Emmanuel, on US churches

MY INTRODUCTION TO PARTICIPANT OBSERVATION

Armed with the wisdom of my ethnography class, I set off one
Sunday morning in late summer for my debut as a participant
observer. My professor, a seasoned anthropologist with fieldwork in
India and West Virginia coal mines, had an uncanny capacity for
'seeing' the fascinating grain of the ordinary. Her descriptions of the
quotidian were simply poetry. Now I am eager to emulate her powers
of observation and bring something fresh to theological reflection on
ordinary Christian community. Feminist, race-conscious, progressive wannabe, I am especially zealous to investigate a community that
might have liberatory lessons for the secular society. I think I have

found it in the multiracial community of Good Samaritan United Methodist Church. A dying white Methodist church in a working-class area of a small southern city, Good Samaritan had revived and become one of the few significantly racially mixed churches in the Methodist Conference. Interpreting the story of Philip's witness to an Ethiopian eunuch in Acts 8 as God's call to bring in people 'not like us', the community added African and African American members to their original white nucleus. They further distinguished themselves by seeking out members of nearby group homes to come regularly to worship services.

But back to my first visit. As I look closely for the church along the side of this four-lane street littered with run-down-looking shops, I almost pass it. The sign appears suddenly—white with black lettering—*Good Samaritan UMC*. But no visibly ecclesiastical building can be seen, only a small brick house facing the main road. I turn in the gravel drive and notice a white garage-like structure behind the brick house. It has a bright red-flamed cross on it—the United Methodist symbol—and looks newly painted. A small asphalt parking patch fronts the garage/sanctuary and a portable basketball hoop stands to its side. An olive green shack with a rickety-looking porch sits at the back of the property. No sign of what it is for. Immediately across from the garage/sanctuary is a smaller gray house, which turns out to be the place for Sunday school. To the side of that gray building are a swing and a slide.

I park amidst the other cars and walk to the door of the white converted garage/sanctuary. Inside, the room is rather plain, but sounds of boisterous piano playing fill the small space. People greet one another as they move around finding seats among the rows of metal folding chairs. Some cheery, felt banners hang on the wall, but the rug is a drab green. In an odd contrast with the metal folding chairs and cheap decor are a carved heavy wooden pulpit and communion table, which look like contraband from an old Methodist church—formal in the style of southern Protestant churches of the 1930s and 1940s. While I am expecting a mixed-race group, I am surprised at my own response to all the dark skin in the room. A black woman approaches me. Extending her hand with a bulletin, she introduces herself and welcomes me warmly. I find myself aware of the paleness of my skin as I respond, trying to hide any signs that

I am not used to worshipping with more than a few token black people. The overeager sound of my voice tells me I am probably failing. A good three-fourths of the people gathering to worship are black, or rather, ebony, dark tan, bronze, and shades of color for which I have no names.

Next I notice a thin white man sitting twisted in a wheelchair, parked next to a short man who looks like he has Down syndrome. As I approach the man in the wheelchair, my body feels suddenly awkward and unnatural. When I get in his immediate vicinity, I realize I do not know where to place myself. My height feels excessive and ungainly. I tower over this pale man strapped in the wheelchair. Do I kneel down? Bend down to be face level with him? Speaking to him from above feels patronizing. Or is it the crouching down that would be patronizing? My hand moves to touch his shoulder, as if to communicate, 'I care about you, despite your mildly frightening, contorted body and guttural gurgling sounds.' But I withdraw my hand quickly, wondering if this, too, would be a sign of condescension. What was it like to be unable to command a safe space with your presence, to be vulnerable to the groping of other people's hands?[1]

A WORLDLY CHURCH: IN SEARCH OF THEOLOGY FOR THE ORDINARY

I begin with a brief description of my first encounter with Good Samaritan Church to raise questions about the shape and subject matter of Christian theological reflection. In the two and a half years of my participant observation at Good Samaritan, I was to learn much about this unusual and vibrant community. Successful at bringing together people usually divided by class, race, and ability, Good Samaritan is an occasion to celebrate. This gathering of 'people who are different' included conservative white working-class folks, white liberal university students, African Americans with liberal social and traditional religious views, and members from a variety

---

[1] This description comes from notes I made as a participant observer at Good Samaritan UMC from 1996 to 1999.

of African countries. People from two different group homes came regularly to the Sunday services and to monthly services organized especially for them.

Good Samaritan, however, is not just a success story. My reactions of discomfort in the presence of darker and 'disabled' bodies signal something more complicated than simple 'good news'. My unaccustomedness to being outnumbered by people 'not like me' has social analogues in a society still largely segregated by race, a society where group homes are zoned out of many neighborhoods. As I later learn, church members' claims to welcome outsiders covered over forms of dis-ease and imbalances of power. Along with its joys and accomplishments, the church had crises and moments of transition, including the replacement of their founding white pastor with a Bahamian man of color. Good Samaritan was a church characterized by gospel conviction and ambiguity, pain and joy, hospitality and aversion, and plenty of unsaid along with the sharing. It was a worldly church.

To do theological justice to this community will be to write about its people, about its habits and idiosyncrasies, its mistakes and its blindness, as well as its moments of honesty and grace. That requires attention to the markers of difference, the role of bodies, and visceral responses. These are as much a part of the ambiguity and grace—the 'worldliness' of this faith community—as the Bible studies and the preaching. All of this is crucial to making theological sense of the community.

Success at this kind of theological representation is no small challenge. Theological framing can easily miss or obscure this worldliness. From overly cognitive and orthodox definitions of Christian faithfulness to concepts of practice that ignore the contribution of bodies and desire, prominent theological options risk overlooking both the worldly way that communities live out their faith and the worldly way that God is among us. The very conviction of God's redemptive presence tempts the theologian to map sense and order onto the worldly. The zeal to find good news can slip easily into the desire to smooth out the tangle called 'community', rendering it amenable to the correct theological categories.

That very conviction of God-with-us, however, can compel in a different direction. It can provoke theology to ever-fuller attention to the complexity of the world.

By such a 'worldly theology', of course I do not mean an empirical,) !!
'objective' analysis of this community. Even anthropologists have ' ''
long given up that ideal. Instead I propose an inquiry for a theological frame that will be adequate to the full-bodied reality that is
Good Samaritan, one capable of displaying its ambiguity, its implication in the banal and opaque realities of ordinary existence, even as
it allows for testimony to God's redemptive reality. I envision a
theology that thematizes the complex and dense subject matter of
contemporary *situation*. Attention to the worldly, situational character of Christian faith directs me to the task of practical theology.

TOWARD A PRACTICAL THEOLOGY:
DEFINING SITUATION

While all theology is practical and situated (just as any academic
endeavor is a practice), it is still useful to foreground a dimension of
theological reflection as its practical task.[2] Practical theology
'describes the critical reflection that is done about the meaning of
faith and action in the world'.[3] In contrast with the definition of
normative memory or systematic and philosophical judgment, the
practical theological task has to do with the way Christian faith
occurs as a contemporary situation.[4] For this focus it is simply not
helpful to ask whether Good Samaritan is 'biblical' or properly
creedal. Instead, the complexity of Good Samaritan must be taken

[2] Everything has a situational character, viz., a historian's situation will shape his/
her notion of what counts as a historical event. The focus on situation with which I am
concerned, however, is the present-oriented, synchronic lived response.

[3] James N. Poling and Donald E. Miller, *Foundations for a Practical Theology of
Ministry* (Nashville: Abingdon, 1985), 33. Much contemporary practical theology
focuses on the shape of contemporary faithful practice. See Friedrich Schweitzer
and Johannes A. van der Ven (eds.), *Practical Theology: International Perspectives*
(New York: Peter Lang, 1999).

[4] David Tracy defines practical theology as 'the mutually critical correlation of the
interpreted theory and praxis of the Christian faith with the interpreted theory and
praxis of the contemporary situation'. David Tracy, 'The Foundations of Practical
Theology', in Don Browning (ed.), *Practical Theology: The Emerging Field in Theology,
Church, and World* (New York: Harper & Row, 1983), 76.

seriously as a 'situation of faith'. Group home members' forms of communication, the racialized habituations of members, not to mention their cultural, regional, and religious shaping—all of these complexities must be factored into a theological reading of Good Samaritan.

Questions about situatedness are certainly interrelated with the tasks of normative memory and systematic/philosophical judgment. Indeed, each task of theological reflection assumes some version of the others; each has implications for the others. Just as it matters whether this contemporary community stands in continuity with biblical traditions or how its soteriology is related to its Christology, it also matters that results of the practical inquiry have an impact on what and how those traditions are read and which, if any, doctrinal questions are judged to be relevant. Proper framing of this situation may very well (re)formulate the link to origins and systematic ways of thinking, a subject of later discussion. I begin, though, with the challenge of presenting Good Samaritan as a contemporary situation. More specifically, what emerges from my opening anecdote and its connection to larger social problems is the task of *framing* this faith community as a situation that is bodied and visceral as well as biblically shaped and doctrinally traditioned.

The task of framing a contemporary situation is not about its every detail, but the identification of certain patterns that characterize it. And not all of the patterns to be found in the phenomenon of faith are pertinent. Systematics, for example, is relevant to theological reflection, but not as a way to frame the complex configuration of the lived situation. Kathryn Tanner rightly observes that 'belief and value commitments' are usually left underdeveloped and 'ambiguous' in the ordinary practice of faith, and the pattern of a dogmatic system will occlude the contradictory way commitments occur.[5] Nor does this mean that 'situation' is simply chaotic. Rather, situation has 'structure' and pattern as 'the way various items, powers, and events in the environment gather to evoke responses from participants'. I propose that 'situation' helps image what needs to be foregrounded about

<hr>

[5] Kathryn Tanner, 'Theological Reflection and Christian Practices', in Miroslav Volf and Dorothy C. Bass (eds.), *Practicing Theology: Beliefs and Practices in Christian Life* (Grand Rapids, MI: Eerdmans, 2002), 230.

Good Samaritan.[6] The framing of contemporary situation involves the question not only of 'what to do', but equally what constitutes the relevant 'items, powers, and events' and how to understand a contemporary environment as that which demands a response.

To define practical theology as a theological reading of contemporary situation is not a new idea. Most accounts of academic theology assume that its ultimate end is contemporary lived faith, sometimes defined as 'ethics'. However, by addressing the question of how 'situation' is thematized I make some distinct moves in relation to the theological task. Most obviously, this definition is an alternative to the 'trickle-down' theory of applied theology.[7] The notion that faith is something found in authoritative texts such as Scripture or doctrine and then 'applied' in contemporary life situations is a much-critiqued but popular version of practical theology.[8] Falling far short of describing the full density of lived faith as a situation, this greatly underdescribes the character of situations. The model suggests that response is individualistic and highly cognitive and renders invisible most of the elements that characterize situations, such as the socially produced and affective responses signaled in my opening anecdote.[9] It renders invisible the way in which traditions have always already shaped a situation, however invisibly, and will affect the way other elements 'gather together' to evoke a response.

[6] According to Edward Farley's definition, practical theology's task is filling in the frame of the 'situational' character of lived faith. Successful at teaching how to interpret texts, historical events, and doctrines, theological education problematically assumes that one can simply bring them to bear on a context. As Farley puts it, this 'bypasses most of the structural elements in the situation of the believer and, therefore, suppresses most of the acts in which communities interpret their own lives and situations'. Edward Farley, 'Interpreting Situations: An Inquiry into the Nature of Practical Theology', in *Practicing Gospel: Unconventional Thoughts on the Church's Ministry* (Louisville, KY: Westminster John Knox, 2003), 38, 36.

[7] For an old sampling of virtually unanimous rejection of this language, see Browning, *Practical Theology*. Lewis Mudge and James Poling (eds.), *Formation and Reflection: The Promise of Practical Theology* (Philadelphia: Fortress, 1987), p. xxiii.

[8] The dominant fourfold pattern, treating three 'fields' (Bible, church history, and theology/ethics) as the theoretical disciplines that are then 'applied' in a division typically characterized by the study of clerical practices, helps keep this thinking alive.

[9] I am primarily speaking of academic theology here, but there are clear parallels with the reflection of the lived faith of the ordinary believer.

The lenses I brought as a systematic theologian were akin to the 'application' model, and ultimately inadequate to the task of attending to this situation. Drawn to the church because of its diversity, I began with a primary interest in members' beliefs and how they articulated their convictions about why they should welcome those who are different. The yield, however, was pretty slim. Not only did members not speak the social justice language I had expected, few used explicit theological terms when it came to explaining what they did. Typical of an oral culture, many spoke in aphorisms and trite sayings that simply did not qualify as 'theological', at least according to academic definitions. Nor could my belief litmus take seriously the members from group homes with whom I could not communicate. Finally, subtle reactions to bodies—like my own responses—seemed important, but were not reflected in the beliefs articulated about 'not seeing color'. I found that my frame for thinking about what mattered was too intellectualist to capture what seemed important in the community.

Alternatives to the application model and its focus on beliefs are the accounts of practical or pastoral theology that focus on a practice-oriented subject matter.[10] There are more situational elements in such practices as preaching, liturgy, education, and pastoral care than simply articulatable convictions.[11] An early metaphor of the subject matter of pastoral care, the 'living human document', indicates the continuum of human experience that constitutes contemporary situations.[12] Important expansions of that living web to include the

[10] For different overviews of practical theology, see Randy L. Maddox, 'Practical Theology: A Discipline in Search of a Definition', *Perspectives in Religious Studies*, 18 (1991), 159–69; Gijsbert D. J. Dingemans, 'Practical Theology in the Academy: A Contemporary Overview', *Journal of Religion*, 76 (1996), 82–96; Kathleen A. Cahalan, 'Three Approaches to Practical Theology, Theological Education, and the Church's Ministry', *International Journal of Practical Theology*, 9 (2005), 63–94.

[11] For a historical account of the 'clerical paradigm', see Edward Farley, *Theologia: The Fragmentation and Unity of Theological Education* (Philadelphia: Fortress, 1983). For pastoral care's shift from clerical activities to broader notions of lived Christian faith, see Elaine L. Graham, *Transforming Practice: Pastoral Theology in an Age of Uncertainty* (London: Mowbray, 1996), 11 n. 1, 38–111.

[12] This, Anton Boisen's image, was important for the development of Clinical Pastoral Education. Cited by C. V. Gerkin, *The Living Human Document: Revisioning Pastoral Counseling in a Hermeneutical Mode* (Nashville: Abingdon, 1984), 37. Thanks to Bonnie Miller-McLemore for calling my attention to this.

complex political and social constituents of human life have helped move much of practical/pastoral theology away from individual-focused subject matter.[13] The work of theologians on the structure of practical reasoning in communities, for example, attends to the variety of activities that make up faith's situational character as well as ways of reflecting practically on being faithful in a parish.[14] Theologians have recently broadened the category 'Christian practices' to include the corporately produced and shared practices that address 'fundamental human needs and conditions', such as 'embodiment, temporality, relationship, the use of language, and mortality'.[15]

In the spirit of this increasing turn to the complexities of contemporary lived situation, practical theology must seek out a patterning of the community that can yield the continuum of experience I have identified. A wide spectrum of 'elements and items' must be recognized as constituting a situation, one that includes hidden inheritances, habituated bodies with desires and, implicitly, affective and visceral reactions. Finally the 'powers'—the local and the political, as well as the global—that constitute situations must be factored in. An adequate patterning must foreground the complexity and selectivity of items, the way they come together, and the complex way they impinge to evoke a response.

Crucial for such a framing are the important resources of cultural anthropology, which attends to rituals, behaviors, kinship relationships, and much more than beliefs or ecclesiastically defined practices.[16] Basic to this project is my ethnographic research, from which

[13] Bonnie Miller-McLemore, 'Pastoral Theology as Public Theology: Revolutions in the "Fourth Area" ', in Nancy J. Ramsay (ed.), *Pastoral Care and Counseling: Redefining the Paradigms* (Nashville: Abingdon, 2004), 44–64. Pastoral care theologians such as Elaine L. Graham, Nancy Ramsay, and Dale Andrews, whose work takes gender and race seriously, develop practical/pastoral theology's range.

[14] A founding figure is Don Browning. See his *A Fundamental Practical Theology: Descriptive and Strategic Proposals* (Minneapolis: Fortress, 1991); and id., *Practical Theology.*

[15] Craig Dykstra and Dorothy C. Bass, 'A Theological Understanding of Christian Practices', in Volf and Bass (eds.), *Practicing Theology*, 22.

[16] Congregational Studies and recent focus on 'lived religion' attend to broader activities than beliefs. See Carl S. Dudley and Nancy T. Ammerman, *Congregations in Transition: A Guide for Analyzing, Assessing, and Adapting in Changing Communities* (San Francisco: Jossey-Bass, 2002); and David D. Hall, *Lived Religion in America: Toward a History of Practice* (Princeton: Princeton University Press, 1997).

I develop thick descriptions of the church's life. As a participant observer I have done interviews with most of the active members and ministers, attended worship services, Bible studies, meetings, and every kind of church event.[17] From this fieldwork come the stories, symbols, habits, and patterns that characterize Good Samaritan.[18]

Arguing that an adequate frame is found by thematizing situation in a complex way, I have, however, suggested only part of what is needed to read Good Samaritan theologically. As important as it is to display the community as a dense, bodied, and, therefore, worldly reality, more is necessary to convey fully what a theological reading is to indicate about this worldliness. It remains to explore how a complex reality is not only full of ambiguity and complexity, but also of traces of God's redemptive presence. I move to an image for theological reflection on this community more suggestive of a worldly God.

THEOLOGY AS RESPONSE TO A WOUND

Thus far I have argued for what some call the first task of practical theology, that is, the task of describing a situation. Whether it be

---

[17] This research was carried out between 1996 and 1999. Participant observation is a research strategy aimed at understanding the culture and worldview of groups; it involves living with or participating in the group's life, interviews, group discussions, study of practices, and just 'hanging out'. See H. Russell Bernard, *Research Methods in Anthropology: Qualitative and Quantitative Approaches* (London: Sage, 1994), 136–64. For one of many critiques of its historic power relations, see James V. Spickard, 'The Epistemology of Post-Colonial Ethnography', in James V. Spickard, J. Shawn Landres, and Meredith B. McGuire (eds.), *Personal Knowledge and Beyond: Reshaping the Ethnography of Religion* (New York: New York University Press, 2002), 237–52.

[18] Even though my research has provided me with elements to construct coherence, no culture can be taken as a neatly identified whole, whether in the form of a symbolic consensus or structuralist system. James Clifford and George E. Marcus, *Writing Culture: The Poetics and Politics of Ethnography* (Berkeley and Los Angeles: University of California Press, 1986); George E. Marcus and Michael M. J. Fischer, *Anthropology as Cultural Critique: An Experimental Moment in the Human Sciences* (Chicago: University of Chicago Press, 1986); and James Clifford, *The Predicament of Culture: Twentieth-Century Ethnography, Literature, and Art* (Cambridge, MA: Harvard University Press, 1999). Kathryn Tanner relates this discovery to theology. See her *Theories of Culture: A New Agenda for Theology*, Guides to Theological Inquiry (Minneapolis: Fortress, 1997).

description of what Browning calls 'contemporary theory-laden practices' or simply of 'lived experience', as say Poling and Miller, these theologians rightly wish to generate theological issues from the dilemmas of contemporary life.[19] However, theological reflection is not something brought in after a situation has been described; it is a sensibility that initiates the inquiry at the outset. As such, theology reflection does not begin with a full-blown doctrine of God or of the church. Such a method misses that strange, often unremarked thing that *compels* a theological response—how it is that theological reasoning is provoked at all.[20] With reference to this level of reflection, my construal of Good Samaritan is already theological.

Theologies that matter arise out of dilemmas—out of situations that matter. The generative process of theological understanding is a process provoked, not confined to preconceived, fixed categories. Rather, as Charles Winquist is reported to have said, creative thinking originates at the scene of a wound. Wounds generate new thinking. Disjunctions birth invention—from a disjuncture in logic, where reasoning is compelled to find new connections in thought, to brokenness in existence, where creativity is compelled to search for possibilities of reconciliation.[21] Like a wound, theological thinking is

[19] I am not suggesting that they represent this descriptive task as 'objective' or narrowly empirical. Browning insists that even a sociological analysis has preunderstandings, is value-laden, and has a religious dimension. Poling and Miller initiate their discussion of description with language that resonates with my account. However, I want to make more explicit the theological shaping of the task. Browning, *Fundamental Theology*, 47–9; Poling and Miller, *Foundations*, 69, 70–7. The same goes for congregational studies, with its underdeveloped admission that description is theological. Nancy T. Ammerman, Jackson W. Carroll, Carl S. Dudley, and William McKinney (eds.), *Studying Congregations: A New Handbook* (Nashville: Abingdon, 1998), 16, 25–6.

[20] Even theologies that are successful at hiding their 'scene of origin' are still constituted by intersections with other texts and their convictions, as Wesley A. Kort shows. See his *Bound to Differ: The Dynamics of Theological Discourses* (State College, PA: Penn State University Press, 1992). This is an important sense in which theologies are nonfoundational; even when they ascribe an a priori unquestioned normativity to certain concepts, they are in truth writings compelled by concerns that may not be fully articulatable.

[21] Walter Lowe speaks of the 'wound of reason' as that fracture of reason compelled by the memory of suffering. This wound demands 'that the justification of suffering be nothing less than the redemption of suffering'. Walter Lowe, *Theology and Difference: The Wound of Reason* (Bloomington, IN: Indiana University Press, 1993), 9–10.

generated by a sometimes inchoate sense that something *must* be addressed.[22]

Such a process itself is defined by an a priori logic of transformation. More precisely, transformation is inherent in the image of the wound, for it invokes a sense of something wrong—of a fracture in things that should be joined or whole. The very sense of harm implies an impulse toward remedy—a kind of longing for it to be otherwise. In a provocative reference to such a nonfoundational sensibility, Mark Taylor speaks of a liberatory a priori that compels emancipatory thinking. A desire for freedom 'haunts' this thinking.[23] For the theologian this impulse is produced, however unconsciously, in tandem with some sense of ultimate reality—of God. My reading of what matters, what needs addressing in Good Samaritan, comes together with convictions about the ultimate, however underdeveloped. These sensibilities function as 'stipulations of relevance' that give a sense of what deserves attention—of what is out of place, of what is broken and needs to be fixed, as well as of what is good and compels thanksgiving.[24]

This is still not to say that theologies must 'begin' with either a concept of God or with a clearly defined problem and then move in a linear fashion to conclusions. These senses are co-constitutive, just as the production of a sense of the world and a theologian's sense of faith can never be separated. Just like the ordinary believer, the academic's faith has a cognitivity prior to explicit theological reasoning. As a kind of 'belief-full knowing', convictions about who God is/what God does are entailed in judgments about just which situations compel a response, and vice versa.[25] Defined this way, what is an implicit theological process is already at work in my reading of Good Samaritan.

[22] Wounds like the idolatries of the German church compelled Karl Barth to articulate a theology of the Word; falsely universal white theologies in a context of deeply entrenched racism compelled James Cone to write black theology.

[23] Mark Taylor, 'Subalternity and Advocacy as *Kairos* for Theology', in Joerg Rieger (ed.), *Opting for the Margins: Postmodernity and Liberation in Christian Theology* (Oxford: Oxford University Press, 2003), 8.

[24] This is Stanley Fish's term. See his 'Change', *South Atlantic Quarterly*, 86/4 (Fall, 1987), 423–4.

[25] Farley, *Theologia*, 156.

The very selectivity of the description of Good Samaritan offered thus far is the emerging articulation of a wound as well as an incipient impulse for change. I have foregrounded the racialized and bodied density of the community. By selecting particular elements to take most seriously, my account of the subject matter for theological reflection already frames the issue as a woundedness that must be traced out. As a sense of what mattered and a kind of nonfoundational 'foundation' for this theological reflection, my description is only suggestive. The generative wound might be defined in terms of those whose bodies are marked as the 'different' and the 'Other' in my account—all who suffer the wounds of racism and able-ism in the US. It might include the larger social segregations that have made this church so unusual. The harm that needs tracing, however, includes but goes beyond even these injustices. That harm also concerns a level of contemporary social *obliviousness* that not only disregards the marginalizing forces of racism and able-ism, but represses complicity in the/my production of 'difference'. It is an obliviousness symbolized by my first visit's discomfort.

Let me explain. My feeling of strangeness in response to the unaccustomed 'blackness' of the place and the presence of people with disabilities at that first visit suggests that my conscious commitments to inclusiveness were not completely correlated with my habituated sense of the normal. My posture 'confessed' a disruption of the dominant world I inhabit, signaling an implicit break between my convictions and these perceptions. This tacit sense that surprised me when I became self-conscious of my whiteness and my able-bodiedness suggests forms of occlusion operating in my own internalized sense of the world. Evidence of a broader social 'unaccustomedness' to black and disabled bodies, this discomfort has significance far beyond my own sense of dis-ease. It is an unaccustomedness and obliviousness with widespread parallels, not only at Good Samaritan, but in the larger society as well. It is an obliviousness that comes with dominance, and it foreshadows fracture in the smooth veneer of welcome and Christly inclusivity in the church as well.

Despite the fact that for a number of years now most white Americans have been saying they are in favor of racial integration and equal opportunity, '[w]hat has changed in recent years', in

Andrew Hacker's words, is not living patterns, but only 'the way people speak in public'.[26] It has been reported that 90 per cent of white US citizens have never been in an African American home, and recent studies indicate signs of increasing segregation in schools.[27] The percentage of significantly interracial Protestant churches is amazingly low: only 6 per cent of evangelical churches and 2.5 per cent of mainline churches are communities in which no more than 80 per cent of the membership identifies as the same race.[28] The more highly educated and progressive-sounding US whites are, the less likely they are to be in racially mixed churches or neighborhoods.[29] But there is more.

Consider Tim, the man in the wheelchair whose disability made me uncomfortable. My sense of awkwardness in relation to him also signifies something larger than personal idiosyncrasy. So common are such reactions from the 'able-bodied' to people with disabilities that they have been given a name. Erving Goffman calls them rituals of degradation.[30] Few churches welcome such noisy and frightening(!) people as those who live in group homes and mental institutions. In Rosemary Garland-Thomson's stark terms, they are often experienced as grotesque or 'freaks'.[31] Churchly conventions of sacred silence, decorum, and physical inaccessibility help reproduce the larger society's ghettoizing of these 'special needs' people. At their very

[26] Andrew Hacker, *Two Nations: Black and White, Separate, Hostile, Unequal* (New York: Scribner, 1992), 52.

[27] A recent study based upon 2000 data of segregation in 'moderate to large sized public school districts' reveals a trend that 'virtually all' the 239 districts analyzed 'are becoming more segregated for black and Latino students'. See 'Race in American Public Schools: Rapidly Resegregating School Districts', Press release, 8 Aug. 2002, from the report of Harvard University's Civil Rights Project, 'Race in American Public Schools: Rapidly Resegregating School Districts'.

[28] Michael Emerson, e-mail communication, 23 Oct. 2001. See Michael Emerson and Christian Smith, *Divided by Faith: Evangelical Religion and the Problem of Race in America* (New York: Oxford University Press, 2000), 10.

[29] Emerson and Smith, ibid.

[30] This from social scientist of disability Erving Goffman's theory of stigma, cited in Nancy L. Eiesland, *The Disabled God: Toward a Liberatory Theology of Disability* (Nashville: Abingdon, 1994), 92–3. I put 'able-bodied' in quotes because it is really a misdescription, suggesting a clear line between so-called normal and abnormal. In reality, all human beings are on a continuum of disability.

[31] Rosemary Garland-Thomson (ed.), *Freakery: Cultural Spectacles of the Extraordinary Body* (New York: New York University Press, 1996).

best, the majority of church-related disability organizations are only working on access rather than attitudinal change.[32] Furthermore, group homes are most likely to be found in low-income neighborhoods due to the power of wealth and influence in the control of residential zoning. The conditions for continued obliviousness, of power-related willing-not-to-see, are widespread.

Two things follow. First, that I am not alone in my visceral responses to the differences at Good Samaritan is a sign that the worldliness of the community—its woundedness—is a social phenomenon. While Good Samaritan is distinctive in bringing together very different populations, these populations will bring with them the habituations of the wider social reality. Some will correspond to my reactions, a wound of the dominant; some will correspond to the wounds of being marked as different. Since the majority of Christians in the United States are 'traditioned' or habituated into the faith in racially homogeneous communities and are isolated from those with physical and mental disabilities, the argument for a complex framing of Good Samaritan is, in effect, a recognition of a woundedness much larger than this faith community. This suggests that we may think of Good Samaritan as a complex text about difference and a variety of positionings in relation to difference—about 'whiteness' as well as 'color', and 'normal' and 'not-normal', at the very least.

Second, my reading of the community is already a construal of Good Samaritan as a place that demands response in a particular way. The demand for a frame for the community's full-bodied worldliness is not a wish for complexity for complexity's sake. Surfacing the density of Good Samaritan aims to uncover more fully the brokenness in human life. By reading it as a wound—a situation characterized by interpersonal forms of obliviousness and aversiveness marked and sustained by larger social-political processes— I understand Good Samaritan as *a situation characterized by harm that demands redress.*

The precise character of the brokenness that 'haunts' this situation, however, is not immediately apparent. It demands attendance

---

[32] See Nancy L. Eiesland, 'Barriers and Bridges: Relating the Disability Rights Movement and Religious Organizations', in Nancy L. Eiesland and Don E. Saliers (eds.), *Human Disability and the Service of God: Reassessing Religious Practice* (Nashville: Abingdon, 1998), 200–29.

to bodiliness and how it is that having 'race' and 'disability' evoke bodiliness in ways that being white or normal-bodied do not, at least in the perception of a dominant such as myself. Somewhat reminiscent of associations of bodies with femaleness and rationality with maleness, the marked character of certain bodies and not others is a sure signal of power differentials. (To construe the wound as obliviousness is, admittedly, already a reflection of my own subject position.) Whatever harms are experienced by different members of Good Samaritan and however deeply they are connected, the brokenness of whiteness and that of being marked as bodied and 'different' cannot be collapsed.

TOWARD A PLACE FOR APPEARING

If interpreting Good Samaritan as I have invokes a need for some kind of change, at the same time it suggests a critical lens for displaying Good Samaritan. This dense situation of differences must be framed in a way that not only brings its complexity into view, but also assesses its moves to redeem the realities associated with these harms. How do the beliefs, different forms of communication, and activities of Good Samaritans converge with the enculturated bodily habits and affective sensibilities of its members? And how are they connected to both the diminishing of human well-being and its flourishing? Such questions will guide the display of Good Samaritan. To do that well, however, requires more clarity about the kind of change needed.

While the terms of redress will extend beyond this chapter into the argument of the book, what can be said about obliviousness—the not-seeing that characterizes far too much of North American society—suggests important hints about what kind of change is at stake. The obliviousness that afflicts the community is not so much a cognitive problem on the part of the dominant, as, for example, in racist or ableist *beliefs*. Nor is it primarily found in the malice that characterizes these 'isms'. Indeed, like the majority of North Americans, members of Good Samaritan understood themselves to be welcoming of, not prejudiced toward, those who are marked as different.

However, obliviousness is a form of not-seeing that is not primarily intentional but reflexive. As such, it occurs on an experiential continuum ranging from benign to a subconscious or repressed protection of power. Non-innocent obliviousness is founded in the power of the visceral, the 'pulse of attraction and aversion' that characterizes all human interactions, says political theorist Iris Young.[33] It is this visceral register where fear, anxiety, and disgust occur, those responses that all too often characterize human reactions to those who are different. This level of consciousness fertilizes the more intentional, overt forms of oppression and does so by nurturing apprehensions that fund various ways of dispensing with the other.[34] Persisting through cultural constructions of bodies as racialized, gendered, sexualized, and marked as 'normal/abnormal', these constructions ascribe and project all manner of fears and anxieties onto 'Othered' bodies. Taking form in rationalizations that justify resulting marginalizations, they leave some bodies as unmarked and designated 'normal'.

In short, such visceral responses create the possibility for aversive 'isms'.[35] Aversive forms of response (what Glenn C. Loury calls the effect of stigma) have the potential to create and solidify 'Others', and they modulate all of our interactions. Speaking of a taxi driver's refusal to pick up a black man at night, for example, Loury says that 'the subject becomes an "invisible man" precisely because of the visibility, and the social meaning, of his stigmata'. Ironically, his visibility as a reviled and feared black man effectively means we who are white do not 'see' him. In a word, we substitute social stereotypes for knowledge of particular individuals.[36]

---

[33] See Iris Marion Young, *Justice and the Politics of Difference* (Princeton: Princeton University Press, 1990), 123; and William Connolly, *Why I Am Not a Secularist* (Minneapolis: University of Minnesota Press: 1999), 19–29.

[34] In an analysis of social obliviousness, political theorist Kimberley Curtis argues that a kind of disregard, both experiential and geographical, forms the a priori condition of widely acknowledged forms of injustice. Kimberley Curtis, *Our Sense of the Real: Aesthetic Experience and Arendtian Politics* (Ithaca, NY: Cornell University Press, 1999).

[35] Young, *Justice*, 142–3, 124.

[36] Explaining stigma, Loury says, 'The symbols we call "race" have through time been infused with social meanings bearing on the identity, the status, and the humanity of those who carry them. Once established, these meanings can come to be taken for granted, enduring unchallenged for generations. In a hierarchical society,

Ellis Cose describes parallels between the discomfort white people have with race and with disabled people. In reaction to these discomforts, whites frequently claim to 'not see difference'. Ignoring race with black people (such as not mentioning slavery or the race of a famous figure) is comparable to 'that [behavior] exhibited by certain people on encountering someone with a visible physical handicap. They pretend not to notice that the handicap exists and hope, thereby, to minimize discomfort.'[37] Indeed, as Toni Morrison points out, 'the habit of ignoring race is understood to be a graceful, even generous, liberal gesture'.[38] Yet the will to 'not see' these differences, Cose insists, is a costly 'solution'.[39] Aversive reactions eventuate in practices of avoidance and group isolation, providing supports for an obliviousness that is a denied, thus repressed, will-to-disregard.[40] This obliviousness, importantly, can co-exist with belief in equality and (Christian) inclusiveness.

The alteration of conditions of obliviousness and its related harms will require that accounts of social oppression be linked with this experiential field upon which the visceral register plays. Thus, a primary focus in my analysis will be 'everyday practices'—the level of interactions within the local community that consists of more

a correspondence may develop between a person's social position and the physical marks taken by that society to signify race. . . . When the meanings connoted by race-symbols undermine an observing agent's ability to see their bearer as a person possessing a common humanity with the observer—as "someone not unlike the rest of us"—then I will say that person is "racially stigmatized," and that the group to which he belongs suffers a "spoiled collective identity." ' Glenn C. Loury, *The Anatomy of Racial Inequality* (Cambridge, MA: Harvard University Press, 2002), 65, 66–7.

[37] The conclusion was that although the 'color-blind perspective' might 'ease initial tensions and minimize the frequency of overt conflict', it did so at a high price. Ellis Cose, *Color-Blind: Seeing beyond Race in a Race-Obsessed World* (New York: Harper Collins, 1998), 189–90.

[38] Toni Morrison, *Playing in the Dark: Whiteness and the Literary Imagination* (New York: Vintage, 1993), 9–11.

[39] Young argues that blacks do not construct whites as the abjected other, which is not to say that blacks do not have internalized problematic aversions toward whites, simply that the power dimensions are radically different in cultural imperialism. Young, *Justice*, 147, 123. Since neither argument nor facts can bring about such change, Connolly speaks of the 'arts of the self', whereby constructive work, a 'selective desanctification' of elements in the dominant identity, is done as a way to alter this visceral register in relation to the rejected other. Connolly, *Why*, 67–8, 143–52.

[40] Young, *Justice*, 122–3.

than ideas or convictions to welcome the other. For the 'wound' of obliviousness for those who are white and able-bodied occurs as a continuum of experience, extending from beliefs to desire and visceral reaction to embodied others. The wounds of those victimized by obliviousness are not identical, but complexly experienced. Changes in consciousness, then, not simply rational commitments, will be necessary to address these supports for oppression, particularly changes in the consciousness of dominant subjects. Supports for transformation will require attention to the registers of affect, visceral response, and fear.

More will be needed to characterize the terms of redress as my theological reading of Good Samaritan develops. However, at this point, transformation of obliviousness and its social harms is best imaged as the creation of its opposite: 'a shared space of appearance', as political theorist Kimberley Curtis puts it.[41] What is needed to counter the diminishment and harm associated with obliviousness is a *place to appear*, a place to be seen, to be recognized and to recognize the other. Being seen and heard by others, being acknowledged by others—these are said to be essential to the political life; my point is that they are also essential to a community of faith as an honoring of the shared image of God. How is Good Samaritan a place where people of different races and abilities 'appear' in significant ways to one another? How do those with the power to disregard become able to recognize? How do these 'items, powers, and events' of situation gather and evoke responses that can also alter supporting social forces so that all can recognize and be recognized?

In this introductory chapter, I have argued that practical theology, the task of theological reflection upon this contemporary situation, is at least two things. It is, first of all, full attention to the structure of situation, its shape and demand, in such a way that the complex of racialized, normalized, and otherwise enculturated bodies and desire are as much a part of the analysis as the presence of biblical and doctrinal elements. Such attention is crucial to the full honoring of the created worldly place that is Good Samaritan UMC. Equally

---

[41] Curtis, *Our Sense*, 14. As an aesthetic notion of redemptive alteration, a place of appearing opens up a wide continuum for what 'appearing' means—not simply visual or aural, it is being recognized.

important is the way reading this situation as a wound implicitly assumes an emancipatory interest and demands a response of change. Thus practical theology is also a particular way of attending to the structure of situation; *it is an inquiry shaped by a logic of transformation.*

While thus far this logic entails nothing explicitly 'theological' in the sense of recognized conventional languages of the inscribed tradition, its evaluative character does distinguish my reading from an interpretation confined to mere description and/or institutional functionality.[42] The logic of interpretation will open later into more explicit theological thematization. To interpret this community in the fullest theological sense will be to use the language of 'redeemed' and mean by that 'sustained by God'. But this reading of the theonomy, or God-dependence, of the situation that is Good Samaritan must advance in a way that resists letting the claims about the transcendent falsify the density of the worldly wounds.

To say that the subject matter of practical theology is contemporary situation and to define situation as 'the way various items, powers, and events in the environment gather to evoke responses from participants' is still a very formal way of thinking about Good Samaritan. To avoid the inadequate (modernist) model of Christian community as a coherent system of beliefs, the next move in the argument is a proposal to frame Good Samaritan with the categories of postmodern place theory, a framing that will further specify these items, powers, and events, their gathering and evoking of response in such a way that brings to focus the social problem of obliviousness as well as the means of its redress. A much improved alternative to the charting of beliefs, or activities or attempts to cobble them together, postmodern place theory allows for a needed expansion of the results of my ethnographic research, which, despite its thickness, does not represent the continuum of human experience that is needed. Most importantly it offers a crucial counter to the modern prioritizing of

---

[42] Postmodern anthropology has recognized the located, interpretive character of anthropological description for several decades. James Clifford's account of the function of allegory in ethnographic writing has some similarity with what I am arguing. But in contrast to Clifford, I am sketching out a logic that has goods and ends. James Clifford, 'On Ethnographic Allegory', in Clifford and Marcus (eds.), *Writing Culture*, 98–121.

space that overlooks the bodied way in which culturally shaped places come to be. As such, it allows for recognition of the role of bodily habituation in the making of a shared communal reality as well as the traditioning of that reality by authoritative Christian texts.

As Chapter 2 will argue, place theory makes practices central to the imagining of the faith community as contemporary situation, but extends the definition of practices with a complex account of the role of bodies, desire, power, and nonsymbolic forms of communication.

Drawing upon the notion of place as convergences of practices, in Part II I display the community of Good Samaritan with chapters on the various practices that constitute its identity—from formation practices (Chapter 3) to worship practices (Chapter 4), home-making practices (Chapter 5), and practices of biblical interpretation (Chapter 6). In Part III (Chapters 7 and 8), I discuss the kind of places that are constructed by these practices—the unity of the place called Good Samaritan UMC and how its places of appearing are redemptive and political. Finally, I discuss the implication of this account for thinking about theological tasks of normative remembering and systematic/philosophical judgment. For if the place of faith is to take seriously our continuum of experience and forms of communication, our accounts of faithful remembering will no doubt have to broaden and deepen.

2

Postmodern Place: A Frame for Appearing

> the lived body—which is perhaps what human beings take to be the most self-enclosed and intimate thing they experience—shows itself to be continually conjoined with place, however impersonal and public in status it may be in given instances. The conjunction itself, however, is made possible precisely because the body is already social and public in its formation and destiny... while places for their part are idiosyncratic in their constitution and appearance. Just as sedimentation and reactivation are both bodily and placial, so the public and the private realms realize themselves in body and place alike.

> place is not entitative—as a foundation has to be—but eventmental, something in process, something unconfinable to a thing. Or to a simple location.

> Edward Casey, Fate of Place

To propose that the term 'place' will provide the frame for thinking about contemporary situation will seem odd, particularly when the problem is how to 'make appear' the complexities and intersections of bodied, visceral, and encultured habituation in a faith community. Place is, after all, a reference to some location, a 'here' or a 'there'. The place of Good Samaritan United Methodist Church lies in a city located in Durham County, North Carolina, the US, the northern hemisphere, and the globe. Place tells us where something is relative to something else. I live on that dot labeled 'Hillsborough, NC', which is 200 miles from the Atlantic Ocean and 15 or so miles from Good Samaritan UMC. Thus, place is a specification, a marker within the infinite extension that is space. Such a thin manner of locating something seems an unlikely way to frame Good Samaritan as a public place of appearing for a variety of marginalized populations.

Indeed, since what is of interest about Good Samaritan is the bodied, visceral, and interconnectional, such spare identification as site seems the opposite of what is needed. Place as site suggests a pinpoint location in an empty, measurable nowhere. Even the *relational* character of its locating, that it tells us where Good Samaritan is in relation to someplace else, is thin—an abstraction that does not help situate the dense practices conducive to obliviousness. For a map to be useful I must know where I am situated bodily. Place seems inadequate for the task at hand, particularly when that task is to provide a thickened account of *situation* for theological reflection.

Or is it? Just such a conception of place as site has come under serious scrutiny of late, or, more accurately, the modern concept of space that underlies it. Postmodern geography contests the modern concept of space as a vacuum—an infinite extension only to be measured or filled—and its implication that place is simply a site or pinpoint marker on that extension.[1] In redefining place as a structure of lived, corporate, and *bodied* experience, such theories argue that place is primary and this modern concept of space is a secondary abstraction.[2] When understood as *bodied ingression into the world*, place is truly fundamental in generating knowledge. For it is the body, with its corporeal bifurcation, that *provides* orientation in the world (left-right, up-down, front-back) and thus the basic ingredients of place.[3] The world *takes shape* through our bodies.

[1] For a brief account of this, see Edward S. Casey, *The Fate of Place: A Philosophical History* (Berkeley and Los Angeles: University of California Press, 1998), 197–201.

[2] 'Humanist geography' began in the 1970s, when the concern to move from the abstract framework of geometric spatial relationships to the meaning-worlds led to the insistence that the meaning-world is a place-world. Such theorists as Yi-Fu Tuan, *Space and Place: The Perspective of Experience* (Minneapolis: University of Minnesota Press, 1977, 2001); E. C. Relph, *Place and Placelessness: Research in Planning and Design* (London: Routledge, Kegan, and Paul, 1976); J. Nicholas Entrikin, *The Betweenness of Place: Towards a Geography of Modernity* (Baltimore: Johns Hopkins Press, 1991). More recently, 'cultural geography' brings together humanist and Marxist cultural studies: Peter Jackson, *Maps of Meaning: An Introduction to Cultural Geography* (London: Routledge, 1989); K. Anderson and F. Gale (eds.), *Inventing Places: Studies in Cultural Geography* (Melbourne: Longman Cheshire, 1992).

[3] Despite his later work supporting modern constructs of absolute space-time, it was Kant who argued for the priority of place through embodied experience. In a 1768 essay he contested the adequacy of the notion of relational space, insisting that without orientation, there is no way to locate anything. See Casey, *Fate of Place*, 202–10. Kant's 1768 essay is 'On the First Ground of the Distinction of Material Regions in Space'.

Suggesting something quite different from the idea that Good
Samaritan is a site on a city street map, place theory turns our
attention to the density of location. Place is a structure of lived,
corporate, bodied experience and, as such, contests the view from
nowhere.[4] 'We don't live in an abstract framework of geometric
spatial relationships, but in a world of meaning—existing in and
surrounded by places, neither totally material or mental,' as one
theorist puts it.[5] Postmodern place theory mandates that as agents,
'we are always "in place", much as we are always "in culture"', as
theorist Entrikin argues.[6] Place will be a category that characterizes
all knowledge—a structuring of corporate understanding that joins
enculturated bodies to larger social matrixes.[7]

This chapter will explore postmodern place as a constructive way
to think about Good Samaritan UMC. I will draw upon examples of
places and go on to explore what is distinctive about faith community as place. The goal is to show that place theory provides a frame
through which the complexities of the worldly character of the faith
community can appear. The categories of place, in short, are best
designed to display the shape of faith as a lived *situation*, that is, 'the
way various items, powers, and events in the environment gather to
evoke responses from participants'.[8]

---

[4] Arif Dirlik argues that obliviousness to place is key to ignoring the realities of
gender, race, and ethnicity. Arif Dirlik, 'Globalism and the Politics of Place', *Development*, 41/2 (June 1998), 10. Postcolonialist theorists of place argue that the modern
notion of space as infinite extension helps authorize imperialist invasions because
vast continents can be read as empty space, ripe for colonization.

[5] Tim Cresswell, *In Place/Out of Place: Geography, Ideology and Transgression*
(Minneapolis: University of Minnesota Press, 1996), 13.

[6] Entrikin, *Betweenness of Place*, 1.

[7] Developments in postmodern geography include Yi-Fu Tuan's founding work in
humanist geography in the 1970s, an attempt to recapture the lived world of place
and its construction by human interest, employing phenomenological, ethnographic, and hermeneutical methods. More recent incorporation into place theory
of cultural and social theories, including the race, class, and gender theories, have
complicated humanisms. See Paul C. Adams, Steven Hoelscher, and Karen E. Till,
'Place in Context: Rethinking Humanist Geographies', in Paul C. Adams, Steven
Hoelscher, and Karen E. Till (eds.), *Textures of Place: Exploring Humanist Geographies*
(Minneapolis: University of Minnesota Press, 2001), pp. xiii–xxxiii.

[8] Edward Farley, 'Interpreting Situations: An Inquiry into the Nature of Practical
Theology', in *Practicing Gospel: Unconventional Thoughts on the Church's Ministry*
(Louisville, KY: Westminster John Knox, 2003), 38.

DEFINING PLACE

So how to think about place in this postmodern way? Attention to the lived body is not new. Analyses such as Merleau-Ponty's phenomenology of the body as a world-relation have shown that a human being experiences the world through the oriented body.[9] But a postmodern notion of place is more than simply the appreciation of the lived body, for the concepts of 'here' and 'there' are still central to place. To get a sense of how such localizing directives as these do not simply bring us back to thinking of place only as a mappable entity, let us look at how place might have a unity and an enduring character, that is how it exists though time. I turn now to examples.

The place called 'hometown', to take one example, illustrates important features of a postmodern conception of place. To begin with, place transcends the dualisms of mind-body, mental-physical, and self-world.[10] Hometown is constructed by the people of a particular geographically defined reality—from family and friends to the strangers who make up our environment and its past and present. Hometown is our surroundings in the fullest aesthetic and experiential sense. Particular buildings—our family home, school, church, the park—make up the place, but so do their associations (as spacious or cramped, light or dark, safe or dangerous). Reducible neither to the geographical boundaries on a map, nor to our projections onto an ostensible physical 'outside', then, the place hometown is better described as a matrix of feelings that a place 'releases' to us.[11] It is this matrix or constellation, this 'territory of meaning' that

---

[9] M. Merleau-Ponty, *The Phenomenology of Perception*, trans. C. Smith (New York: Humanities, 1962).

[10] Mind–body dualism assumes that the self has no constitutive relation to place. On such accounts, '[p]lace belongs entirely to the physical world, the self to the realm of consciousness, and the twain supposedly never meet'. Edward S. Casey, 'Body, Self, and Landscape: A Geophilosophical Inquiry into the Place-World', in Adams et al. (eds.), *Textures of Place*, 405.

[11] Edward S. Casey, 'How to Get from Space to Place in a Fairly Short Stretch of Time', in Steven Feld and Keith H. Basso (eds.), *Senses of Place* (Santa Fe, NM: School of American Research Press, 1996), 25.

constructs place—suggesting another feature, a way of imagining the unity of a place.[12]

Understood as a territory of meaning, the unity of place is a kind of *gathering*, says Casey. Places 'gather reality'. Hometown is well described as a 'holding together in a particular configuration' of the experiences, subjects, landscapes, histories, and expectations associated with it.[13] Its elements come together or converge to create some kind of unified reality. While this postmodern notion will mean that place is clearly constituted by the past, a feature to be explored more fully later, here the important point is the *synchronic* shape of its unity. A holding of such elements in the present, place is thus a frame for *contemporary situation*, a way to understand the living environment out of which and to which we respond.

Given that place frames situation, how do we think about the *ordering* of elements that make a situation? For as a *gathering*, to use Casey's term, place is a *selecting* of subjects, memories, smells, and landscape. Not every detail, every person, or every piece of landscape in our chronological past constructs the place of our hometown. Just as we do not experience our past as simply disconnected moments, undistinguished one from the other, we do not experience place as every imaginable detail collected in some random way. To order this infinite mass of detail, something connects some pieces of our landscapes, creating affinities for some elements over others.

A first form of connecting has to do with the affective character of human experience and is best described with the acoustical term *resonances*. Defined as the 'intensification and prolongation of sound produced by sympathetic vibration', resonances suggest modes of connecting that are indirect but tangible and strong.[14] Pleasant sympathetic vibrations between positive school experience and

---

[12] E. C. Relph, 'Place', in Ian Douglas, Richard Huggett, and Mike Robinson (eds.), *Companion Encyclopedia of Geography: The Environment and Humankind* (New York: Routledge, 1996), 907–8.

[13] Casey, 'How to Get,' 24 ff.

[14] For use of this concept to explore the Religious Right's success with connecting different social issues together in the public imagination, see Linda Kintz, *Between Jesus and the Market: The Emotions that Matter in Right-Wing America* (Durham, NC: Duke University Press, 1997), 6.

reading may go into the making of hometown as place, as well as more complex resonances of unfulfilled desire—the unattainable crush, the parent one could never please. Given the unpredictability of resonances, such communications of meaning, then, are not direct. As one scholar puts it, communication is 'strewn with previous claims that slow up, distort, refract the intention of the word'.[15] We might say that 'previous claims' in our hometown, indeed, in each and every place, function as refracting media. They snag and route and reroute the meanings of that place by refracting communications through the affective resonances—the hopes, fears, and multiple feelings—to which they connect.

A second kind of ordering of place happens through more reflective genres, such as stories. Narratives move resonances to the level of conscious interpretation. From a kaleidoscope of elements we 'make sense' of our hometown—'an ideal place to grow up, full of caring adults and old-time values', or 'a place of hardship and desperation, where mere survival was the central occupation'. Even as it orders, however, interpretive connecting does not domesticate every detail. Sympathetic resonances may link memories of childhood friends and good times with kindly adult mentors. Contrary incidents—violence, sexual abuse, for example—can co-exist with the sense-making elements of a place, however, and prove resistant to neat incorporation into a narrative of one kind or another.

The unity of place, then, holds conflict and contradiction. Place cannot demand seamlessness or homogeneity in its unity. So understood, the identity of a hometown has horizonal boundaries.[16] Like

---

[15] 'Every word is like a ray of light or a trajectory to both an object and a receiver. Both paths are strewn with previous claims that slow up, distort, refract the intention of the word.' Michael Holquist is describing this refracting in relation to the work of M. M. Bakhtin in *The Dialogic Imagination: Four Essays by M. M. Bakhtin*, ed. Michael Holquist, trans. Caryl Emerson and Michael Holquist (Austin: University of Texas Press, 1981), 432.

[16] Expanding Kant's appreciation of the directional way we experience, Casey points to the way our perception as bodied subjects is characterized by depth and horizons. Perception is perspectival, characterized by near and far, wide and deep. It is a located worldly sensing that has distinctive boundaries. Its *horizonal boundaries* are distinctive modes of limiting something; by virtue of that peculiar limiting they grant unity to perception. Horizonal boundaries are permeable; one cannot mark exactly where a horizon starts and where it ends.

the edges of located perception, the outlines of place are never sharply demarcated. On the one hand, our hometown is never the same. The constellation of its resonances—the elements that connect—and the disjunctive pieces of the place shift in relation to each other. Provocations of many-layered memories serve up new versions of the hometown at different periods. What 'gathers' to make place is unavoidably fluid. Thus, the boundaries of place are always permeable, modulating over the years and continuing to change. When we visit our hometown, we could even say that we find it a *new* place. On the other hand, we always know there is a clear *something* referred to by this place we call hometown, even if only because we say it is no longer 'the same place'.

Good Samaritan UMC has the unity of a place. As such it is not constituted simply by its building, the renovated garage with the Methodist flame and cross, or by its distance from the tall-steepled, brick Baptist church down the road from it. But neither is this place simply a bunch of ideas in its members' heads. As a 'territory of meaning' it will be the buildings, the land, *and* the forms of meaning produced by its participants.

The place called Good Samaritan occurs as a gathering—a coalescing of language, rituals, stories, and tacit understandings as well as bodies, habits, buildings, and memories. The Praise Songs will matter as much as the sermons, the face-to-face meetings, and the shared meals in the making of Good Samaritan. Memories of other churches, other ministers will matter as will associations around whiteness and blackness, around guilt and forgiveness. Even as the 'what' that gathers is always fluid, as place this community is thus a constellation with specificity—you can tell 'church' when you have been there. As for the ordering of this constellation, the role of interpretive genres and the more unruly affective prove equally important in selecting what matters in this 'gathering'.

In addition to traditional creedal affirmations that 'order' the place, Good Samaritan's racial and cultural diversity generates stories and traditions from different kinds of Christianities. Aphorisms and the other genres associated with oral cultures will have a prominent function in the production of meaning; the special needs participants will create even more complexity. The verbal interpretation of a biblical text in a sermon, for example, may be the least important form of communication for group home members, many of whom use nonsymbolic modes of communication, such as body movements, gestures, facial expressions, and touching.[17]

Important to the process of ordering are the resonances of communications—our affective associations. As noted, such associations occur through 'refracting media', and in the faith community, as in the hometown, these media are multiple. While experience is a refracting medium—for example, stories of God's family will refract through experiences of families—a refracting medium that focuses experience is *bodies*. Resonances around gendered, raced, classed, and sexualized bodies in a society historically shaped by a variety of segregations will be inevitable. As desiring, feeling, and fearful creatures, church members respond affectively to the world, and their responses to that which is different or 'Other' are grounded in visceral reactions to bodies.

In sum, as place Good Samaritan has a unity analogous to that of the hometown. As experiences, histories, and expectations associated with the place come together, like 'hometown' this place of faith will be made up of the resonances of different people, their bodies, events, and physical things—from welcoming habits, the character of the preaching, to the racial histories and subtexts of its participants. What 'gathers' to make this place will be ordered by way of refracting media and their resonances as well as by the explicit interpretive acts used to make sense out of this Christian community. Its unity will be complex and multilayered, like that of a hometown; its boundaries will never be fixed. But it will be just as real.

---

[17] I am relying upon a theory of communication that seems most respectful of persons with disabilities, where '[s]ymbolic modes of communication rely on forms that represent, or stand for, something else, such as the word *shoe*, spoken or signed, referring to the shoe that you put on this morning. Combining the words *my* and *new* with the spoken or signed word *shoe* requires understanding of the formal rules of language.' Educators have discovered other modes of communication employed by persons with a range of disabilities. These modes include bodily, vocal, affective, and other behaviors. Ellin Siegel and Amy Wetherby, 'Enhancing Nonsymbolic Communication', in Martha E. Snell and Fredda Brown (eds.), *Instruction of Students with Severe Disabilities*, 5th edn. (Upper Saddle River, NJ: Prentice-Hall, 2000), 409.

CONSTITUTION BY PRACTICES

The notions of 'gathering' or 'holding together in a particular configuration' are helpful images to think about the unity of place in terms of its synchronic identity. But since place describes situation, and almost anything, however fleeting, can count as a 'situation', another necessary determinant of place is longevity and endurance. The diachronic identity of place, its duration through time, is defined by ongoing *practices*.

For the role of practices, we turn to postmodern place theorist Michael Curry's discussion of 'North America' as place. The unity of 'North America' as place could be defined as a gathering of meanings just as we described hometown. However, a look at its diachronic identity highlights the role of reiterated practices in the constitution of place in a particularly striking way.

'North America' did not simply exist, argues Curry, it was *made*. And that making involved a great number of practices by which Europeans conquered and recreated the Western hemisphere. Take the actions of Hernando Cortez, sixteenth-century Spanish explorer. Five of Cortez's practices, Curry argues, were not simply activities, they were *place-making functions* crucial to the production of the place, 'New World'. To create the New World (or 'New Spain' on his terms), Cortez publicly pronounced the territory for Spain, a ritual-ization of place. He raised a national flag, linking a symbol to the place. By building structures from local trees he changed the natural landscape; measuring the terrain made it a mapped reality. Finally, Cortez's institution of a penal system created laws to control the place. All of these practices together brought into being a new place, which continued to exist—was reproduced—as long as the Spanish engaged in them.[18]

Because they included aggressive physical and symbolic marking, maintenance, and legislative control, these Spanish practices may seem more distinctive than those that reproduce the hometown. New Spain came into being through a conquering takeover of

[18] Michael R. Curry, '"Hereness" and the Normativity of Place,' in James D. Proctor and David M. Smith (eds.), *Geography and Ethics: Journeys in a Moral Terrain* (New York: Routledge, 1999), 98.

preexisting places; it included indigenous resistance from such groups as the Aztecs and colonializing force. In comparison, the endurance of the hometown seems rather tame; occupants just keep showing up.

However, the two are more alike than may first appear. Like Cortez's flag claiming territory for Spain, symbolic markers produce the place hometown. Buildings not only alter the natural landscape of a town, as inscribed with cultural meanings they also announce and sustain the class and race boundaries of place. From the gated community, the practices of redlining and 'whites only' signs of Jim Crow to the more subtle contemporary economic segregation of housing, contemporary geographical markings are practices of claiming territory. As Cortez's lawmaking practices controlled the place of the New World, state laws and city ordinances control the place hometown. The creation of mixed, residential, and industrial zones produces place. Ordinances prohibiting beggars or the homeless from occupying public space, laws protecting wealthy suburbs from the incursion of halfway houses, public housing, or group homes—all are place-producing practices.

Places have many layers. Benignly this means that places overlap. My hometown overlaps with that of many others with similar class and race profiles. Habituated not to see whiteness as race, growing up we saw race as a trait exclusive to African Americans.[19] Consequently *our* hometown was/is a place with few if any racial memories, save for what were viewed as disruptions by others if we grew up in the 1960s. A different 'we' was produced for those from the same geographical area who required a double consciousness due to their racial status, a consciousness both of their own reality and that of the dominant race.[20] For this 'we', hometown was/is fraught with (previously) dangerous boundaries, some safe places, and places of conflict. Only home on the other side of the segregation line felt safe, as bell hooks puts it.[21] While residents of the 'white side' and 'black side' of

[19] Others would have had race for us (Latinos, Mexican Americans, etc.), but African Americans dominated that category in our southern town.

[20] W. E. B. Du Bois, *The Souls of Black Folks* (1903; repr. New York: Vintage Books, 1990), pp. xii, 7–9.

[21] bell hooks, *Black Looks: Race and Representation* (Boston: South End, 1992), 175; ead., 'Homeplace: A Site of Resistance', in *Yearning: Race, Gender, and Cultural Politics* (Boston: South End, 1990).

town shared the same hometown in the sense of a designated site on a map, our implacements were radically different.[22]

Despite their contrasting resonances, however, these differently racialized hometowns *do* overlap, particularly as the realities of one place begin to be shared by the other, say, with the development of civil rights sensibilities. Such overlappings create the possibility for new practices, even new places, and indicate the social and shared character of place.

The convergence of different places also entails relations of power. The Cortez example illustrates overlappings that colonized indigenous populations. Whatever new practices came into being as this New World, they were marked by the preexistent place, both as something to be exploited and as something to be, in many ways, erased. Overlapping is not simply a synchronic phenomenon. It requires the recognition that places are not produced upon 'empty space'. History and its power dynamics are as crucial to place as are its synchronic elements. Places are *emergent* realities or practices. Dependent upon elements of previous places and times, places contain these elements as *residuals* in their new synchronic formation.[23]

The presence of residuals, elements of the past in the present, makes place somewhat like the *palimpsest* or ancient manuscript marked by erasures. Like a palimpsest, place has the past 'scrawled upon it' in a variety of ways, a past that is not completely visible. Like the unconscious, it exists in various modes of accessibility. The palimpsestic character of place also refers to the conflicts held in a memory of place. Nostalgia for past joys in one's sense of hometown, for example, can co-exist with buried memories of abuse. As 'previous claims' or refracting media, the latter can 'slow up, distort, refract' any meanings that are new, affecting how they shape the present place.

---

[22] For accounts of different associations for whites and blacks in the same places, see David K. Shipler, *A Country of Strangers: Blacks and Whites in America* (New York: Alfred A. Knopf, 1997).

[23] For complexities of race and memory, see Karen Fields, 'What One Cannot Remember Mistakenly', in Genevieve Fabre and Robert O'Meally (eds.), *History and Memory in African-American Culture* (New York: Oxford University Press, 1994), 150–63.

Two concluding features render explicit what has been implied all along about place. First, that place is produced through practices assumes that it is not simply the lived experience of an individual. Practices such as those that produced North America are best understood as *habitus*. As agents are 'socially informed bod[ies]', practices, according to Bourdieu, are a social enculturation. What is more, they operate along the continuum of human experience as 'a system of lasting, transposable dispositions which, integrating past experiences, functions at every moment as a *matrix of perceptions, appreciations, and actions* and makes possible the achievement of infinitely diversified tasks'—durable dispositions that reexternalize social cultures in ever-new ways.[24] One sees this habituation of subjects in the gendering and racialization of practices I have foregrounded. It means that the overlapping of places makes place political, too, and even global. Shaped by the cultural-economic forces of a society, of global capitalism, and so on, one is produced by a 'mangle of practice', as one theorist puts it. 'We are always in more than one place at once.'[25]

A second implication of the social character of place has to do with its constant fluidity. The overlappings of places have a temporal character. Never static, they create the possibility for the emergence of new places in the form of the *centripetal* and *centrifugal* forces that constitute place. Centripetal forces for unity, for the gathering that emerges out of overlapping habituations—say, a shared loyalty to the Spanish crown by new settlers—will be in dialectical relationship with the pull of the various centrifugal forces that direct away— longing for the Old Country, or destruction by new invading armies. Differently habituated members in Good Samaritan are drawn together by various forces, as we will see, and they are also pulled apart by social forces.

Finally, then, no place is ever a fixed entity; a place is always in process. The terms 'centripetal' and 'centrifugal' allow us to describe this transience in terms of larger forces—political, global, and so

[24] Pierre Bourdieu, *Outline of a Theory of Practice*, trans. Richard Nice, Cambridge Studies in Social Anthropology, Jack Goody (general ed.) (1972; repr. Cambridge: Cambridge University Press, 1977), 16–17.

[25] Reference to Andrew Pickering, author of the *The Mangle of Practice: Time, Agency, and Science*, in Curry, ' "Hereness" ', 96.

forth—that are constantly in play in the construction of place. On the one hand, strong centripetal forces show that the process character of place is conducive to its integrity; on the other, when overcome by centrifugal forces, process may entail a shift or the dissolution of a place.

Let us review. A postmodern framing of place allows the densities of embodied human being-in-the-world as synchronic situation to come into focus. Identifiable solely with neither the so-called physical realities nor the mental, place is a gathering of meanings that endures through practices. Bodied habituations, these practices are culturally shaped and thus social in multiple senses. The unity of place holds conflict as well as residual memory. It is affectively and reflectively ordered, temporary and multilayered, and imbricated in power relations. With horizonal boundaries subject to shifts, the diachronic identity of place is a process constructed out of centripetal and centrifugal forces. Not only can one go back to 'the same place', it is precisely this complexity, this density, this fragility, and this fluidity that make place real. To think of Good Samaritan as place will entail much more complexity than a dot on the map.

Not unlike practices producing New Spain or the hometown, those producing Good Samaritan have been regularized, indeed, have become a revered tradition. But defining practices for Christian community are authorized in ways that other places often are not by virtue of the normative power accorded them.[26] Such practices as proclamation, interpretation of Scripture, and sacramental activities have long been understood not only to constitute church as a distinctive place, but also to play a defining role in the creation of Christian community. While 'normative' is traditionally designated through some form of divine authorization, its material form has to do specifically with ensuring faithfulness to the ends of Christian community, what we can call 'faithfulness to Jesus'.

If place requires attending to the unavoidable 'messiness' of situations, the next question is how its features apply to an identity founded in

---

[26] This is not an absolute contrast between religious practices/traditions and the practices/traditions that construct other places. What is considered the 'tradition' and related practices of being a patriotic member of the place 'America' can not only be regulated, but can be construed as authorized by God as well.

a normative historic (salvific) event. How should the life, death, and resurrection of Jesus Christ and the literatures that witness to those events shape their continued reenactment? How can Good Samaritan be understood such that the features of place—what it means to call it a *situation*—and the importance of faithfulness to Jesus are both taken into account? While a fuller theological accounting of these issues awaits development in a later chapter, we move now to a preliminary account of normative tradition.

PRODUCING CHRISTIAN PLACE: TRADITION AND PRACTICES

The most basic terms of evaluation for Good Samaritan's practices come from linking the contemporary community to the defining events of the community, the faith of Israel and the life, death, and resurrection of Jesus Christ. This linkage is accomplished by Christian tradition, 'the whole way of life of a people as it is transmitted from generation to generation', as J. P. Mackey puts it.[27] As a 'way of life' and not simply the transmission of belief, tradition is a *communicative process best imagined as participatory, vision-shaped practices.*[28] Recognition of the complexities of the activities that produce and sustain place mandates that our account of tradition be adequate to that 'communicative process'. There must be an ecclesial vision, but it will necessarily be refracted, multiply routed and rerouted in the manner of the meanings of hometown.

We must identify ways of being faithful that continue, enhance, even expand such a vision, yet do not escape the messiness of place. The question is how normative memories of the Christian tradition intersect with that constellation that is a *situation*, or, in the language of my frame, how the 'various items, powers, and events in the environment' of Good Samaritan 'gather to evoke responses from participants' that can be called faithful.[29] Place theory insists that the

---

27 J. P. Mackey, *Tradition and Change in the Church* (Dayton, OH: Pflaum, 1968), p. x.
28 Terrence W. Tilley, *Inventing Catholic Tradition* (Maryknoll, NY: Orbis, 2000).
29 Farley, 'Interpreting Situations', in *Practicing Gospel*, 38.

various items and events in this environment will be imbricated in power relations and will include more than Scripture, doctrine, and official religious items. It means that these items will 'gather' complexly as well as systematically, conflictually as often as harmoniously. Responses to that 'gathering' will be visceral and affective as well as cognitive, nonsymbolic as well as symbolic.[30]

How, then, do the authoritative texts and traditions of Christianity have a 'normative' effect in this mix that is situation? How might they further the vision of Good Samaritan to create a place for all 'to appear'? Such questions require an account of ends, their source, and form of mediation. Then we will see how these three come together in a way that respects the situational shape of human experience.

Pierre Bourdieu's notion of bodied *habitus* has been important to the postmodern concept of place as bodied ingression into world. But for thinking about normative evaluation, Alasdair MacIntyre provides a helpful supplement appropriate to the temporal and changing nature of place. Arguing that an intelligible action is defined by its comprehensibility in a story, MacIntyre privileges a genre that makes sense of the temporal change inherent in life by marking and connecting its various moments with regard to particular ends. As a part makes sense only in a larger whole, he says, individual actions can only be made intelligible in terms of larger contexts. My act makes sense in the larger story of my life, which is embedded in many larger stories. Its 'making sense' has to do with a notion of *ends*, which come from the stock of stories that constitute my life. To evaluate a life, then, requires connecting its chronological pieces through narrative and using the concept of the good to put a sort of moral trace on behavior.[31]

The *source* of the good, MacIntyre continues, is not simply an individual's history; this temporal tracing of what he calls 'character' evolves from *communal* wisdom. Just as a human life has unity

---

[30] Tilley recognizes these basic ingredients when he defines tradition as 'a nexus of vision (belief), attitude (dispositions, affections), and style (pattern of action) constituting complex practices'. Tilley refers to Connerton's work, but does not develop what I am going to discuss later as incorporative practices. Tilley, *Inventing Catholic Tradition*, 55, 86.

[31] Alasdair MacIntyre, *After Virtue: A Study in Moral Theory*, 2nd edn. (Notre Dame, IN: Notre Dame University Press, 1984), 204–25.

through story, tradition unifies a corporate life through stories as well. My story is embedded in a community's story, the history of stories that MacIntyre calls tradition. Not just any past, of course, but a communal past that is 'an historically extended, socially embodied argument, and an argument precisely in part about the goods which constitute that tradition'.[32] Such a tradition is a necessary source for the good and for media with which to assess the achievement of that good. Such a tradition and its stories, according to this view, would have been the source of ends with which to evaluate how Cortez's America continued to be faithful to its founder. It will be the source of ends with which to evaluate how Good Samaritan lives out its commitment to inclusion.

More explicit evaluation, however, requires attention to the *mediation* of ends, which are found according to MacIntyre in the *practices* of a tradition. His widely used definition of practice describes activities which can instantiate and extend the goods of a tradition. A practice is

any coherent and complex form of socially established cooperative human activity through which goods internal to that form of activity are realized in the course of trying to achieve those standards of excellence that are appropriate to, and partially definitive of, that form of activity, with the result that human powers to achieve excellence, and human conceptions of the ends and goods involved, are systematically extended.[33]

Not just anything can count as a practice; what raises an activity to the status of a practice is its intelligibility in the terms of a *communal narrative* tradition. Further, for MacInytre, practices involve the *participatory development of a good*. To do a practice well is to enhance one's capacities and to realize goods internal to the practice. In this way practices function to pass on the proper ends of a community—to tradition it—when they make sense in relation to the goods of that tradition. And when they do, practitioners' abilities to do that good are extended.

MacIntyre's terms are helpful for normatively interpreting Good Samaritan. With a notion of *ends*, the ordering of the complex

[32] Ibid. 222.

[33] MacIntyre's view also includes an account of virtues as the human qualities which 'enable us to achieve those goods which are internal to practices'. They contribute to the common good. Ibid. 187, 191.

circulation of meaning in a place such as Good Samaritan has more explicit focus, providing a way to evaluate what otherwise sounds like random discursive journeyings. We would expect that narratives of the Christian tradition, with its highly text- and Word-centered media for gospel, serve to direct the reflective ordering of Christian practices at this place of faith. Such biblical stories as Jesus's ministry to the outcast along with a host of related traditions will offer ends that help corroborate Good Samaritan's vision to welcome those who are different. MacIntyre's terms are also consonant with the change entailed in the production of place, both in the refusal to absolutize a practice—it must instantiate a good in order to qualify—and the insistence that its very performance involves change—by way of enhancement of capacities.

However, hermeneutical practices (such as Jesus stories) as the sole media for evaluating Good Samaritan are insufficient. If a considerable part of the problem is obliviousness and the communal end is creation of a shared world where all may appear, an account of tradition and practices must take seriously the full continuum of human experience, particularly the nondiscursive ordering that constitutes place. Resistance to and achievement of such ends as a shared world where all may appear connect to power, affectivity, and the body. Telling the morally relevant story may not be adequate to the enhancing and reforming of the 'sins' of obliviousness.

Take Daphne and other members of group homes at Good Samaritan who do not have language capacities. Daphne cannot tell stories, nor is her behavior likely to qualify for a 'coherent and complex form of socially established cooperative human activit[y]', as the definition of practice requires. Indeed, taking Daphne's practices seriously is not itself a long-practiced habit in the US; the 'tradition' regarding people with disabilities is filled with derisive designations, ranging from 'idiot' and 'imbecile' (two favorite medical terms prior to the nineteenth century), the turn-of-the-century worry in the US about 'the menace of the feebleminded', to more recent accounts that such people are harmless mental retards engaging in disruptive behavior.[34] The Christian tradition has generated much in the way

---

[34] See Peter L. Tyor and Leland V. Bell, *Caring for the Retarded in America: A History*, Contributions in Medical History 15 (Westport, CT: Greenwood, 1984), pp. 6, xiii.

of exclusionary and dehumanizing practices, as well, ranging from demonizing disability, identifying it with sin, to making it an object of pity or virtuous suffering.[35]

More recent study by educators, however, concludes that individuals with severe disabilities communicate (like infants) at the presymbolic (perlocutionary) level, that is, their communications have an effect on listeners. The illocutionary component of communication, its intended *purpose*, is discernible in human responses even when the agent has no language, particularly when the listener develops a *habitus* of careful and reciprocal attending to the agent.[36] In other words, even though she cannot talk, Daphne's squeals in the service are messages. She is communicating. To count her as a potential contributor to tradition, however, requires changes in the categories, including what counts as a practice.[37]

This is to say that tracing the faithfulness of Good Samaritan demands taking seriously more forms of ends-mediation (or practice) than typically come into view with linguistically defined accounts. In one sense that means an account of tradition that includes the *contributions* of bodies. However, written traditions are not only in need

---

[35] For a review of important recent literature, see Sharon V. Betcher, 'Rehabilitating Religious Discourse: Bringing Disability Studies to the Theological Venue', *Religious Studies Review*, 27/4 (Oct. 2001), 341–7.

[36] Adapting Austin and Searle's speech act theory, this 'pragmatics' theory of communication focuses on use rather than concern with language and stretches 'use' beyond the symbolic. A speech act has three components: 'a) the "perlocution," which is the effect of the message on the listener; b) the "illocution," which is the purpose of the message as planned or intended by the speaker, and c) the "locution," which is the referential meaning of the message and includes the proposition (new information or explicit content) and the presupposition (assumed information or implicit content) of the message'. Nonsymbolic acts communicate by including illocution and function, even when intention cannot be expressed in language. The importance of this shift is that crucial attending to persons without language led to the discovery of ways to elicit, understand, and develop such communication. Siegel and Wetherby, 'Enhancing Nonsymbolic Communication', 413–17.

[37] MacIntyre's definitions do not *explicitly* exclude agents without symbolic capacities. Her parents' interpretation could count as reasons for her squeals and enhancement of some excellence. He has no illusion that traditions are problem-free; that is why argument is necessary. John Horton and Susan Mendus (eds.), *After MacIntyre: Critical Perspectives on the Work of Alasdair MacIntyre* (Notre Dame, IN: Notre Dame University Press, 1994), 290. It is only in his later work that he recognizes the need to attend to persons with disabilities. Alasdair MacIntyre, *Dependent Rational Animals: Why Human Beings Need the Virtues*, The Paul Carus Lectures, 20 (Chicago: Open Court, 1999), 136–54.

of *supplementation* by interpreting bodily practices. A definition of tradition must itself reflect the wider character of communication. With this proviso I am arguing that the situation of Good Samaritan mandates an altered view of tradition. The judgment that people like Daphne are not insane or disruptive emerged as a challenge to centuries of tradition. And that challenge was provoked by a reading of the situation—'items' such as the nature of autism or Down syndrome, 'powers and events' such as who has the power to decide what is human and where to put resources—not simply as the faithful repetition and advancement of the ends of a tradition. While it is in some sense the ends of Christian tradition that open up the possibility of discerning its inadequacies, my point is that the very definition of faithfulness and tradition must include a way to think about continuity as more than the *repetition* of tradition.

In short, we need to know how to evaluate the community of Good Samaritan not only in terms of its ends, their source in the tradition, and their mediation through practices, but how this is all in response to the spectrum of 'items, power, and events' of the environment. For it is only in the reading of a situation that we have the full sense of what faithfulness might require, namely, a critical response to and correction of the given tradition.[38] We turn now to an account of tradition that takes seriously bodily contributions and to a final definitional element, the terms of responding to a situation, that is, *situational competence*.

TRADITION AS INSCRIPTION AND INCORPORATION

Bourdieu's enculturated *habitus* assumes that traditioning of participants in the community—for example, the habituations that gender,

---

[38] MacIntyre acknowledges this need for correction insofar as a tradition is a history of arguments. My point is that traditioning is more about bodily communications than he seems to allow, both the harmful incorporative practices like racialization and the creative kind like nonsymbolic communication. The capacity to argue (even shaped by the virtue of generosity) seems rather thin as a way to define normative control of a tradition. More promising are his recent gestures toward including people with disabilities as those we can learn from (especially about our vulnerability and dependence) and who need to be represented. And his call for developing the virtues of vulnerability. *Dependent*, 139, 141.

sexualize, and racialize subjects—does not happen in isolation from bodies. But I have said that an additional distinction is necessary to respect the contribution of the *habitus* as bodily. For all members of Good Samaritan to be considered practitioners, that is, potential contributors to and not simply passive objects of traditioning, bodily 'wisdom' is crucial to the concepts of practice and tradition. Bodily knowledges cannot be collapsed into explicitly held ends and commitments. While corporate memory is born in 'inscribed' or storable memory, which we know primarily as our written traditions, this memory is also born in 'incorporative' practices, where the messages are bodily performances.³⁹ To explore the implications of these more complex accounts of tradition, we move from Bourdieu's bodied *habitus* to Paul Connerton's additional twist on incorporative practices.

The familiar 'inscribed' form of tradition is illustrated by culture as it shapes the social world through memorized values and mores, or in the way Christian communities maintain a faithful identity by 'remembering Jesus'. But as Bourdieu argues, agents also bear culture (and faith) as 'socially informed bod[ies]'.⁴⁰ From the most naturalized conventions of how to walk properly for one's gender or class to the more explicit knowledges about how to play a sport well, internalized bodily wisdom accumulates from earliest childhood. By choosing the term *habitus* instead of habit, which connotes invariant behavior, Bourdieu describes a knowledge that is imprecise, yet effective and cumulative.⁴¹ As *corporeal knowledge, habitus* signals a range of understanding from the tacit to the explicit—'a knowledge and a remembering in the hands and in the body'.⁴²

Typical examples of this corporeal knowledge are explicitly learned skills, such as fencing or tennis. A *habitus* can also emerge from the requirements of polite conversation, such as skills of 'unceasing vigilance' for proper participation in the game, such as 'the art of playing

³⁹ These categories are Paul Connerton's, *How Societies Remember* (Cambridge: Cambridge University Press, 1989).

⁴⁰ See Craig Calhoun, '*Habitus*, Field, and Capital: The Question of Historical Specificity', in Craig J. Calhoun, Edward Lipuma, and Moishe Postone (eds.), *Bourdieu: Critical Perspectives* (Chicago: University of Chicago Press, 1983), 74.

⁴¹ See Claudia Strauss and Naomi Quinn, *A Cognitive Theory of Cultural Meaning* (Cambridge: Cambridge University Press, 1997), 44.

⁴² Connerton, *How Societies Remember*, 95.

on the equivocations, innuendoes and unspoken implications of gestural or verbal symbolism ... required, whenever the right object-ive distance is in question'.[43] Similarly a *habitus* can develop from the attentive presence of a parent or teacher to a child who lacks symbolic capabilities. The adult can strengthen a sensibility that becomes a *habitus* of 'being aware and receptive to the subtle cues' of the child, from her use of conventional movements, such as pointing, to her subtle facial expressions. Developing such a disposition includes reflective reasoning, but is fundamentally a bodily skill as well, enabling the parent—and in response, the child—to know when to wait, when to augment, when to intervene, and thereby to solicit new communication.[44]

Another 'bodily wisdom' relevant to Good Samaritan is found in survival traditions. The hegemonic power relation between the white owner class and the black bodies of slaves required the development of certain bodily habituations for slaves. Postures of submission—from bowed heads, shuffling gaits, and other attempts at invisibility—were widely shared incorporative practices of a population whose survival and well-being depended upon their being perceived as docile and obedient. Writing on a variety of black nonverbal communication patterns, Kenneth Johnson notes that 'not to look white males in the eye was really a survival pattern in the South'.[45]

Racialized incorporative practices are not merely history, of course. African American writer Toi Derricotte invokes such bodily know-ledge when she describes an immediate awareness as she wanders the all-white streets of a new town—'*I'm not supposed to be here*'.[46]

---

[43] Pierre Bourdieu, *The Logic of Practice*, trans. Richard Nice (Stanford, CA: Stanford University Press, 1980), 80–1.

[44] Siegal and Wetherby, 'Enhancing Nonsymbolic Communication', 437, 43 ff., 441.

[45] Kenneth R. Johnson, 'Black Kinesics: Some Non-Verbal Communication Patterns in the Black Culture', in Ronald L. Jackson II (ed.), *African American Communication and Identities: Essential Readings* (Thousand Oaks, CA: Sage, 2004), 41. Johnson identifies a host of other forms of nonverbal communication that would seem to qualify as incorporative practices. The bodily practices characteristic of traditional African American worship are some of many good examples.

[46] Derricotte also charts the experience of being a light-skinned African American and the constant fear of not being a 'real' black person. Toi Derricotte, *The Black Notebooks: An Interior Journey* (New York: W. W. Norton, 1997), 33, 18.

Modern racialized incorporative practices constitute the maneuvering knowledge to survive in a racist society, requiring 'knowledge of language, norms, customs and rules, and knowledge to use the means and resources that make living possible (or successful) in a given environment' as it is determined by the matrix of social relations of race, class, ethnicity, and gender.[47]

Maneuvering knowledges also develop in response to rituals of degradation, which are performed regularly on persons with disabilities. Interpersonal distancing, averting of the eyes, and patronizing speech are only a few examples of the many forms of social rejection enacted by so-called normal-bodied persons when in the presence of those with disabilities.[48] Stigmatized persons can respond in a variety of ways, from postures of defensive cowering to those of hyper-performance—the feeling of being 'on'.[49]

These examples suggest that, whether born of self-preservation, privilege, or the creative impulses of pleasure, a bodily *habitus* has an ongoing regularity. It is also inherently flexible, reflecting the changing texture of lived experience itself.[50] Derricotte's everyday knowledge about the safe way to be in a predominantly white world—learned over time, 'in the bones'—is capable of display in different situations. Such flexibility displays respect for the changing and complex character of human existence and suggests something key to this kind of 'wisdom'. The conditions that enable a successful practice, says Bourdieu, must be made a part of its definition.[51] Thus it is competence that matters—not simply of an abstract sort,

---

[47] Philomena Essed, *Understanding Everyday Racism: An Interdisciplinary Theory* (London: Sage, 1991), 48–9.

[48] Lerita M. Coleman, 'Stigma: An Enigma Demystified', in Lennard J. Davis (ed.), *The Disability Studies Reader* (New York: Routledge, 1997), 224. Erving Goffman, 'Selections from *Stigma*', in *The Disability Studies Reader*, 203–15.

[49] Goffman, 'Selections from *Stigma*', 203–15.

[50] While 'rules' might be developed to describe the character of good practice, as Bourdieu points out, this is after-the-fact, secondary reflection, not constitutive of *habitus* itself. It abstracts from and invites the overlooking of that crucial incorporate aspect of social identity. *Outline*, 22–30. Charles Taylor, 'To Follow a Rule', in Calhoun et al. (eds.), *Bourdieu*, 45–60.

[51] Pierre Bourdieu, *Language and Symbolic Power*, ed. and introd. John B. Thompson, trans. Gino Raymond and Matthew Adamson (Cambridge, MA: Harvard University Press, 1991), 37–65.

but the competence to communicate or respond *to a situation.*[52] While refering specifically to language exchange, Bourdieu's point has wider application. From playing a sport to a *habitus* for racial justice, competence for responding to a situation is inherent in distinguishing a successful *habitus.* Just as books about boxing are not enough to make a good boxer, a *habitus* of justice is not adequately defined by knowledge of principles (or stories) of love, or of what the church or even Jesus have said in the past. Any such *habitus* requires a feel for and grasp of the 'items, events, and power' of an environment and how they 'gather', to use the earlier language of situation; *situational competence* is fundamental to the successful continuity of a practice.

A final move extends Bourdieu's notion of the *habitus* as bodily wisdom to its relevance for tradition. The true significance of such wisdoms are seen in their role as incorporative practices that mediate communal identity. This is to say that practices of inscription, or the sedimented meanings of a community's tradition, are not the only sources of identity. Certain long-established bodily *habitus* merit the status of tradition as well, argues Paul Connerton. The distinction goes beyond Bourdieu's, for 'incorporative' practices *convey their own meaning in the performance;* contemporary bodily activity is itself the communication. As Connerton says, 'The transmission occur[s] only during the time that . . . bodies are present to sustain that particular activity.'[53] Not an ideational model of agency whereby bodies are simply *expressing* or *enacting* the values of a community in a second-ary way, the concept of *habitus,* as one scholar puts it, assumes a notion of the 'body as an assemblage of embodied aptitudes, not as a medium of symbolic meanings'.[54] As an incorporative practice,

---

[52] Practical theologian Charles R. Foster speaks of 'communicative competence' in his *Embracing Diversity: Leadership in Multicultural Congregations* (Bethesda, MD: Alban Institute, 1997), 79.

[53] Connerton, *How Societies Remember,* 72. This point is made more explictly by Connerton than Bourdieu.

[54] This view of body as medium of symbols, in contrast, relies upon what Connerton calls inscription practices and simply means that bodily practices pass on written or otherwise saved or stored meaning. This would seem to be all that MacIntyre suggests. Talal Asad, *Genealogies of Religion: Discipline and Reasons of Power in Christianity and Islam* (Baltimore: Johns Hopkins University Press, 1993), 75.

it is an active, presentist communication through bodies, both as the sending and receipt of messages.[55]

If the continuity of practices and, thus, of a tradition, requires enculturated bodily habituation with its learned everyday wisdoms and their entailed competence for ever-changing situations, what might be said about normative theological judgments at this point? Of course, traditioning cannot happen without practices of inscription. Stories and other verbal articulations of ends and vision are essential to the identity of a community. The point here, however, is that the wisdom suggested by the *habitus* requires a shift away from a rule- or content-driven model for normative thinking about traditioning.[56] The kind of 'knowledge' at stake here combines flexibility with identity in a way best described as *improvisational*. As Bourdieu puts it, the *habitus* entails the ability to do a thing in a new way in a new situation, that is, 'regulated improvisation'.[57] Whether it is in public speaking, the continual creation of ever more well-developed sentences—as we see in the capacity to preach extemporaneously— or the long-developed racialized incorporative strategies where reading the situation is essential to survival, neither wisdom can be assessed by a continued reproduction of the same thing. Not only is improvisation a fluid way to think about continuity, it is also dependent upon the bodily character of practice as well.

In sum, the 'understanding' of *habitus* is, first, a *competence*, one that is productive and creative. Importantly, the social and bodily character of this competence gives it a particular character, distinguishing it from certain kinds of abstract productivities. It is, as Essed says, an 'everyday' knowledge.[58] It will draw from inscribed traditions, from ends and visions available, but it may outrun them and

---

[55] Connerton, *How Societies Remember*, 73. The contrast entailed in the distinction begun with the notion of inscribing practices is not between signifying and prelinguistic bodies, but between practices in which this storage is the primary way to pass on the communal memory and practices that focus primarily upon the passing on that occurs in face-to-face bodied encounters (which itself can include inscripted communication)–incorporative practices.

[56] There is, as Tilley puts it, a 'priority of practice over rules' or any other kind of belief or content. Tilley, *Inventing Catholic Tradition*, 107.

[57] Bourdieu, *Language*, 78.

[58] Essed's work defines 'everyday' knowledge as structured and therefore identifiable, *Understanding Everyday Racism*.

reconfigure them. Second, its wisdom is a capacity to respond improvisationally to a *situation*; it is competence to do or say something well *for a circumstance*.[59] Third, while shaped by inscribing practices of a culture, *habitus* as incorporative practice is a distinctively presentist and performed bodily way of communicating meaning as well.

COMPLICATING THE NORMATIVE: ASSESSING FAITHFUL PRACTICES

This broader understanding of practice has implications for how to make normative judgments about the practices that make Good Samaritan a *faithful* place. First, it suggests more complex reasons for an already familiar truism, that is, that candidates for faithful practices will not be confined to cognitive activities. Faithfulness is not displayed simply in what Christians believe. Something more affectively and situationally rich and embodied will be involved. That 'something more' is not just the claim that theological judgments need pay attention to lived faith as well as belief. It has to do with a more complex relation between the two.

The faithfulness of a *habitus* will not be evaluated in terms of its success at a mental search for the correct Christian teaching or doctrine to 'apply' to or direct a situation. Nor does the model that Christian practices must be 'grounded' on 'adequate beliefs' prove sufficient to the dynamic and experiential nature of faithfulness and the necessarily changing character of the discourse that qualifies as 'belief' or inscribed tradition. Bourdieu's *habitus* entails a level of wisdom that cannot be reduced to such second-order reflection and precludes prescribed, fixed forms of normative discourse.[60] It

---

[59] This argument is developed in the context of a criticism of both Saussure and Chomsky. See Bourdieu, *Language*, 32–3, 43–4, 54–5.

[60] Mark Taylor, 'Subalternity and Advocacy as *Kairos* for Theology', in Joerg Rieger (ed.), *Postmodernity and Liberation in Christian Theology* (Oxford: Oxford University Press, 2003), 50: 'To know how to type is neither to know the place of each letter among the keys, nor to have acquired a conditioned reflex for each letter, which is set in motion by each letter as it comes before the eye. We know where the letters are on

provides a way to think constructively about continuity in the role of bodied traditioning, which leads to recognition of the distinctive communicative force of bodies.

Thus, the second implication of this broader account of practice is that the body, too, is an essential condition of competence. Specifically, the continuity or identity of a practice depends upon the degree to which bodily messages are part of and congruent with the ends of a practice.[61] That bodies matter in a practice may seem obvious in the example of racialized bodily messages picked up by Derricotte on her walk. However, this factor also means that competence in communicating gospel cannot be evaluated simply by attention to the verbal message. 'Jesus loves everyone', for example, will not be a successful communication of welcome in a situation characterized by inherited, racialized visceral reactions without attention to the bodily messages that will inevitably accompany it.

Because practice refers to bodily as well as cognitive shaping, habituation into Christian faith is always accompanied by bodily habituations, from the proprieties of 'proper' body movement in a culture to its techniques and rituals. Bodily memory is not simply a potentially positive improvisatory skill; as noted it may also produce messages at odds with good intentions. However, it is an inevitable factor in traditioning. Whatever form of gospel one learns, racialized incorporative practices will accompany it, whether for Christians habituated as 'whites' or those habituated as 'blacks'. Everyday knowledge, the wisdom to maneuver, is racialized. In the case of Good Samaritans, as we will see, people 'of color' from outside the US will

---

the typewriter as we know where one of our limbs is. We remember this thru knowledge bred of familiarity in our lived space. The movement of the typist's fingers may be describable; yet it's not present to the typist as a trajectory through space that can be described, but as a certain adjustment of the typist's mobility.' Connerton, *How Societies Remember*, 95: 'Here a meaningful practice does not coincide with a sign; meaning cannot be reduced to a sign which exists on a separate "level" outside the immediate sphere of the body's acts.'

[61] I am extending Bourdieu's focus on language to the fuller sense of communication implicit in his notion of *habitus*. While designed at one level to recover local dialects, Bourdieu's critique requires that language be understood as a *sub-set of the dispositions* which make up a *habitus*. Insofar as practice is inevitably a communication, like good speaking it cannot be conceived as a message that is communicated by the proper execution of a grammatical system.

be racially habituated in very different ways from African Americans. Whites will have been habituated into illusory proprieties that, being 'without race', they are simply human beings.[62] All of these racialized habituations will be gendered as well. Many of the participants, black and white, will have been habituated into bodily proprieties, every-day knowledges, around 'normal-bodiedness'. They will, in other words, most likely participate, however unconsciously, in aversive postures toward people with disabilities.

The third implication of an account of practice along the lines of Bourdieu and Connerton concerns the definition and functioning of Christian tradition in theological assessments of Good Samaritan's practices. The vision or *telos* of the community, the creation of a place for all to appear, will be rooted in an inscribed tradition—the authoritative written and stored memories of Christian communities that are found in Scripture, catholic creeds, and denominational commitments. But Connerton's point is that tradition—social memory—is not just comprised of these practices of inscription, but of distinctive bodily practices as well.

Now it is premature to say that Christian faith itself has any explicitly normative incorporative practices (although kneeling and bowed heads are certainly important incorporative practices of humility), but the traditioning of any Christian through Scripture and other normative texts will always converge with existent incorporative practices. Thus to determine what counts as complex enough to be a practice will require attention to the ceaseless interplay between the messages of bodies and the messages of explicit discourse. And this interplay is as necessary a 'text' for theological reading as any attention to circulation of biblical themes. Hence, the vision of the good that comes from inscribed tradition and its terms of evaluation must be broader than explicitly theological terms or the 'fit' between systematic beliefs.

To assess 'remembering Jesus' in this newly expanded sense will mean that practices with no traditional Christian markers may very well be exemplary displays of the *telos* of the community. For example, certain kinds of 'nontraditional' practices with participants from the group homes will prove crucial to fulfilling the end of Good

---

[62] Thus other particularities, like gender for women, can become totally defining.

Samaritan, namely, the creation of a place for all to appear and be seen. Insofar as competence for a situation is sometimes a crucial source of criticism of the received tradition, our evaluation of Good Samaritan may well unearth practices that have not previously counted in the normative Christian tradition.

Finally, it is important to recognize that practices, both incorporative and inscribed, allow for the enhancement of capacities when they advance the end of the community. MacIntyre would describe this as the instantiation of ends and the resulting extension of excellences and capacities through faithful enactment of the pertinent virtues. Bourdieu calls it a skill of improvisation that improves with use. While not exactly the same thing, they suggest a social source—traditions are internalized and intersect with bodily wisdom—that is in dialectical relation to subjects' contributions, contributions from a context that may itself enhance or alter what counts as tradition. The ongoing endurance or temporal identity of Good Samaritan as place, then, is a function of its practices. The ongoing faithfulness of those practices has to do not only with the complex criteria attending bodily and inscribed social memory, but with the enhancement of relevant capacities as well.

The purpose of this chapter has been to move closer to a model for framing faith that can do justice to the complexities of a worldly church, complexities symbolized in the deceptively simple claim that being Christian is an identity that suffices for color-blindness. I have argued that such a model is found by conceiving of faith as a place-world. Postmodern place frames contemporary situation in a way that brings a number of the complexities of bodied, visceral, local, and global environment into view. Despite the fact that theologies have always acknowledged the stuff of place insofar as they understand that every discourse of faith must come to rest ultimately in a *context*, my argument is that adequacy to the worldliness of faith requires that this texture be articulated in the determining of continuities and not relegated to the (secondary) context. The frame of place has served to highlight that shifting, fluid, and affective shape of a Christian community, which will help in making sense of it as a lived world that produces both forms of obliviousness and possibilities for appearing, the double meaning of 'not seeing color'.

Framing complexity, of course, brings with it new difficulties for theological judgments. Place as constitutive of and constituted by deeply internalized social and cultural discourse means that there is more to track than simply the traditional media of biblical narrative, sacramental activity, and doctrinal beliefs. This chapter has provided a way to *theorize* the complexity of Good Samaritan as place. My next task is to *display* Good Samaritan as place, the subject of Part II.

In the next chapter, we turn to the *formation practices*, that is, the activities that brought Good Samaritan into being, namely, the practice of starting and defining a new church, or, more accurately, revitalizing and redefining a dying community. For a sense of that defining vision, we must now 'place' Good Samaritan.

Part II

The Practices that Make Place

3

Placing Good Samaritan: Formation Practices

It is a living metaphor of the reign of God extant. At any given time, you can find black and white, men and women, living, sleeping, eating, worshipping together.... The special needs community at Good Samaritan makes churches which are full of the homogeneous crowds of 'normal' people look like spiritual dwarfs, if you ask me. For me they are a powerful word of judgment against a divided church.

Gerald, successor to Dan Weaver as pastor of Good Samaritan

one of the best kept secrets in the United Methodist church . . . a model church that reminds us of what we should be.

United Methodist District Superintendent, 1997

That's just the way it was then [on Durham's history of segregation].

Ivy Reese, Good Samaritan parishioner

Successful evangelism to a eunuch. Now there's a founding vision. According to Pastor Dan Weaver, it all began with a hermeneutical insight. In July of 1988, a group of ten people met in the Weavers' living room for Bible study. The passage for the evening was from Acts, a book about the emergence of the early Christian community under conditions of persecution. Feeling rather marginal themselves, this group of ten was the remnant of a dying white church in a medium-size southern city. Pastor Weaver directed their attention to chapter 8, which told of the scattering of the disciples into the world to preach. What caught the group's imagination, however, was an encounter of the disciple Philip with an Ethiopian eunuch.

Directed by the Holy Spirit to approach the eunuch as he traveled toward Samaria, the text reports that Philip shared the good news of Jesus and baptized the eunuch, who 'went on his way rejoicing'.

The small group of struggling southern Christians heard the biblical story as an invitation to go and do likewise. Not to search for castrated men from Africa, of course, although their obliviousness to the problematic connotations of the image cannot go unremarked. Nor were they especially interested in baptizing strangers or saving souls. What church members began to plot was evangelism with a difference. God was calling this failed white congregation, or so they thought, to 'go and find people like the Ethiopian eunuch'—'people who aren't like us', in the vernacular of east Durham. Taking 'Ethiopian eunuch' to mean people of different races, different nationalities, and physical abilities, this remnant group went on a mission. And in what followed, all sorts of people 'not like us' were 'found' and, for a while at least, accounted for traces of redemption at the place called Good Samaritan United Methodist Church.

In this chapter we will look at the events that brought the community of Good Samaritan into being. Of particular interest are the *formation practices*, of which the opening story is a significant piece. Who did the community understand itself to be? What did it understand itself to be called to do? As activities of self-definition, formation practices create signs that can coalesce into a claimed identity. And since identity always undergoes renegotiation, there will be no absolute boundary between formation practices and those practices that sustain the community—between the origin and dispersal of an identity. Even so, there are clear early articulations of Good Samaritan's self-understanding, and it is to the emergence of that vision that I now turn.

First, preliminary placement of Good Samaritan.

A PLACE CALLED DURHAM

An account of the emergence of the place called Durham, North Carolina, would be misleading if told as the sudden appearance of a village called Durham Station, as it was called earlier. 'Discovery' stories or those that imply the construction of a town on empty space simply echo a colonialist logic incapable of acknowledging what is already there. As any good history would show, it is better to describe a place as the gradual shifting of boundaries instigated by the introduction of new practices. Like a palimpsest, Durham has the past 'scrawled upon it' in a variety of ways. Like those scrawlings, as a kind of deep subconscious, that past is not consistently visible. Partially erased, it exists in various modes of accessibility. Innumerable precedents haunt the place that is present-day Durham. What will matter, of course, are those residuals that leave lasting marks, however faint, on its contemporary shape.

Good Samaritan UMC came into being in a southern city in North Carolina, located in the southern section of Durham County, itself almost 300 square miles of varied terrain 200 miles from the Atlantic coast. Durham became an incorporated city in the state of North Carolina in the US in the nineteenth century. Lying on a ridge running through a Triassic basin formed almost 400 million years ago, its land modulates from higher, hilly elevation in the north and northwestern areas of town to a lower sandy and marshy area in the south. The social-archeological past of the area includes Native American places (Ahkontshuck, Akenatzy, Oenocks, Enoes, and Tuscarora tribes among others) that are still evident in Native American burial grounds.[1]

If the presence of Native Americans in the area was mostly erased in the period of European conquest, in this ancient history there were some (admittedly minor) alternatives to the racisms still to come. A local historian describes a period somewhere between 1600 and 1750, when the newly arrived Europeans lived in a 'libertarian, live-and-let-live society', a compromise between Native American and African American cultures. This included a kind of egalitarian social interaction that elicited the strong disapproval of a nearby Virginia governor.[2] Indeed, in early colonial America race was less a factor

---

[1] For 'residual', see Raymond Williams, *Marxism and Literature* (Oxford: Oxford University Press, 1977), 121–7. My account of residuals in NC will focus primarily on race relations. I have not found adequate information on the history of treatment of persons with disabilities.

[2] See Jim Wise, *Durham: A Bull City Story*, The Making of America Series (Charleston, SC: Arcadia Publishing, 2002), 17–18.

in the indentured servant class, where an intermingling of races included interracial marriage and integration in some churches.[3]

While these social tolerations lie at best in some deep subconscious of the place that would someday be North Carolina, more accessible to Methodist memory is the most important early North American Methodist missionary, Francis Asbury, who helped plant the Methodist church in the area. Asbury's denomination formally adopted John Wesley's 1743 official declaration against slavery. In the face of deepening racism in the 1700s, Methodist church revivals sometimes had the effect of bringing African Americans and whites together in worship.[4] These and other such hints of an alternative social imagination find symbolic if not direct descendents in later formations such as Good Samaritan, even as much that is contradictory will succeed them.

Residuals with even more conscious impact on modern-day Durham come from its recent history of race relations. Durham has not been just any southern city when it comes to race relations, or so Durham would like to think. Though policed and segregated, African American agency and creativity have been crucial to the formation of the place. Tobacco was a major source of wealth and industry for key white families and their inheritors, as well as a resource for a major southern university. However, it was Stephen, an African American blacksmith, who in 1839 invented one of the most lucrative curing processes for brightleaf tobacco. A slave on a Caswell County, NC, plantation, Stephen created what was to become a multi-million-dollar commodity out of brightleaf. A business with more immediate capital for African Americans was also the invention of a (former) slave. In 1898, John Merrick founded North Carolina Mutual Insurance Company, which was to become the largest African American company in the US. Under the later governance of Charles Clinton Spaulding, NC Mutual carved out a successful financial and social space that made it possible

---

[3] Curtiss Paul DeYoung, Michael O. Emerson, George Yancey, and Karen Chai Kim, *United by Faith: The Multiracial Congregation as an Answer to the Problem of Race* (New York: Oxford University Press, 2003), 43 ff. Also Lerone Bennett, Jr, *Before the Mayflower: A History of Black America*, 6th rev. edn. (New York: Penguin Books, 1962, 1993).

[4] Bennett, *Before the Mayflower*, 46 ff.

for other black businesses, typically doomed in the world of white-controlled capitalism, to begin to flourish.

NC Mutual also spawned a network of support and inspiration for the African American population in general that went far beyond the contributions of even the most community-friendly business. Across the tracks from Durham's white community was a thriving, self-supporting 'Colored Community', called Hayti. Its name was supposedly a corruption of 'Haiti', the country noted for its African slave revolution against the French colonialists. Indeed, the name was used by a number of African American communities during Reconstruction. Dating from what became 1880s business successes, this 'town within a town', as Dorothy Phelps Jones describes it, provided the place for Durham blacks to create their own culture, businesses, churches, and social life. Hayti became known as the 'Capital of the black Middle Class'.[5] Although all entrepreneurial success was not literally confined to this community, Hayti sponsored permanent and productive alliances long past its physical existence, which ended with 1970s urban renewal.

It is not just African American agency and creativity that makes Durham distinctive, since, whether acknowledged or not, such agency would be extant in any southern town. What set this town apart was the *reputation* it got for being progressive on race issues, at least for the South. Indeed, there was enough real success among blacks that the town became particularly renowned among southern blacks. Booker T. Washington and W. E. B. Du Bois visited the African American community of Hayti and agreed upon how remarkably race-hospitable Durham was.[6] Prominent southern newspapers, black and white, reported on the positive race climate, as illustrated by this praise from *The Atlanta Independent* in 1921: 'There is more grace, grit, and greenback among the Negroes in Durham and more harmony between the races than in any city in

---

[5] The gendered extension of this ethos, Jones relates, is seen in stories of the many black Durham women who defied the convention that 'women's place is in the home'. Dorothy Phelps Jones, *The End of an Era* (Durham, NC: Brown Enterprises, 2001), 58–67. See 'Symbols of Hayti's Grand Past Re-Emerge', *Durham Herald-Sun* (4 Nov. 2001).

[6] Reported by Osha Gray Davidson, *The Best of Enemies: Race and Redemption in the New South* (New York: Scribner, 1996), 23 ff.

America.' Durham was long known nationally and internationally as 'the Jewel of the New South' and the 'Black Middle-Class Capital of the South'.[7]

But to place Durham with residuals of southern white racism and African American agency and heroism is still too simple. It would be better to say that these and other events too extensive to include here linger, making up a social reality threaded with ambiguity. Take black civil rights activism. As early as 1942 southern black leaders gathered in Durham to make a public declaration for full equality. A 1957 sit-in led by local Methodist minister Douglas E. Moore at Durham's Royal Ice Cream Company happened three years before the more famous Greensboro lunch counter sit-in.[8] And the agency and activism of black activists would continue throughout the decades as the realities of racism continued to evade resolution. Durham's proud heritage of black financial success was coupled with a history of standing for justice.

The activism of Pastor Moore and others such as lawyer Floyd McKissick and newspaperman Louis Austin looked a bit different from the perspective of some of the elite African Americans, however. Purportedly their success in Durham put them in a relation with white power brokers that would be threatened by some of the black activist movement. The stability of this 'Black Middle-Class Capital', the future of black business interests, and political influence with the white elite would be at great risk when the fate and interests of the poorest blacks were made part of the civil rights vision. Some charge that the black elite contributed to the slow-down of desegregation, choosing to allow the processes of circumvention that delayed it until the 1970s.[9] The place where desegregation would seem most likely to

---

[7] See William H. Chafe, *Civilities and Civil Rights: Greensboro, North Carolina, and the Black Struggle for Freedom* (New York: Oxford University Press, 1981, repr.).

[8] The minister who initiated the sit-in, Douglas E. Moore, pastored Asbury Temple Methodist Church, the church with which Good Samaritan was finally combined in 2000. Moore represented the more 'radical' of the black pastors. See Davidson, *Best of Enemies*, 87–94.

[9] This general assessment is founded on more specific accounts. See Davidson, *Best of Enemies*, esp. 71–110. Also two Duke University honors theses: Chris D. Howard, 'Keep Your Eyes on the Prize: The Black Struggle for Civic Equality in Durham, N.C., 1954–1963', Duke University dept. of history, 1983; Devon Amanda O'Rorke-Wieneke, 'Mobilizing the Myth of Immoral Black Motherhood: How

happen with reasonable dispatch turned out to be a place where white racism and its quite explicit self-interest was aided by elite black self-interest.

The realities of oppression and liberation were connected in a messy way. The story of racist white Durham is threaded not only with the exploits of the Klu Klux Klan but with white apathy. Realities of class and gender oppression left working-class white women and men misdirecting their resentment and hatred at working-class African Americans.[10] If 'man' was a false universal that rendered white women invisible, 'African American' could function similarly for black women. The more connections that are made, the more ambiguity comes into view, the more inherited conditions for aversion and obliviousness.

Of course, recognition of multiple levels of complicity and agency does not level the playing field. The traces of countercultural behavior in the long-ago past of North Carolina were overridden by those with more power. The more recent agency and public status achieved by black elites were gained by hard work and sacrifice in a racist society, making white activism look easy by comparison. Complicity was not equally shared.[11] Similar dynamics work in groups disadvantaged by class. Unskilled white workers in east Durham continued to see blacks as an ever-present economic threat. As one commentator put it, 'Any setback, disappointment, or reversal was easily and perfunctorily blamed on those dark-skinned residents living just beyond the railroad tracks.'[12]

As true as it is that ambiguity threads all stories of villains and victims, the legacies that make up Durham are marked by profound imbalances of power, whether due to the invisible privilege of

Southern Segregationists Prevented School Desegregation, 1954–1970', Duke University Program II, 2001.

[10] Davidson says, 'The Big Men of Durham learned an important lesson from the Populist affair: the best way to preserve the status quo was to keep blacks and whites fighting each other. It was clear that if workers of the two races ever united they could challenge the industrialists' rule.' Davidson, *Best of Enemies*, 67.

[11] As bell hooks says, 'The prejudicial feelings some blacks may express about whites are in no way linked to a system of domination that affords us any power to coercively control the lives and well-being of white folks.' hooks, *Black Looks: Race and Representation* (Boston: South End, 1992), 15.

[12] Davidson, *Best of Enemies*, 68.

whiteness or the more complex convergences of race with gender, class, and sexuality. And like the history of its regional surroundings, Good Samaritan will inherit, however indirectly, a social ethos characterized by both this ambiguity and (always) by this imbalance.

Good Samaritan UMC thus came into being in a complicated environment with quite divergent impulses rooted in historical residuals that would continue to shape its present—a town with deeply embedded habits of racial separation in its history, faint traces of social alternatives from long ago, a public tradition of black success, and class and gender lines that have only begun to be factored into the picture. The church's story will need to be told so as to reflect these ambiguities and power imbalances of social reality.

GOOD SAMARITAN EMERGES

The more immediate dynamics of the church's formation are seen in the legacies of contemporary United Methodism and the immediate precursor to Good Samaritan, an all-white Methodist church called Wellspring UMC. United Methodists have long been one of the mainline Christian denominations in the US. With about 8.5 million members in the US (and 1.5 million outside of the US), they constitute the third largest church following Roman Catholics and Southern Baptists. Rooted in the Methodist and Wesleyan traditions of John and Charles Wesley's renewal of the Church of England in the mid-eighteenth century, North American Methodism was originally a lay-led movement that spread with great success 'to reform the nation, particularly the church, and to spread scriptural holiness over the land'.[13] While most growth today is to be found in Africa and the Philippines, contemporary churches in the US are predominantly white, with only 6 per cent nonwhite members (more about that shortly). Most United Methodist churches, like Good Samaritan, are small congregations.

---

[13] *The Book of Discipline of the United Methodist Church* (Nashville: United Methodist Publishing House, 1996), 60, p. 43.

They tend to occupy the middle: middle and lower middle class, middle-range social views. More pious than most Protestants, but less so than evangelicals, Methodists are also in the middle of the Protestant mainline and the larger society on religious commitment.[14]

Wellspring UMC, the congregation that immediately preceded Good Samaritan, was typically Methodist. Started in 1957 in east Durham, Wellspring was part of a larger growth plan engineered by the Conference bishop. It was a successful plan: Wellspring was one of some ninety-four churches that sprang up in the conference over the next couple of decades. Located in a part of the city inhabited by a lower socioeconomic population, the congregation was one of predominantly small to moderate all-white churches that characterize the denomination, and it mirrored much of white east Durham. In the midst of this moderately depressed part of town it managed to remain successful for almost thirty years.

Looking back, one of the members speaks fondly of Wellspring. It was the church where Mrs Ivy Reese raised her children. Now a grandmother in her seventies, she speaks of how central the church was in the life of her extended family—her parents were charter members when they moved to Durham from Salisbury. She remembers Wellspring members meeting in the basement of her home before the growing congregation was finally able to build a beautiful and spacious sanctuary with space for three Sunday school rooms. It was a church made up of largely middle-and working-class white families, which, back in the 1970s and 1980s, meant incomes in the upper teens and lower twenties.[15]

As well as Wellspring did, this area of Durham became increasingly racially mixed over the next few decades. The predominantly white residents moved farther and farther out as the African American population grew in east Durham. With white flight, an aging

[14] See John C. Green and James L. Guth, 'United Methodists and American Culture: A Statistical Portrait', in William B. Laurence, Dennis M. Campbell, and Russell E. Richey (eds.), *The People(s) Called Methodist: Forms and Reforms of Their Life, United Methodism and American Culture*, ii (Nashville: Abingdon, 1998), 27–52.

[15] Conversations with Dr Stephen Compton, Office of Congregational Development, North Carolina Conference, on the demographics of closing down Wellspring UMC and starting Good Shepherd.

membership, and racial transition in its surrounding neighborhoods, the congregation of Wellspring shrank. The church's continued failure to reflect the racial diversity of its surroundings did nothing to halt its shrinking rolls. In this it followed the larger denomination, which was 94 per cent white in this period.[16] The mid-1980s found Wellspring in its last days. Things had changed from the old days, reports one of the elderly members, when the church had lots of young people. It got so that 'after kids left for school they didn't come back', she said. By 1987 worship attendance was down from a peak of one hundred and thirty or so members to about ten.

Despite this ecclesial downturn, the Office of the United Methodist Conference had hopes for a rebirth. The 1980s had brought an increase in job opportunities in the nearby Research Triangle area, which meant an emergent new suburban middle-class white population was to be found at the outer edge of the east Durham area. Through feasibility studies, the Office judged that this group of computer, research, and science professionals might be included with the primary target, the working-class whites in the area.[17] There was, they hoped, the potential for a resurrection of Wellspring United Methodist. All they needed was a new minister with a great deal of energy and commitment. When the conference decided to sell the building in 1986, Dan Weaver was charged with developing a new church in east Durham out of the small group of faithful who remained.

INTERPRETING THE EUNUCH

Reading the life cycles of cities, however, is only relevant up to a point when a vision appears. The white-bread successor to Wellspring United Methodist was not to be, for Dan Weaver saw something else in that multiracial area, something that feasibility studies simply could not predict. Under his leadership the small group that still called itself a Methodist church decided that their very make-up

---

[16]   I am drawing on information from the period of the 1980s. See Green and Guth, 'United Methodists', 29, 35.

[17]   Ibid.

would contradict the sociological truisms behind feasibility.[18] They would be defined by difference and not homogeneity. With the story of the eunuch, the remnant of Wellspring UMC got a new founding biblical narrative.

In the fall of 1988 former members of Wellspring began meeting regularly for worship in a local elementary school building, and the deliberations continued. What would it mean to find people like Ethiopian eunuchs in Durham? 'What it would take to *do* that and not just say it?' These were the questions they asked themselves, remembers Dan of those first meetings. The eunuch became a symbol to them for those 'people who are different from us, people who usually are looked over and passed over, that regular established church folks would pass on the street' and never think of in relation to their church.

But what a strange founding story. The dictionary defines a eunuch as 'a castrated man in charge of an Oriental harem or employed as a chamberlain or high officer by an Oriental potentate' (*Webster's New World Dictionary*). For Dan and his small congregation the term took on a life of its own, a life that proved ultimately creative. The Ethiopian, as some authors explain the New Testament passage, 'symbolized how far the church would expand its reach beyond Jerusalem'.[19] We might call Dan's an interpretive 'catachresis'—a resignification that indicates how a biblical story gains new meaning through a performative excess of meaning.[20] However, this image also bore with it the very marks of racialization and unacknowledged power, as will be seen, marks that would haunt the developing community itself.

The resources for imagining and forming such a community were complex. Dan reports that the name, Good Samaritan, was chosen a

[18] One of these truisms is that people want to be with people who are most like them. See Michael O. Emerson and Christian Smith, *Divided by Faith: Evangelical Religion and the Problem of Race in America* (New York: Oxford University Press, 2000), ch. 7.

[19] A recent book on multiracial congregations includes this story in its chapter on 'Biblical Antecedents for Multiracial Congregations', but identifies the Ethiopian as 'the Ethiopian finance minister from Queen Candace's Nubian Empire'. DeYoung et al., *United by Faith*, 24–5.

[20] Jose Medina, 'Identity Trouble: Disidentification and the Problem of Difference', *Philosophy and Social Criticism*, 29/6 (2003), 655–80.

year later to proclaim the founding identity. 'God is calling us to be like the good Samaritan,' he says, 'to go out and find the lost by the side of the road—not just lost spiritually, but kind of lost in the crowd, in the shuffle...those not usually reached out to.' This creative exegesis matched well with the church's location, which was ripe with 'those who are not like us'. The area around what was to become Good Samaritan United Methodist Church was fairly well integrated, especially compared to the larger county.[21] Good Samaritan would be located only a couple of miles away from the inner urban neighborhoods known as areas of high crime and poverty; its area is more residential—but only a bit.

In addition to its founding biblical story and physical location, Good Samaritan's emerging self-identity was denominationally shaped. The most explicit tradition was, of course, the United Methodist. Methodism, as mentioned earlier, had a strong history in the area. Francis Asbury's preaching visit to the area in 1780 had helped galvanize white Methodism, which began to grow in surrounding counties. North Carolina had its share of the revivalism that spread through the Appalachian area into the Carolinas and on toward Ohio, solid preparation for reception of the Great Awakening of the early nineteenth century.

Yet these earlier vestiges of Methodism are less vivid as residual shapers of the contemporary community. While not erased, the heritage of this historic form of Protestantism for Good Samaritan is better described as faint, particularly when it comes to a consciously claimed identity. Explicit avowal of Methodist beliefs and practices is minimally evident in many Methodist churches, according to sociological studies, even in churches with native-born Methodists.[22] That

---

[21] Figures for 2000: Within a 1-mile radius the figures were about 52% of whites compared to 42% of African Americans. At a 2-mile radius the percentages were 40.25% white and 53.15% African American (with 8.16% Latino). Within the surrounding 5-mile radius, the rate of African Americans increased to just over 60%. This is compared to Durham County, made up of 51% white and about 39% African American. These figures were prepared for the Ormond Center, Duke University Divinity School.

[22] Jackson W. Carroll and Wade Clark Roof, 'United Methodist Congregations in North Carolina and California: Regional and Generational Trends', in Laurence et al. (eds.), *The People(s) Called Methodist* ii. 60–5, 79.

most of Good Samaritan's members were from churches in other traditions simply intensifies this lack. For the emerging congregation, the Methodist hymnbook and polity and founding theological themes, such as personal religion of the heart and the focus on 'spreading scriptural holiness over the land', did not have enormous impact. Indeed, a United Methodist clergywoman who was a chaplain at a local hospital attended Good Samaritan for a couple of years and later claimed that there was practically nothing Methodist about the place.

Although Dan's successor would introduce the liturgy of *Word and Table* and some discussion of the Methodist *Discipline*, the Methodist hymnbook was rarely used during his ministry. Most members had some version of a religion of the heart, but were as likely to have gotten it in its Baptist or black evangelical forms. The styles of worship that came to characterize Good Samaritan oscillated between interactive ritual, which was more dependent upon group participation, and 'mass ritual', which was dependent upon a controlling authority figure. Both of these are conceivable within Methodism but are just as likely a result of the varied non-Methodist denominational traditions of the two pastors who would serve the church.[23]

Some residuals of historic United Methodist theology did take on a more contemporary shape. Mrs Reese's earlier-mentioned appreciation for Wellspring is a tradition that continues to shape most contemporary churches. Even if church is no longer the central reality in people's lives as it was when she was young, interest in the relationships and family-like atmosphere of a community is frequently a primary draw in local Methodist churches in this part of North Carolina.[24] The current face of the Methodist tradition may be seen in the 'freedom, diversity, openness, inclusiveness' that

[23] Michael H. Ducey, *Sunday Morning: Aspects of Urban Ritual* (New York: Free Press, 1977), 157, quoted in Keith Roberts, 'Ritual and the Transmission of a Cultural Tradition', in Jackson W. Carroll and Wade Clark Roof (eds.), *Beyond Establishment: Protestant Identity in a Post Protestant Age* (Louisville, KY: John Knox, 1993), 80. I thank Jeanne Allen for pointing out these features. 'Redeemer United Methodist Church: A Case Study', 30 Apr. 1999.

[24] This concern is cited in portraits of several Methodist churches in the area of Good Samaritan and in California in Carroll and Roof, 'United Methodist Congregations', 55–83.

characterized this church determined to open its door to the different, even if there was little evidence of explicit avowal of the Methodist teaching to justify this openness. The North American Methodist adoption of John Wesley's 1743 official declaration against slavery and occasional joint revival worship of African Americans and whites were not invoked to authorize the new ministry of Good Samaritan. Rather than identifying the spread of 'scriptural holiness' or 'practical divinity' as its distinctive marks, we are much more likely to find statements about the church's family-like ethos, its casual and friendly feeling, and its welcoming of different beliefs— 'the church doesn't tell you what you have to believe', as several will say.[25] Other than the Methodist board's financial support of this struggling community, admittedly no small thing, a bright curling red flame on a brown cross would be the only visible sign that the humble buildings that later housed the community constituted a Methodist church.

There were, however, two other features of Methodist organization that would shape the community. What they have in common (indirectly) is race. A first is the Methodist practice of ministerial itinerancy. After almost eight years, the district superintendent moved Dan and Linda to another church, replacing them with Gerald, a United Methodist minister originally from the Bahamas. The significance of this move had to do with Gerald's perceived race; the church went from being led by a white man to being led by a man judged to be black.[26] As we will see, this shift of ministers led to some important crises in the community's self-understanding.

The other impacting Methodist traditions on this place have to do with its race history. On this count the contemporary racial situation is mixed. Besides the early brush meetings of slavery times, the first distinctively African American churches in the US were Methodist. Some moments in the history of Methodism commend it as a supportive tradition for this small community organizing around

[25] Ibid. Carroll and Roof describe the effect of this lack of Methodist (or other denominational) traditioning as 'self-authoring' or '*à la carte*' religion; other versions are 'golden rule Christianity' or 'lay liberalism'. As seen later, I will find its bricolage character of less concern.

[26] I say 'judged to be black', because the perception of Gerald and his wife Dina as black is more characteristic of the US as we will see.

difference in the late twentieth century.[27] It is probable that the founding Methodist evangelical worship style and concern for the poor helped draw new North American converts in those earliest years. Even more so, the previously mentioned early antislavery position of the Methodist church made it attractive to blacks, both slave and free, and the possibility emerged for black and white to claim a place in the same family of God.

However, it is not clear that this residual in the place that became Good Samaritan had a powerful effect. In 1844 slavery divided the church into northern and southern branches. This later 'backsliding' of the denomination on race issues meant that black Methodists were forced to create their own versions of Methodism—African Methodist Episcopal (AME), African Methodist Episcopal Zion (AMEZ), and Christian Methodist Episcopal (CME)—which continue as lively communities of faith today. One of Durham's earliest African American Methodist churches was St Joseph's AME congregation, founded in 1870 by a former slave who led brush arbor meetings (safe places for slaves to worship). Edian Markham's small band of worshippers turned into one of the most prominent African American churches in the city. What with segregated black annual conferences and white annual conferences, Good Samaritan came into being in a contemporary denomination with residuals of century-old arrangements. And even as the official black conferences have been abolished, as Lincoln and Mamiya observe, the practice of black Methodists has been relatively autonomous.[28] As for the white Methodist church, it is said to have used the presence of these separate African American Methodist churches, located mostly in eastern North Carolina, as an excuse not to do much interracial work.[29] And in the first decades of the century, says historian Timothy Tyson, eastern North Carolina was where '[m]ost white Christians believed that white supremacy was the will of God'.[30]

[27] See C. Eric Lincoln and Lawrence H. Mamiya, 'The Black Methodists: The Institutionalization of Black Religious Independence', in *The Black Church in the African American Experience* (Durham, NC: Duke University Press, 1991), 47–75.

[28] Ibid. 67. This is symbolized by a black caucus within the church that is a 'counterpart' to the independent black churches.

[29] Conversation with Compton, Office of Congregational Development.

[30] Timothy B. Tyson, *Blood Done Sign My Name* (New York: Three Rivers, 2004), 182.

Truth to tell, the current state of institutionalized interracial and otherwise diverse community in the Conference is unimpressive. While the last fifteen years have seen a considerable amount of intentional work to bring different populations together—black and white, Latino and Asian, Native American—the total number of significantly multiracial congregations is two.[31] This fits rather well with the larger national scene, where the percentage of significantly mixed-race churches in mainline denominations remains in single digits. Nine out of ten religious communities in the US are made up of at least 90 per cent of one so-called race.[32]

Given this context for a new 'place'—complex racial inheritances along with the thin and rewritten influences of historic Methodism—the band of Christians at Wellspring had quite a challenge ahead. Dan and Linda wasted no time. And as it turned out, any hypothetically Methodist ethos in the community had less to do with faithfulness to the past than with Dan and Linda's *production* of a Methodism that was a creatively alive and welcoming form of faith.

MOVING ON OUT

Considerable discussion followed that defining Bible study. What, they wondered, did this call to go to people 'not like us' mean? How in the world could it be carried out? Dan and Linda took a first step. They convinced Betty, the African American woman who cared for their two girls, to keep the nursery at Good Samaritan at the local elementary school where it began to meet on Sundays. This was no casual decision. Betty grew up in a nurturing all-black community in Laurinburg, NC, that provided much-needed protection from the hostility of the surrounding white world. Raised in the black Baptist church from her earliest years, Betty was currently attending a large

[31] Currently there are two in process: one starting up with Asian, Hispanic, and some Anglo members with a Filippino pastor; the other (unchartered) is mainly Anglo and African American.

[32] Brad Christenson and Michael O. Emerson, 'The Costs of Diversity in Religious Organizations: An In-Depth Case Study', Sept. 2001, p. 1, unpublished paper. The authors quote Mark Chaves's 1998 National Congregations Survey.

black Baptist church in Durham. Later she would confess to her distrust of white people, a distrust that began with her experience of being suddenly placed in a predominantly white school during school integration. She describes her defensive reaction as 'putting up walls and defenses, sort of to protect myself and to make myself feel good about myself. I began to stereotype all white people the same—they hate us and they were dumb.'

Yet Betty was intrigued by the invitation. Finding herself less than satisfied with the cold impersonal size of her current church 'where nobody knew your name', as she said, Betty agreed to do some of the child care at Good Samaritan. More to the point, Betty decided to take Dan's invitation seriously as a way to explore her dislike of white people. From helping with child care, it was not long before she was singing 'specials' at the service. Then she and her family started coming as regular participants. In less than a year, her picture appeared on a leaflet advertising Good Samaritan: 'I'm not just there to give a tithe or just be a number,' Betty is quoted as saying, 'the warmth and acceptance I feel here really drew me into the fellowship.'

Soon Dan's ministerial connections snagged a missionary couple. The husband, Robert Dube was Liberian and the wife, Marion, African American, and they got Dan quite interested in church connections with Africa. Pleased by his growing interest, the Dubes soon became regulars in the church, and they brought another Liberian couple, Harold and Frances Mwaura, who also became stalwarts of the community. The attraction of Good Samaritan to these members is perhaps a bit more obvious than that of an all-white church for a southern African American such as Betty. Liberia has a long history of revolution. Founded in 1822 by freed US slaves, the capital itself bears the mark of a special relationship to the US: Monrovia was named after President James Monroe. Although Robert and Marion came to the US during a period of Liberian peace, their families and friends were later caught in the turmoil that was the routine experience of Liberia's 3 million people. Following the 1980 civil war led by rebel sergeant Samuel Doe, raping, robbing, torture, and killings were commonplace. The cycle simply repeated itself when Charles Taylor, another rebel, took control of Liberia in the 1990s.

After such grim, unrelieved suffering, it was the warmth of the exuberant Dan and Linda Weaver more than Methodism that attracted the Liberians who found their way to Good Samaritan. Elizabeth was another exile who came to the church through a member of the Dube family. Barely escaping with her life during one of Taylor's insurrections in 1989, Elizabeth tells of her joy at finding a community where she was not only welcomed as a refugee, but also where the particularity of her African experience was taken seriously. A single woman who found herself cleaning houses as she struggled to create a new life, Elizabeth became a regular at Good Samaritan.

Gradually but steadily the community began to lose its 'whiteness'. As it did, the importance of visceral reactions to the increasingly multiracial hue of the place was not lost on its membership. Some regulars noticed that unsuspecting white visitors seemed caught off guard when they walked into the worship space, surprised to discover the racial mix. Seeking to respond to this, members of Good Samaritan began targeting its outreach with flyers that pictured smiling faces in a mix of hues. They sent members out in pairs of white and black to knock on doors and invite people to worship. The community was determined to welcome whoever turned up—'even Yankees', as one member put it. And in this way a visual message was delivered of God's work in this new place.

In a bit the flyers began to pay off, particularly for those whose own experiences were at odds with the majority of homogeneously raced congregations that constitute American Christianity. Zelda Ramirez, African American, and her Puerto Rican husband, Stephan, noticed the church flyer. After visiting they were drawn to Good Samaritan because of its hospitality toward their interracial marriage. Zelda's black Baptist community had offered only hostility to their family, and the other Baptist options they could find were completely homogeneous congregations, either all-white or all-black. It was seeing the images of multihued faces on the flyer, Zelda reports, that drew them to the church. Echoing the judgment that the warmth and inclusiveness of Good Samaritan were its most compelling features, the Ramirez family was an early addition to the evolving palette of colors in the community. While Stephan's work driving a truck kept him away more than he would have liked, Zelda was actively involved, and she particularly appreciated the personal size of the church, since the only other multicultural congregations in the area were a couple of mega-churches.

After worshipping at the elementary school for about six months, a change at the school forced Good Samaritan to move into some rooms in a shopping center across the street. There the community continued to grow with outreach to local people, internationals as well as native-born. Edgar, the youngest of the original white members, reports that reaching out to people of all races continued to motivate the community. 'That's what God really had in mind when He started the church. That's really what Christianity is supposed to be about,' he explains. In the fall of 1989 this spirit led to the next application of the founding hermeneutic, the eunuch story. A new population was attracted to the church.

IMPROVISING

As Dan tells it, that September he saw the possibility for a new form of ministry. During his regular drive to work, Dan noticed a group playing football in a grassy field. Closer inspection revealed the players were people with a variety of disabilities. A couple of wheelchair-bound figures were parked off to the side of the action, and figures waiting in the background were attendants at a group home. Upon inquiring, Dan found that New Hope, the group home, was delighted to attract the interest of a pastor. Its residents' experiences at two local churches had been less than positive, the supervisor told Dan. At one, a group member's wheelchair had gotten mud on the new carpet. At another church a member had a seizure and urinated on himself and the furniture. Unwelcome as they were in most churches, the supervisor said, they were in real need of some kind of worship. So Dan began to visit the group home regularly to lead devotions. Soon, folks at Good Samaritan got wind of his new activity. Appealing to their founding story, the church council determined that just as they had sought people of different races, Good Samaritan should welcome the group home community to their regular worship.

Within a week, a group of six New Hope residents came to Sunday worship at Good Samaritan, and that number quickly expanded to twenty-odd participants. And odd is the right way to put it, at least at first. For these new additions included people whose sensibilities and forms of communication were unlike those of any other member of the congregation. There was Danny, who rocked slowly and steadily back and forth in his chair. Lucy's excited squealing punctuated the service according to a logic of its own. And Tim, frozen and twisted in his wheelchair, spoke with slurred and guttural noises. Diane had a grin for everybody. Soon a local Mennonite family whose daughter, Daphne, had Down syndrome began to attend the bi-monthly Thursday night services for the 'special needs' participants. In her wheelchair Daphne was an exuberant and vociferous fan of any and all songs.

The expansion of the church to include what congregation members came to call special needs folks was productive almost immediately.[33] Not only did the residents of New Hope and, later, a group home called Westside, add their own distinct mass to the bodies that gathered in the place called Good Samaritan, other locals whose children had special needs soon came as well. As its membership took this new turn, the dimensions of communal hospitality deepened. Now not only were people of different races and nationalities greeted with warmth, an ambiance of welcome began to develop that extended to the unexpected shriek, the disruptive movement, and the unsightly body. Liana, a single mother from Uganda, started coming to the church because her daughter had a severe case of autism. Only at Good Samaritan, said Liana, could she rest easy with her daughter's repetitive movements and sudden outbursts.

Then there was Liana's friend Pam, an African American single mother, who found no church, black or white, that would make welcoming space for her autistic son Billy. Until she visited Good Samaritan that is, where the community had begun to get comfortable with these new energy patterns and was starting to learn alternative forms of communication. Liana and Pam were two of the parents who were drawn to the church because of its expanding cast of 'those who are not like us'.

---

[33] The phrase 'special needs' is contested, but I use it because it is the language of most of the community.

COST AND CLARIFICATION

When it came time to get a building of their own, however, the visceral reactions to difference that were taken account of in Good Samaritan's evangelism came to matter more than members ever expected. After a while, the shopping center became less adequate for the community's needs, and members began to look for a way to buy property for their own church buildings. When the spot on US Highway 22 came to their attention, they were on the verge of going ahead. Its location would likely never draw a high-income crowd. Car lots dot the side of the highway that cuts through central east Durham. Much of the drive is rather bleak—lots of gas stations, little stores and businesses apparent only by a cheap sign on a small frame house. A girlie-show place on the right is followed by housing projects on the left. A nursing home sits right beyond where the future new home of the church would be, and a small restaurant directly across the street boasts 'Family Style Cooking'. The farther out one drives the less commercial it becomes, with signs of older white residents from some earlier, more segregated time.

However, this east Durham site was affordable and seemed to pose no problems. A small brick house close to the road could function as the minister's office, provide a church kitchen and rooms for meetings. With more work, a reconstructed garage could serve well for a sanctuary, and two smaller buildings would be adequate for Sunday school classes and other activities. The property was quite modest, but given the congregation's limited means, it was perfect. There seemed to be no problem. To be safe, church members made efforts to visit the few neighbors who lived in this mixed-zone area to confirm their tolerance of a multiracial community. No one made any objection.

When a hearing was scheduled to review the granting of a permit for the building of a church on the property, however, a number of neighbors showed up. To the surprise of all, their reactions were less than supportive. A white retired minister and several white women expressed objections to the church. The property's immediate next door neighbor was negative as well. When asked whether they wouldn't prefer a church to a massage parlor, the response, as Dan tells it, was 'not *that* church'. The traffic would drastically increase with the building of the church, they complained, and they feared a rise in theft. But the more chilling response, as Olive remembers it, was that they confessed to feeling uncomfortable with 'that kind of people' in the neighborhood.

Local Ku Klux Klan members were part of the forces lined up to protest granting of the permit, and when the county commissioners postponed the vote on permit approval, Klan members made personal contacts. Rita, the white organist, remembers a Confederate flag was found at the church site, and bricks were thrown through Dan's car window and he received threatening telephone calls. In an attempt to counter the harassment, Linda organized a 'witness' by the church aimed at displaying members' care and concern for the community. But visits to neighbors with gifts of cakes and pies did not alleviate all the threatening behavior. Another window was broken, more phone calls. The residuals of racism were deeply embedded.

The fact that some residents seemed amenable when contacted earlier by church members seemed strangely at odds with the turnout at the hearing and completely contradictory to the appearance of a handful of Klansmen. However, the experience of Good Samaritan may reflect the continued ambivalence that characterizes race relations in the US. Andrew Hacker notes that when they are asked, most Americans say they believe in the equality of the races. In addition whites seem unwilling to admit they do not want black neighbors. However, the fact that it is now illegal to use race as a factor in refusing to rent or sell residences has not changed practice very much. Even if most whites say a black family would be acceptable, says Hacker, they still prefer predominantly white neighborhoods. Some 'will say they would like a black family nearby, if only to be able to report that their area is integrated'. But not many, he reports. 'Most white Americans do not move in circles where racial integration wins social or moral credit.'[34]

And North Carolina had long practice in slowing down or 'moderating' actual racial integration. Its response to Brown v. Board of

---

[34] Andrew Hacker, *Two Nations: Black and White, Separate, Hostile, Unequal* (New York: Scribner, 1992), 35.

Education, the landmark Supreme Court decision against segregated education, was astoundingly and deviously successful in almost bringing school desegregation to a complete halt. In the early 1960s, North Carolina's desegregation rate lagged behind Virginia, Arkansas, Tennessee, and Texas at a mere 0.026 per cent.[35] However, something was slowly creating space for alternatives.

It is not clear what tipped the balance for Good Samaritan. It would be nice to think that traces of those ancient regional practices of tolerance stirred in east Durham's unconscious. Perhaps it had something to do with the lessening of organized racial violence in the US—racialized ambivalences of society are highly problematic, but they are not equal to the state-backed racism of earlier decades. Or perhaps the church tapped into the goodwill that did exist amidst the conflicted racial tensions that shaped east Durham. Maybe their efforts made a difference. It is hard to say what accounts for the fact that at the final permit hearing a respectable crowd of supporters rallied around the faith community. But rally they did, and Dan remembers with pleasure that a large number of people sporting 'I Support Good Samaritan' badges showed up. The vote went the young church's way.[36]

The small plot of land on US 22 soon became Good Samaritan UMC, and a large welcoming sign announced the name and the times of services. With new paint and a lot of work inside, the members turned the garage on the property into a sanctuary. Its modest frame construction turned a gleaming white. A bright red flame curling around the brown Methodist cross was painted in the upper corner. Inside the big square space, folding chairs filled half the room and a large heavyset oak pulpit and communion table took center stage. The plain white door at the entrance disguised any former signs of a garage, and a small asphalt parking space for the group home vans fronted the worship space. Nearer to the highway, the small brick home on the property served as the church offices and

---

[35] Christenson and Emerson, 'Costs of Diversity'. NC Governor Luther Hodges resisted desegregation with the 'politics of moderation'. William H. Chafe, *The Unfinished Journey: America since World War II* (New York: Oxford University Press, 1986), 157–61.

[36] See 'A Confrontation with Love', *Virginia United Methodist Advocate* (5 Nov. 1998), 3–5.

a meeting place for adults. Farther back on the property, a small plain building served as Sunday school space for the children. And soon bright yellow, red, and blue playground equipment appeared in the adjacent grassy space.

At its high point the church would have about 130 official members. A third of those were Anglo, a third African American, and a third African members. Small numbers of Korean and other Asian families became members as well. Sunday morning services averaged from sixty to ninety participants, and the special Thursday night worship for group home members could typically attract forty or so participants. Dan estimates that about half the church earned less than thirty thousand dollars a year—more likely closer to twenty thousand, and Emmanuel, the wealthiest member, made around seventy thousand as the head of the state department of transportation in the nearby capital city.[37]

Good Samaritan was not a church of professionals. There were a couple of members who were either on welfare or worked for minimal wages, and one was reputed to go without food sometimes. A number of members were teachers; there was a pharmacist, a dietician, and at one time a sheriff. Some of the women cleaned houses; a number had secretarial and mid-level computer jobs. Several of the men were electricians; one developed a cleaning service during his time at Good Samaritan. Another was a truck driver, an occupation that frequently meant he was not in church on Sunday. More than a couple of men had to get a second job during Christmas season in order to afford extra spending for the holidays.

To be in the place-world of Good Samaritan was to be simultaneously in a host of other places. It was to be in the racialized nation of the US, a place that values certain kinds of bodies as 'normal'. It was to be in a place where the long-term effects of urbanization, white flight, and redefining property use make it more and more difficult to care

---

[37] In the period of transition, the late 1980s, the average household income was around 40,000–45,000 dollars in newer areas, with low twenties in the older sections (Compton, conversation). Household income level in the area nearest the church was well distributed between 15,000 and 60,000 dollars in 1990, with some increase by 2001, when 61.6% of households made between 40,000 and 99,000 dollars. For the county there were clusters of higher income, particularly in 2001 when almost 22% of households made between 60,000 and 100,000 dollars.

for the disabled in the home, and the distribution of power/influence prevents their presence in economically desirable residential areas. Insofar as we can identify the force of capital investment and labor organization to make special kinds of places—'factory towns', 'gentrifying urban neighborhoods', 'deindustrializing regions'—Good Samaritan was also in the place of globalized capitalism.[38] As the shifting of centers and boundaries of economic power and commerce away from local sites and nation states, globalization refers to the resulting radically altered way that money and capital flow. As one scholar puts it, money and commodities now 'unendingly chase each other around the world'.[39] The resulting 'deterritorialization' created a very distinctive 'ethnoscape', a world map constituted by movement and migration.[40]

Not only is the flow of capital and goods de-linked from local sites of production and loyalties, but people are dislodged as well. Good Samaritan was a place of global displacement—the Africans' sense of 'home' and where they belonged was multiple. (And their sense of where they owed money would not coincide with the minister's.) Combined with several civil wars, global capitalism brought exiles from Liberia, such as Elizabeth and other members of the church, into the area. These globalizing forces bring and create workers from specific territories to occupy the lower-class sectors of wealthier nations. A Kenyan trained as a civil engineer, Emmanuel was one of the few Africans who were able to make a lateral work move upon coming to the US. Most were forced to take lower paying and lower skilled jobs than the ones they had left in their home countries. The place of church members Beatrice, Dina, and Elizabeth was also the place of a gendered capitalism that defines productivity in terms of commodities and marketable labor, thereby excluding the

[38] See Sharon Zukin, *Landscapes of Power: From Detroit to Disney World* (Berkeley and Los Angeles: University of California Press, 1991), 12.

[39] Arjun Appadurai, 'Global Ethnoscapes: Notes and Queries for a Transnational Anthropology', in Richard G. Fox (ed.), *Recapturing Anthropology: Working in the Present* (Santa Fe, NM: School of American Research Press, 1991), 194.

[40] Ethnoscape is 'the landscape of persons who make up the shifting world in which we live: tourists, immigrants, refugees, exiles, guest-workers, and other moving groups and persons constitute an essential feature of the world and appear to affect the politics between nations to a hitherto unprecedented degree'. Ibid. 192.

domestic work these women did in their own homes, as well as others'.[41] This devaluation of women's work kept their pay for work as domestics in other homes below the minimum wage.[42]

While rarely explicit, through such effects globalization was part of the background 'powers and events' that made up Good Samaritan's environment. With members from north Durham, a few from Chapel Hill, the South Square Mall area, north Raleigh, and Creedmoor, Good Samaritan was not only a regional rather than neighborhood church, this Methodist community was also a global church.

CONSOLIDATING IDENTITY

As time went on, the church community developed habits of welcoming the outsider. Its story of origin began to consolidate. That exegesis of the welcoming of a eunuch led a small number of white southerners to welcome persons of other 'races'. That they extended the status of the welcomed outsider to residents from group homes was important not only to the staying power of this identity but as a test of its flexibility as well. This extension was important because it suggests an ability to improvise, or, in Bourdieu's terms, to 'do the same thing' in a very different way, and to do it in response to a new situation. As such, the extension of a behavior or pattern is not just about conscious reasoning; it requires internalized habits as well.

Of course this internalized *habitus* of 'welcoming eunuchs' cannot be attributed to the church activities alone. Nor can I say that all members developed such dispositions, or how deeply habituated members were. With the variety of enculturations and accompanying visceral associations that characterized this growing group of members and the extended amount of time required to be habituated into new practices, some of the capacity to improvise in Good Samaritan

[41] Barbara Ehrenreich and Arlie Russell Hoschschild (eds.), *Global Woman: Nannies, Maids, and Sex Workers in the New Economy* (New York: Henry Holt, 2002).

[42] Geraldine Pratt and Susan Hanson, 'Geography and the Construction of Difference', in *Gender, Place and Culture*, 1/1 (1994), 3.

would have to be accounted for by members' previous communities, the most immediate residuals. It is just these variances that later chapters will explore. However, it is crucial to note the constitutive role of habituation, because, as it turned out, the *belief* that the church should welcome those who were different was not sufficient to sustain this identity. The story continues.

It seemed that the pernicious attack from the Ku Klux Klan and hostile neighbors alike would shore up the community's resolve and strengthen member solidarity. For many this seems to have been the case. They tell the stories of the church's successful negotiations with racist resistance with great pride. However, no identity is ever stable or unanimously held. Ambivalences around race continued to plague the community, but this time from within. By 1990, a number of white families who seemed to have accepted and supported the discourses of ministry to 'those not like us' came to different conclusions.

One Sunday when he was out of town, Dan got a call from a white member of the still-all-white administrative council, demanding that he come to their meeting when he returned. 'The church is getting too black', said the member to Dan. For some Good Samaritans there had been a tipping of the color balance. The substitute preacher Dan had provided was a black African man who had invited friends to Good Samaritan that Sunday. For the first time persons of color and internationals outnumbered the white Euro-Americans at worship.

That the limits of hospitality had been reached for some whites must have been signaled by some deeply internal thermometer for what white America had stigmatized as 'difference'. How else to explain what was a numerically fallacious complaint, given that many of the visiting Africans were just that, visitors. To be sure, the combination of African Americans, a couple of Asian families with the Africans amounted to an increase in nonwhite members, but more members who were 'white' had also joined. The numbers of nonwhite had not yet reached the halfway mark; whiteness still dominated. But the member who lodged the complaint said that he could tell that Dan was trying 'to turn this church black'. Another member—a white sheriff—responded to the black African preacher with his racism on full display: 'I ain't coming to no damn church that's gonna get a damn nigger up preaching at me.'

The attribution of excessive blackness from white members is not an idiosyncrasy of some Good Samaritans. It seems to come from something shared by many white North Americans who would disavow racism. Take the significant difference between black and white attitudes toward segregated residential areas. There is striking divergence in the capacity to be comfortable with racial heterogeneity in contemporary society. Only about one in eight blacks prefers predominantly black neighborhoods; most claim to want a mixed-race community. In contrast, 'hardly any whites will live in a neighborhood where one half of the residents are black', says Andrew Hacker. The tipping point in an area that begins to integrate racially is 8 per cent for whites.[43]

That the appearance of extra Africans made Good Samaritan 'too black' for some suggests a similar tipping point in the church and an important marker in its identity formation. Although the response came from a handful of older white members of the generation that lived in a predominantly segregated world, a few who became uncomfortable were in their thirties. Thus 'too black' was not a residual from the quickly disappearing age of legal segregation. And it was a phrase that would be uttered again when Gerald, a Bahamian man of color, succeeded Dan as Good Samaritan's minister. At this point, however, the complaint symbolized a pivotal moment in the identity of the community. Was the welcoming of those 'not like us' to be a carefully modulated practice, where the balance of the 'different' could never outweigh the normative 'us'? Might the church be perceived by those perceived as normal (the 'normate') as 'too disabled' some day? Or was the logic of 'welcoming eunuchs' to be allowed its own course?

'We had to make a very difficult decision which I think any multicultural church has to make,' says Dan; 'that is, you have to let some people go.' And go they did.

What felt like a crisis was a turning point. Linda relates how frightened she and Dan were, thinking that they might not only lose everyone who was white, but also the blacks, who 'were mad

---

[43] Even newly arrived immigrants are preferred over blacks in white neighborhoods. Hacker cites the significant white intolerance for being in the minority. *Two Nations*, 36.

because they heard that it was happening and would leave'. However, the loss was small. They had not realized, Linda reflected later, that some of the members who left had been holding the church back. The payoff for the loss of a few families was a chance to take more seriously the issues of difference and prejudice that inevitably shaped the multihued community.

PRACTICES OF FORMATION FOR THE PLACE GOOD SAMARITAN

As this chapter traced out the elements that constitute the place Good Samaritan United Methodist Church, several features are important. Good Samaritan came into being not out of nowhere, but out of a preexisting community of faith. Thus it is not a completely new place. With the all-white remnant from Wellspring United Methodist as its point of continuity with that preexisting community, it consisted of overlapping places; the remnant was in a sense a residual. As such, the experiences of primarily white working- and middle-class United Methodists contributed to the new reality emerging. Some had not been habituated in such a way that they were comfortable in relation to black bodies. Indeed, the sheriff's response to a black body 'preaching at me' was a vitriolic outrage intimating something more like fear as the underside of obliviousness. Other white members, however, became some of the church's most faithful and central actors in the creation of a new kind of community that emerged from the Bible study. Some carried racial aversions; some did not. Both groups, however, are reminders of the larger social processes that go into creating the palimpsest of Good Samaritan.

How might these founding events be understood as practices of formation? The primary focus of this chapter has been the activity that fits best under a MacIntyrean definition of practice, that is, a defining interpretive event. In the early days of the church's transition, the story in Acts of baptizing an Ethiopian eunuch was interpreted as a call to go to those who are different—'not like us', as the pastor put it. As time goes on, few will remember the imagery of the eunuch. Not all will espouse this communal end; it will be articulated and understood differently by those who do share it. But the results of the Bible study produced a vision for the community that would be a key source of evaluative norms for many in the community.

As such the interpretive event and its rearticulation constitute a practice of inscription. Functioning primarily as a rationale for being a particular kind of church, it will provide reasons to justify other practices, as it did in the case of a ministry with people from group homes. As an interpretive event this judgment to minister to the 'different' was understood to be biblically based and a calling from God. Early on in the church's life descriptions of this communal vision begin to take the more easily repeated form of phrases like ministry to 'the overlooked', and 'the different'—identifications, we note, already inscribed with the positionality of the speaker. Eventually it is expressed by whites in the phrase 'we don't see color here' and proliferates for all members in related images of welcome and inclusiveness. As such the vision is part of the creation of what MacIntyre terms a 'socially established and cooperative human activity'.

What is foregrounded in these activities of self-definition is the linguistic medium; the community's identity takes form as stories, anecdotes, and aphorisms. As such these are practices of inscription. This linguistically mediated identity can be retained—not simply remembered and passed on orally, but written down (on flyers and reports and so forth). However, practices inevitably have incorporative elements, as well; bodies are necessary to convey communications. Indeed, to assess the way in which this community's identity becomes truly embodied as dispositions with the skills associated with habituation will require more attention to the bodied display of this vision. Here the historic residuals of race relations take very specific form. We have already seen that the welcoming practices of Good Samaritans in the community's early formation delivered significant bodily messages, even if unconscious or unintended. The perception of the white families that the church was getting 'too black' is one such example.[44]

---

[44] It reveals my own obliviousness that I failed to get accounts of responses of Africans and African Americans.

As the display of Good Samaritan's practices continues, it is crucial to pay attention to the role of practices that are primarily incorporative along with the practices of inscription, remembering that it is the full-bodied social practices, not simply the beliefs and convictions from Methodism that make place. Already the rudiments of incorporative *practices of propriety* are evident in the community. Practices of propriety are what Connerton identifies as the habituated norms for 'proper behavior' passed on by a society as part of its identity. Not necessarily articulated in explicit ways, these norms are internalized as the respectable way to place and use your body—from table manners, like how to hold a fork, to appropriate postures of deference and the proper place a woman (or man) can be and display her body.

Good Samaritan shows signs of proprieties that were doubtless formed by the history of racism in the US. From the enslavement of Africans to Jim Crow laws to the more recent forms of residential, religious, and work segregation, all of society has been habituated into racialized bodily proprieties. Such practices involve the postures and gestures that are acceptable as well as the places where differently racialized and gendered persons can 'properly' put their bodies. These practices have inevitably shaped most members of the church. Key to these proprieties is the fact that most Americans have grown up in racially homogenous communities.

These proprieties do not constitute separate 'cultures', but link practices for African Americans inextricably with those designated as 'white'. For whites this will mean habituation into being the dominant race. For African Americans this habituation is always already defined with a legacy of marginalization that has led to what W. E. B. Du Bois famously called the 'twoness' of black consciousness.[45] However many other ways being black is differentiated (by gender, class, sexuality), *to have to always be aware* of the dominant race as well as one's own is a key factor in the production of bodily proprieties for African American communities. However many ways being white is otherwise differentiated—and similarly inflected by gender, class, and sexuality—*to be able to be oblivious to* one's own race and the 'Other' are key factors in bodily proprieties

[45] W. E. B. Du Bois, *The Souls of Black Folks* (1903; repr. New York: Vintage Books, 1990), pp. xii, 7–9.

for those called 'white'. (And obliviousness is learned, not a function of ignorance; white people only know their whiteness by the presence of people designated as having race.[46]) For the Africans who need not attend to 'being black' in their home countries, this leads to the discovery that they *have to* attend to it in the US.[47]

While these are well documented as *awarenesses*, the concern here is how they can be articulated as (bodily) incorporative practices of propriety.[48] It is likely that the white members of Good Samaritan are habituated into *a bodily sense of ownership of public or social space.*[49] By that I mean that they can go—their bodies feel comfortable in—most places outside their homes without concern or heightened self-awareness. The domain produced by and productive of this practice is appropriately called 'white space', not only because it suggests the historic dominance of whites, but also because it indicates the continued 'spell' of that dominance even when legal discrimination is mostly a thing of the past. This white incorporative practice is a mode of free and comfortable movement that is possible in a location where either the majority of bodies are white or any black bodies present are somehow displaying 'properly' subservient postures.

African American proprieties range from the subverted gaze and submissive posture of the slave to the messages sent by the uniformed body of the janitor or housekeeper, or other marker of lower status. (Thus in contemporary situations this white ownership of space is not disrupted by a number of black housekeepers gathered for a cigarette break, but it is disrupted by a number of black professionals gathered in conversation.[50]) That I had been habituated into this white ownership of space is indicated by my discomfort when I first

---

[46] Thanks to Maurice Wallace for pointing this out.

[47] This is not saying that Africans don't have ethnicity and race problems, e.g., Hutus and Tutsis in Rwanda.

[48] Examples of the literature on whiteness include David R. Roediger, *The Wages of Whiteness: Race and the Making of the American Working Class* (London: Verso, 1991); Ruth Frankenberg, *The Social Construction of Whiteness: White Women, Race Matters* (Minneapolis: University of Minnesota Press, 1993); David R. Roediger (ed.), *Black on White: Black Writers on What It Means To Be White* (New York: Schocken, 1998); and Thandeka, *Learning to Be White: Money, Race, and God in America* (New York: Continuum, 1999).

[49] I thank William Hart for naming this practice of propriety and helping me understand it.

[50] Thanks to William Hart for this example.

visited Good Samaritan—a discomfort that suggests an underside of fear and threat, on the continuum illustrated by the sheriff.

The African Americans at Good Samaritan are likely habituated into practices of propriety shaped by the double consciousness—a consciousness of white-dominated space that calls for careful placement of their black bodies *and* a consciousness of their own cultures where, whatever else goes into defining 'proper', bodies are less constrained by the dominant race. The latter is a topic of enormous richness, from the proud display and adornment of bodies that came to characterize the Black Church, to all variety of creative proprieties.[51] The former may be characterized for many by what bell hooks calls the 'terror of whiteness'.[52] If not a response to terror, as was often the case in the past, these incorporative practices are still inevitably shaped by African Americans' awareness of the effect of their own presence in 'white space'. Womanist Teresa Fry Brown tells of being raised 'not to act "uppity" in front of whites' or reveal her intelligence or what she really thought. A 'protective device', this bodily propriety involved a repertoire of postures aimed at reassuring whites of their belief in black inferiority.[53]

And theirs is a consciousness that is inseparable from the obliviousness of much white sensibility. As bell hooks puts it, 'White people can "safely" imagine that they are invisible to black people since the power they have historically asserted, and even now collectively assert over black people, accorded them the right to control the black gaze.'[54] There is, then, a linked, if asymmetrical character to these racialized incorporative practices of propriety, and two dynamics seem apparent in Good Samaritan. That there are proper places

---

[51] Harold Dean Trulear says of black worship, its 'first order of business is the celebration of the body'. 'To Make a Wounded Wholeness: Disability and Liturgy in an African American Context', in Nancy L. Eiesland and Don E. Saliers (eds.), *Human Disability and the Service of God: Reassessing Religious Practice* (Nashville: Abingdon, 1998), 238. See Anthony B. Pinn, *Terror and Triumph: The Nature of Black Religion* (Minneapolis: Fortress, 2003).

[52] bell hooks, 'Whiteness in the Black Imagination', in *Killing Rage: Ending Racism* (New York: Henry Holt, 1995), 31–50; ead., 'Homeplace: A Site of Resistance', in *Yearning: Race, Gender, and Cultural Politics* (Boston: South End, 1990), 41.

[53] Teresa L. Fry Brown, *God Don't Like Ugly: African American Women Handing on Spiritual Values* (Nashville: Abingdon, 2000), 53.

[54] hooks, 'Whiteness in the Black Imagination', 35.

and ways to place your body is hardly noticeable for whites; thus these are largely invisible proprieties. (Significantly, since the white incorporative practice of ownership of space is correlated to the invisibility of black bodies, the continued racial segregation of most churches leaves these proprieties intact and unremarked.)

When some white Good Samaritans complained that the church was getting 'too black', they were not making an observation about a literal numerical imbalance. Rather, they were displaying their (normally unconscious) white bodily propriety of ownership of space. That is the first dynamic, and it is a discomfort connected to something like fear, whether of loss of control or aversion and guilt. The second is suggested by what caused the discomfort, the disruption of that space. Black bodies become hypervisible in the white-dominated society when they are not in the minority or they are not marked as subordinate. At Good Samaritan black bodies became hypervisible when they increased in number and were not dressed in uniforms. Thus we see not only an emergence of white consciousness of racialized propriety in the formation of Good Samaritan, but the possibility of its destabilization as well. As such an African American bodily propriety that is other than hypervigilance may be emerging that might aid in the transformation of white-owned space.

The practice of communal self-definition, of course, does not end but continues as the life of the community goes on. Good Samaritan's interpretive activities will proliferate. Its racialized bodily proprieties will continue to shape the community, even after those white members who were most explicitly disturbed have gone. What has yet to surface, at least in such public complaints, are the bodily proprieties of Good Samaritans that are associated with 'normal/abnormal' bodies. Ellis Cose's observation is instructive. Obliviousness and its close cousin aversiveness to race, he said, are comparable to 'that [behavior] exhibited by certain people on encountering someone with a visible physical handicap. They pretend not to notice that the handicap exists and hope, thereby, to minimize discomfort.' It will be important to follow out the practices of the church as they develop or fail to develop these relationships. Welcoming the eunuch, if it will be a *habitus* generating desirable improvisations, should entail more than the not-seeing of disability.

4

Performing Gospel: Worship Practices

This Is a Place for People with:
   ...Hurts as well as hopes...
   ...Doubts as well as beliefs...
   ...Questions as well as answers...
As We All Celebrate & Share God's Love Together

> Bulletin for Dan's services

We are diverse yet united disciples of Jesus Christ, who are called to be faithful and inclusive *NOW* (through *N*urture, *O*utreach and *W*itness)

> Bulletin for Gerald's services

Who's afraid of lightning?
First! Second! Third!
Jesus Loves Me This I Know

Key moments in 'special needs' service

DEFINING WORSHIP

Charles Foster says that worship is 'typically the nerve center of culturally and racially diverse congregations'.[1] Good Samaritan is no exception. Energy put into the services is strong, as are opinions about worship styles. People care quite a bit about the kind of hymns

---

[1] Charles R. Foster, *Embracing Diversity: Leadership in Multicultural Congregations* (Bethesda, MD: Alban Institute, 1997), 79.

sung, as well as the musical selections of the Praise Team. Judgments about the two preachers are diverse, from the African Americans who think approvingly that Dan's preaching is 'more black' than Gerald's, to the university students' widely shared preference for Gerald's 'more intellectual' sermons. Such deep feelings about worship in multiracial and multicultural communities relate to its importance in negotiating identity out of quite different worship traditions. As Foster puts it, worship is a place to nurture and develop 'a common vocabulary and practices for congregational conversation'.[2]

Three distinctive styles of worship provide potential vocabulary and practices for negotiating identity at Good Samaritan. The first is characteristic of Dan, the founding minister, and his wife Linda, a diaconal minister in the United Methodist Church. Their worship services typically include extemporaneous sermons, lots of back-and-forth between minister and congregants, and informality that some associate with evangelical worship. A second style is introduced by Gerald, the Bahamian minister who replaced Dan. While including a form of call and response similar to that initiated by Dan and Linda, Gerald's services are characterized by formal liturgies and sermons preached from a manuscript. A third kind of worship at Good Samaritan occurs in the regular gatherings held every third Thursday night of the month that are designated as 'special needs' services. While group home residents come to Sunday morning services, the Thursday night worship is quite clearly their own—defined by forms of communication most congenial to them.

All three forms of worship are definable as practices. Aimed at forming self-conscious identity in the community, they also rely upon (and help shape) official tradition as well. Interpretive practices of preaching are central to these very Protestant services that intentionally convey inherited inscribed traditions in Scripture, hymns, and liturgies. Along with the traditions conveyed in preaching and in biblical and liturgical texts are messages sent by the praising and celebrating bodies. Incorporative practices consisting primarily of bodily ceremonies or rituals are vital to worship as well.

Appreciation of the full performed and 'sounded word' that is worship requires attention to the style of the ministers, but also to the

---

[2] Ibid.

variety of practices set in motion by their performances.[3] For worship practices are *communal* activities, not simply the work of worship leaders in negotiation with traditions. The role of congregants can be seen through the subject positions or socially located identities that come into being as the preachers create powerful images through which the community can negotiate its identity/identities. Their 'performances' of gospel have the effect of inviting Good Samaritans to take on—to occupy—a variety of self-understandings.[4] Ranging from a position of ordinary folks beloved by God, to that of the forgiven who take God's side with the oppressed, to a position of just being recognized, these performances produce a spectrum of imaginative self-understandings for the congregation.[5]

By subject positions or identities, we do not mean that worship **simply** produces self-understandings in the form of intellectual options for participants. Worship's bodily performances have effects that range far beyond the production of ideas about one's position in the faith, effects that will help reveal how worship practices enhance the ends of the community. For many, the worship performances produce powerful affective experiences. Joy and pleasure are as constitutive of worship practice as enhanced intellect. Since racialized bodily proprieties continue to be a 'given' within which ritual practices occur, worship practices also have a significant effect on racialized and normalized bodily habits at Good Samaritan. Moreover, worship is the main activity that brings together the group home residents with other members of the congregation. Thus, in worship

[3] Mary E. McGann, *A Precious Fountain: Music in the Worship of an African American Catholic Community* (Collegeville, MN: Liturgical Press, 2004), 144.

[4] I am describing what Marxist Louis Althusser called 'interpellation', where a social discourse defines an identity for persons, who take it up as a subject position. The usefulness of this language is to suggest the *relational* character of identity. A subject becomes 'ordinary folks', 'guilty', 'loved by God' in relation to persons and processes that 'position' one in relation to other realities. Place theory, however, will complicate Althusser's too simple account. Louis Althusser, 'Ideology and Ideological State Apparatuses: Notes toward an Investigation', in *Lenin and Philosophy and Other Essays*, trans. Ben Brewster (New York: Monthly Review Press, 1972).

[5] The notion here is akin to what I analyze as register in *Changing the Subject*, a category for indicating that *what* is said is inseparable from *how* it is said. As a register, preaching is a stylized recognizable form of communication. Mary McClintock Fulkerson, *Changing the Subject: Women's Discourses and Feminist Theology* (Minneapolis: Fortress, 1994), 177–82.

we deal explicitly with the reality that most of the community has been habituated into proprieties of 'normal-bodiedness'.

In what follows, I describe three services, highlighting the combination of inscribed and incorporative practices as I experienced them. Following this participatory account comes reflection upon the variety of proffered subject positions and affective resonances of each worship style. What identities are being offered for Good Samaritans in worship, and what goods are enhanced by worship practices? Is a common identity being negotiated out of these very different worship practices? Is there a converging place, and is it a place for all to appear? Mapping the various positions will shape the analysis of this chapter and later be important to the larger project of convergences and divergences in creating the place Good Samaritan.

I begin with worship led by Dan and Linda.

DAN AND LINDA

It is a cold day in January, the Sunday nearest Martin Luther King Jr's official birthday holiday. Hardly anyone is in Good Samaritan's sanctuary at 11.00 a.m. when I enter and sit down in one of the metal folding chairs near Pam. Her son, Billy, wanders around. Cheery felt banners hang on the wall at the front—one with a dark brown Jesus, the other with a multicolored rainbow around the word 'Hallelujah!' in big gold letters. There is little other decoration, aside from the small dark-skinned cloth angel sitting on the window ledge, a leftover from Christmas. The service doesn't start until about 11.15 a.m., but not because of the snowy weather. If there is an 'African time' at Good Samaritan, as some members put it, there is also a 'Good Samaritan time', defined by Dan and Linda's leadership. Things start when they start. Folks gradually drift in—a lot of the regulars with their children. William and Letty with son Carl and their small daughter go right to the front; Liberian Letty looking as beautiful as ever in a stylish dress. Wanda comes in guiding her husband Barry carefully to a seat right down from me. She gives me a cheery hello as she comments on what an ordeal it is to get him seated since a stroke slowed him down. Eventually the whole room is full, black and white, male and female, young and old.

Dan stands at the front making conversation with people as they come in. Dressed in a gray suit and tie, a slightly stocky man of medium height, he speaks in a jovial tone with a bit of a southern accent. Dan comments on the snow, that he is glad folks have come, and, without pausing, moves into a friendly admonition directed to everyone. We shouldn't be here if all we want to do is warm the seats, says Dan. God wants more from us at worship, he continues. And it's not okay to be here and stay passive. If we come just to be fed, we will get fat—overweight!! Everyone laughs. Next comes the weekly Bible verse for memorization. Dan reads Matthew 2: 1, 11 (RSV): 'behold, wise men from the East came to Jerusalem . . . and they fell down and worshiped him.' We all repeat the verses, and Dan asks where the Wise Men come from. William, one of his most frequent partners in repartee, says, 'The Christmas Story!' After a laugh, we pray a short prayer printed in the bulletin.

Thus far things have felt quiet, relatively still for Good Samaritan, almost muffled. Now Linda bursts onto the scene, and the level of energy rises noticeably. With a booming voice that matches her imposing size, Linda announces a hymn from the Praise Songs booklets stuck in the cloth covers on the back of the metal folding chairs. Early in their ministry Dan and Linda chose the Praise Songs over the United Methodist hymnbook, thinking they would appeal to black and white alike.[6] With Dan accompanying on guitar, Linda leads us in three of the wonderfully intense Praise Songs that combine passionate personal piety with equally passionate melodies. Much less staid than most denominational hymnbook selections, these songs are popular in white evangelical churches. Linda thinks they provide a nice compromise between the black gospel style and more stodgy white denominational tastes.[7] With lyrics and music

[6] Praise Music was a product of the Jesus movement of the 1960s and a move away from 'high church' music. Originally developed for rock guitars, it has conversational, repetitive lyrics and usually incorporates biblical phrases. Its success at attracting persons from different racial/ethnic communities is probably indirect. See Gerardo Marti, 'Does Music Determine Diversification?', Paper presented at the Annual Meeting of the Religious Research Association, Nov. 2005.

[7] Not that there is one kind of 'black religious music'. For treatment of some of the differences, see Mellonee V. Burnim, 'Conflict and Controversy in Black Religious

reminiscent of popular love songs, Praise Songs are sung with intense, even physical enjoyment at Good Samaritan. Black and white, African and Western members alike raise arms into the air and sway as they sing. Linda has us repeat a verse or two, making editorial comments as we sing.

who all ?!

This Sunday the national holiday celebrating Martin Luther King Jr's birthday is to be recognized in congregations. Or so says the national UMC. Dan directs us to a responsive reading on Martin Luther King in the bulletin and gets an African American member to lead it. The liberationist language of the liturgy from the national church office sounds a bit foreign. Terms like 'arch supporter of the status quo', 'the church's . . . sanction of things as they are', 'the power structure of the average community', 'our work for justice', and so forth are not typical of Good Samaritan's rhetoric. The deep theological relevance of the events of Martin Luther King Jr's life for the interracial shape of Good Samaritan does not really begin to resonate until Dan moves us into a circle to sing together. Following the directive of the national church's responsive reading to sing 'We Shall Overcome', the congregants make this slightly alien 'liberation' language their own through bodily messages.

We form a weave of handmade connections throughout the crowded room. I am holding two hands on my right—of Wanda and the African man behind me—and one on my left—of Carol, the white university professor. Linda calls out words to each new verse and adds words, such as 'we shall all be one—Africans, Liberians, Chicanos, whites, African Americans'. The feeling is vibrant and warm, the singing loud and lusty; people sway even more with this song. Women holding babies look at one another laughing. Beatrice from Liberia, singing, smiles at Tim, a young white man in a wheelchair. Making his own joyful noises, Tim grins as he looks up at her. We stop to finish the litany and Dan comments that Martin Luther King Jr's vision—and what God calls us to do—has happened right here in this church. As we return to our seats, Wanda wipes tears from her eyes.

Music', in *African-American Religion: Research Problems and Resources for the 1990s* (New York: Schomburg Center for Research in Black Culture, 1992), 82–97. Also, Irene V. Jackson-Brown, 'The Rise of Black Hymnals', in *African-American Religion*, 98–106.

It is 'Children's Time' next, and a number of children gather around Dan to hear a message just for them. While they are in the service, it feels like there are two realities in the room. One is Dan, exhorting, imploring, scolding, and admonishing; the other, folks and their own comings and goings and connectings. Children make movements and noises all during the first part of the service, especially Carl, who sits on the front row with a few other 'special needs' folks. Although there are fewer group home residents at the service today, there are still the occasional squeals from them. Babies and toddlers cry. People come and go at different times, not simply the latecomers (of whom there are plenty); there is also the coming and going of individuals who consult one another and seem oblivious to the front of the room and Dan's performance. There is, then, a kind of force-field of spiritual energy in the room that is multiply located. When the children leave after Dan's sermon, the traveling diminishes quite a bit. Following an offering and special music from a trio, there is quiet, as the remaining adults await the intensity of the sermon. The energy of the room will now be dominated by this performing white male body.

Dan announces the scripture and reads Matthew 2: 1–12, the story of the visit of the Wise Men to the infant Jesus. 'This is about what it means to be wise,' Dan tells us. Working quickly through some 'historical background' about Wise Men, he says he wants to give these Wise Men 'their due'. They really did study hard—were 'very learned'—and traveled and did the best they could. Dan sets up a contrast that will shape the rest of the sermon. There is a 'wise' that fits 'our culture', he tells us, and a different kind of wise that will have to do with understanding Jesus as a different kind of king—not an earthly king, as these 'wise' men saw him. Jesus is God's Son. Developing this contrast, Dan remarks that our society teaches us that wisdom looks like money, power, prestige, house, cars, and so on. 'Who do you think is wise?' he asks us. Coming out from behind the pulpit, he asks again, 'Who does our society say is wise?' 'Newt Gingrich', responds William. People laugh. Someone else says, 'Clinton', and gets even more laughs. Dan continues his banter with William. Others chime in, 'John Hope Franklin'. Wisdom, Dan goes on, is knowledge of God.

Physical movement outside the confines of the pulpit and verbal repartee with members of the congregation are standard features of

Dan's style. Never comfortable standing still, Dan once illustrated a point about the burden of the cross by lurching across the room pretending to carry a huge cross on his back.[8] As he goes on to contrast our society's wisdom and God's, he performs a verbal posture fairly familiar to the community—that of the imploring, warning, scolding, and intensely caring father/older brother. Passionately, Dan sketches out the situation, the false trap our culture has created for us, all the while assuring us that he falls victim to this worldly wisdom, too. The world is always telling us that we should work harder to get more, he says. It is hard to resist. 'I know you know better,' he continues. 'I've seen some of you here and in your jobs. I know you know that it isn't true.'

Raised in Appalachia by working-class parents, Dan freely and often shares his troubled background with the church. His father was an alcoholic, who sold cars on the side when he was employed, and the family struggled to make it financially. In and out of trouble with drugs and alcohol as a youth, it took Dan several tries to get out of high school. Only later after tangles with the law did he (just) make it through a local 'rinky-dink' college, as he puts it. After giving his life to Jesus in response to the personal testimony of an evangelical former Hell's Angel, Dan made attempts to go into ministry in a couple of Baptist churches. However, his predilection for trouble—in this case, reaching out to down-and-outs and challenging the ministers in charge—got him kicked out of at least one. These predilections and their consequences are frequent illustrations in his sermons. This 'ordinary guy' discourse is key to who he is.

'*Real* wisdom—*God's* wisdom—is two words,' Dan says, bringing the sermon to a climax, '*Yes, Lord!*' 'Yes, Lord,' he repeats. 'It is trusting that *God* is the one who knows who is the best partner for you, *God* is the one who knows what kind of house you need, *God* is the one who knows what is best for your family. You must not be convinced by the world that *working* more in order to *get* more is wisdom.' He characterizes this worldly wisdom with a slight edge of disdain in his voice: it is 'coming to church on Sunday—you think

---

[8] This is a practice cited as characteristic of African American preachers. See Geneva Smitherman, *Talkin and Testifyin: The Language of Black America* (Boston: Houghton Mifflin Co., 1977), 150. Such styles surely contribute to Dan's popularity with African American members. As one put it, Dan preaches 'black'.

that's nice—but Monday, Tuesday, Wednesday, Thursday, and Friday you act in a *totally—different—way*. Your Sunday worship doesn't carry over to the rest of your life.'

As Dan talks, getting more worked up as he goes, assenting noises come from many folks: nodding heads, whispered 'yeses' in the back. Dan's bodily display, his performance, pulls in all the attention in the room. What with his popularity with African American members, it is as if a set of black incorporative practices have been artfully appropriated by this white man. A loud, clear African American male voice offers 'hello!'—the basic 'amen' or 'ain't it the truth' characteristic of African American call and response rhetorics.[9]

'I know you've seen this message,' Dan continues. 'It's on posters in people's offices; some ministers even carry this around on cards in their wallets,' he continues. 'Oh yes!' someone calls out. With an aside about the poor quality of many ministers, he closes off with a disparaging comment about himself. Back on track, Dan continues, 'The recent version of this wisdom of the world is "don't work harder, work smarter!"' More assent. A few arms wave. Again, voice raising, he commands us, 'But the real wisdom is found in two words. What is real wisdom?' The response is full and immediate. We all cry, 'Yes, Lord!'

Dan's regular style slips in and out of a 'liturgical voice'. His alternative, a 'chatty voice', provides informal segues between different parts of the service but can also occur at almost any point in the service. When reciting the liturgy for the Lord's Supper, he will add asides to the formal language of the Methodist liturgy, when he occasionally uses it, offering commentary on the text as well as soliciting our consent. With the next part of the service, however, a kind of 'evangelist' register takes over. As Dan's sermon moves seamlessly to a hymn of invitation, his solicitation gets more concrete. With a speech he gives every week at this point in the service, Dan implores us to come down to the front and rededicate our faith. 'I have preached the gospel as best as I know how. Now it's time for

⁹ Adisa A. Alkebulan, 'The Spiritual Essence of African American Rhetoric', in Ronald L. Jackson II and Elaine B. Richardson (eds.), *Understanding African American Rhetoric: Classical Origins to Contemporary Innovations* (New York: Routledge, 2003), 23–40.

you to decide if there is something you need to do—you don't have to come, but I feel like there may be something you need to talk or pray about.'

We sing a 'Hymn of Invitation to Christian Discipleship' to create the space for those ripe for (re)commitment to come forward. A black man I have never seen before comes forward. Dan continues to talk, going back and forth between imploring us to come and assuring us that there is no pressure. 'Don't hold back. But don't just come for me. I don't need that to judge whether this has been effective. You can do it at your seat or up here. But don't feel like you have to.' To extend the opportunity a bit longer, Dan has us sing 'Jesus Loves Me', and Letty, with her small baby, finally comes forward.

After soft conversation with each, Dan leads us in prayer. As Letty returns to her seat, Dan announces that Mr Jones, the newcomer, has rededicated his life to Christ and wants to tell us his story. At our murmurs of approval, Mr Jones takes center stage and speaks of God's work in his life this very morning. A series of misfortunes, he says, have brought him to a crisis. Already feeling the loss of his wife, who died a few years ago, he threw himself into trying to make more and more money and slipped away from the church. Commanding the worship space with his black presence, he tells of being held up at gunpoint, and later becoming ill with pneumonia. He has come to realize that he has failed to give back to God and is in great need of Him.

Determined to come to church again, this morning his car broke down on the way. Beatrice and her husband had stopped and offered him, a complete stranger, a ride to Good Samaritan. Laughing, Beatrice volunteers that she would not ordinarily pick up someone on the side of the road, but is so glad they did. Mr Jones ends by dedicating himself again to the church and asks if he might sing. Several voices respond 'yes!' and we are treated to the best music of the day when Mr Jones goes over to the piano. As he plays a jazzed-up spiritual about taking it all to Jesus, his deep beautiful voice takes over the room. 'Jesus will bear the burden!' he sings. Clearly quite talented, Mr Jones is all over the piano, and folks start clapping with the music, nodding and participating in the way people do when they really live into a piece of music. When he finishes, there is loud uproarious applause. Dan and Linda join in the expressions of pleasure at Mr Jones's sharing. As the service ends with announcements and benediction, we all gather in clusters, greeting and expressing our delight at this most recent move of the Spirit.

Assessment

This service conveys themes and postures characteristic of Dan and Linda's worship practices. A first theme is developed in the sermon. Nothing is our doing; all the glory must go to God. Dan puts it most concisely in the command, 'Ask God'. We must always rely upon God, never taking credit for our accomplishments. In the service we hear a second of Dan's favorite topics, celebration of the community's diversity. Dan never allows us to forget that our multihued and abled nature reflects the Kingdom of God. At a Bible study a week later he speaks proudly of the United Methodist Office's judgment that Good Samaritan is the most multicultural church in the whole nation. The gathering of bodies, holding of hands, and other connectings, as well as the visual effects of our differences, constitute a powerful physical display of this valued identity.

A third theme of affirmation is less prominent in this service, but still discernible. Evident in Dan's informal style and his constant 'simplifying' commentary on liturgical events, this theme is God's care for the common person—the person without wealth or status or book learning. Dan regularly invokes some reference to who we are *not.* We are not rich people, not fancy society folks, not intellectuals. His wisdom is not 'book learning', and he is not a fancy preacher. We are all plain old ordinary folks. As he lines out the faults of us ordinary folks, Dan also positions himself as a sinner and a stumbler from way back. The imploring, scolding, cajoling, guilt-inducing style of his altar call as well as his sermon is always accompanied by self-deprecating discourse. All of us, Dan included, are convicted. This combination of interpellations opens up a space of unworthiness for us 'ordinary folks' who fall prey to worldly wisdom. It opens up an identity quite familiar to many, long shaped into moralistic self-understandings. However, as Dan positions it, ours is to be a space of acceptance, not just guilt. God *loves* us as ordinary folks.

The feel and sound of this service—the informality, the traveling, excited bursts of noise, banter, and call-response—are typical of Dan-and-Linda-style worship. Ritual practices of movement with song, especially the erotic aesthetic of Praise Songs, and the constant verbal connections with members of the congregation all produce pleasurable effects. Gathering in a circle and holding hands positions everyone in a face-to-face way, not only as a symbolic leveling of our social differences, but as an affective one as well. Tim's response, nonverbal as it is, in the circle is telling. Performative practices of movement and physical connection along with the pleasure of singing are much more significant to the Wellspring group home residents than the messages of preaching and Bible reading. But the affective and connectional effects of worship practices are important to everyone. The feel and sound of the service have a distinct temporal frame. The bulging out of worship time is a Good Samaritan habit; it is also a characteristic of African American worship, which is never about 'clock time', as one liturgical scholar puts it.[10] That the service lasted over an hour and a half with Mr Jones's testimony is taken as an extension of the Holy Spirit, not the service's running late as several white members would have it.

Finally, the worship practices of Dan and Linda are perhaps best characterized by their relation to the ordinary. There is no narthex or entry hall, no physical arrangement at Good Samaritan for moving from ordinary, secular space into sacred space. To open the door is to be immediately thrust into a bustling room full of folding metal chairs and wandering children. The boundary between the secular and the sacred in this ministerial practice is not a clearly defined physical one. Nor does a shift into formal behavior or liturgy—a procession—signal the transition. The shift that does happen with this worship is a shift Dan moves us through with his non-stop, back-and-forth 'performing of informality', as I will call it. From his repartee with William and his skits about making excuses, to his 'I'm not so hot either' and other identifications with funny, foolish old us, he creates a space of personal intimacy with God for the congregation.[11] As I come to see, however, the themes of ordinary

[10] McGann, *Precious Fountain*, 48.

[11] These are images from different sermons. One striking image of intimacy with God invoked 'sitting in your lap', 17 Mar. 1996.

people, of ordinary faith, which are central to his appeal, are displayed as he *never really takes us out of ordinary space.* This style and message may seem to *stay* ordinary, but that is precisely their contribution. For many, this very honoring of the ordinary is somehow its redemption.

GERALD

One hot muggy day in late May 1998, I arrive a bit late. While the service has not started, I know I am late because six 'special needs' folks already fill up the left side of the room. Usually they arrive after the service has started, and members—typically Richard and Emmanuel—get up to help various ones navigate their way to seats. Today the typical 'disruption' of their arrival is already complete. Gerald has made some changes in worship since Dan and Linda left. He uses liturgical coverings on the altar and pulpit, and both are covered today with red cloths, the appropriate liturgical color for Pentecost Sunday. As Gerald sits in a chair at the front wearing white vestments and the seasonal liturgical stole, someone comes forward and lights the candles on the altar. This style of marking the transition from secular to sacred time and space is more visual than the old one. It does not, however, mean the end of the convivial banter of the minister with arriving members. Particularly good at welcoming the residents of Westside, Gerald calls them each by name as they arrive. His back-and-forth, though, will usually occur sometime during the official welcome, after our space is liturgically lighted. His welcome, indeed his voice, commands a resonant space of its own. A tall, well-built Bahamian man with salt-and-pepper hair and beard, Gerald sounds like a Caribbean James Earl Jones. His slightly British accent adds sophistication to the authoritative reverberations of his deep voice.

The choir, or Praise Team as it is called, is sitting in the front, facing us. In addition to the usual mix of African, African American, and a couple of white members, a white student from the local university has recently joined. But today we will be treated first to the children's choir. Grace's oldest daughter, Betty's two boys, and

Emmanuel's older daughter gather at the front to sing. They are led by Carrie, who is dressed in a sophisticated, lovely sleek white suit with a stylish pin. There are distinct dress differences at Good Samaritan. The African women and African American women are always more dressed up than the white women. Pam swears, though, that in a black church, the women would be wearing matching suits and shoes and hats. In comparison, she says, Good Samaritan blacks are really dressing down. All I know is that we white folks, especially the university students, do not have anything like a comparable church wardrobe.

The children's choir sings 'He's Got the Whole World in His Hands', and the response is immediate. A number of the Wellspring residents come alive. A small, older white woman wearing a golf visor and red dress smiles and claps to the music. Kay, a larger white woman, circles with her arms to the music and gestures to us as if saying, 'You there, the whole world, God's got you in his hands!' Terry, who usually sits with her head bowed and eyes closed, rocking backward and forward, seems to become more alert. She sways and bobs her head in ways that seem in sync with the music. A still younger white man who looks as if he has Down syndrome claps at the end after moving to the music. Tim in his wheelchair grins during this song and manages to clap a bit.

The decision of the Methodist Conference/bishop to bring in a new minister was somewhat of a surprise for the many Good Samaritans who were not raised Methodist. Unaccustomed to the concept of itinerant ministry, many were unfamiliar with connectional denominations, having attended independent churches that called ministers on their own. The transition was difficult for some, especially given strong connections with the founding pastors. Gerald, however, brought new energies and skills to the community. His preaching and liturgical style produced distinctive themes even as he displayed real skill with the group home members. That he was a man 'of color' would mean a new set of incorporative effects as well.

When the children sit down, Gerald leads us in a reading and prayer, which announce and celebrate the coming of the Holy Spirit on the early church. Gerald: '"And in the last days it shall come to pass", God declares, "that I will pour out my Spirit on all flesh."' We respond: '"And your sons and daughters shall prophesy, your old

shall dream dreams, and your young shall see visions." Amen.'
Someone reads passages in Acts on the day of Pentecost. We sing a
hymn from the Methodist hymnal. Following the lectionary readings,
Emmanuel reads from the Psalms and Romans. We stand to hear
from the Gospel of John. Another children's choir performance
receives accompanying responses of delight, and Gerald takes the
pulpit.

Gerald cuts a rather different figure than Dan. Raised Roman
Catholic in the former British Colony of the Bahamas, Gerald
comes from a large family. Middle class in status, his father was a
civil servant in the government of the first black prime minister,
Lynden Pindling. Growing up in the period when the former colony
finally achieved majority rule in 1967, Gerald was influenced by an
emerging indigenous sensibility of independence and agency. He tells
of Pindling's stress on education for the masses as it converged with
the value the Catholic Church placed on learning—influences that
continue to show in Gerald's sermons and their literary allusions.

With the focus of the room now on the sermon, Gerald's voice
takes over. Its compelling rich tones gradually rise in intensity and
volume throughout his performance. Beginning with a James Baldwin story, Gerald pulls out one of the two images with which he will
interpret our situation. Baldwin's narrator tells of the tragedy of his
younger brother's heroin addiction. Although Sonny gets hooked on
smack, it is his older brother who provides Gerald with the primary
image of denial. Having refused to face his brother's true state for
years, the narrator is forced to confront it when Sonny's arrest is
reported in the paper. Baldwin imagines this denial as a great block of
ice settled in his belly. As it melts, yet never quite goes away, he
glimpses his brother as he was in his earlier days of hope and
promise, a young black man in Harlem aspiring to be a jazz musician.
Gerald uses Baldwin's words to describe denial—self-protection,
looking away, and avoidance of painful reality. The capacity to see,
to know truthfully, is frozen within the narrator.

'Touch a thistle timidly', says Gerald, 'and it will prick you; grab it
firmly and its spines crumble.' The cost of timid avoidance is, para-
doxically, much worse than the inevitably traumatic but restorative
facing of the truth. With the paradoxical image of a thistle before us,

Gerald moves to the story of Pentecost. With the figure of the church's birthday, he develops a second image. The outpouring of the Spirit is an inclusive party; it is God's celebration. Describing the disciples as brave, feisty, and empowered by the Holy Spirit, Gerald's voice grows gradually louder as he evokes the turbulence and chaos of the birth of the church. He speaks of empowerment, of gifts for ministry and mission, of the power to 'witness to the mighty acts of God's salvation and not for our own personal glorification'.

Powerfully evoking a force that compelled the disciples to speak, he then moves to a contrast—our likely response to this opportunity. Patiently, Gerald lays out a picture of denial, describing familiar positions in which we can imagine ourselves refusing these 'birthday' opportunities. As he names positions of timidity and denial, the responses in the room begin to multiply. He lists a false concern with politeness, a fear of looking crazy, a notion that faith is private. With each named version of denial, he gets a stronger 'yes!' and another 'say so'.

After sketching out our problematic positions, Gerald moves to a description of the shape of God's Spirit. The Spirit's movement is always outward, he says, and its goal is always renewal. Repeating the prophet Joel's promise that God's Spirit would be poured out on all flesh, Gerald begins a litany of God's renewing acts. God's renewal is toward unity, he says, unity in Christ's body, and it will unite us with others 'across all existing barriers and divisions'. The divisions are cultural; he continues, they are religious and social and economic. And even when they are racial, or class- or gender-based, these divisions will be overcome by the Spirit. 'This is the character of God's work!' Gerald proclaims. As responses to his preaching get more frequent, they become more fervent.

Then Gerald moves to delineate our current divisions with analogous biblical examples: 'Race doesn't matter because we know that our Lord Jesus was born a Jew who also had Gentile blood.... Gender, not an issue, for sons and daughters would prophesy.... Age, not an obstacle, for the old will dream dreams while the young see visions. Class and occupation, of no consequence for there is but one king, and his name is Jesus. We are all his servants. Nationality... doesn't stand a chance in dividing us, because the earth is the Lord's and everything in it and we should be thankful to have been chosen as merely stewards of it.'

With a review of the Pentecostal fellowship of Parthians with Medes, Egyptians with Libyans, Jews with Arabs, Gerald continues to line out our positions of denial. Devout men refused to acknowledge this outpouring of the Spirit then, he roars, and they continue in denial today. We may not scandalize the Parthian or Mede, but we do it to the Hispanic migrant worker. We may not bother the Elamite, but we tolerate the unemployed African American. We may leave the Egyptian alone, but the Native American, the single white mother on welfare or the wheelchair user or 'special needs' child—we are in denial about all of these and the conditions of brokenness between us!

Moving to close, Gerald gets 'amens' and affirmations from most in the room. The responses crescendo with his own rising volume and artful repetition. God, he tells us, is doing this work. The work of God's Spirit is to end these boundaries. This is the birthday party of the church, and everybody is invited. If we have accepted the invitation, he tells us, we are having a good time. 'If you're white, the Spirit is melting that great block of ice in your gut. If you're black . . . you're no longer tasting the cynical trickles of ice water in your veins. Celebrate! Whoever you are . . . know that there is a birthday celebration going on, and the one who makes all things new wants you to be a part of it.' We are all invited, he concludes, and the RSVP is clear. 'For whoever calls on the name of the Lord shall be saved. Thanks be to God!' And many voices chime in with his 'Amen!'

There is clapping when Gerald finishes, and excitement in the air. Then the Praise Team stands up to sing. An African American woman sitting next to me hands off her baby girl to her husband and goes up to join them. 'I Feel the Spirit'—labeled an 'Act of Praise' in the bulletin, the song seems to perform in a full-bodied way the joy and pleasure that the community expressed verbally during the sermon. Betty, the first African American woman to join the church, leads the singing. A back-and-forth between Betty and the rest of the choir gets picked up by many of the worshippers. It is like a different language being spoken—a language of movement that is rhythmic and powerful. We who are white seem less familiar with this 'language'; our bodies do not seem as comfortable with the dance of worship. But it grips almost everyone. The choir sways. Sitting a few seats down from me, Betty's husband, Ronnie, mouths the words and sings along as if it were the most natural thing in the world. Pleasure is palpable in the room.

Gerald's rich, deep voice next moves us to the 'Concerns and Prayers'. Names are offered of relatives who are ill—Edgar's mother in nearby Roxboro and Gerald's stepmother in the Bahamas. Someone lifts up a friend who needs a visa to go to Liberia. Prayers are requested for Minnie at the death of her husband, for families still in Liberia, and for Liana, who is caught, visa-less in England. In the middle of this, Kenny starts clapping. An attendant speaks gently to him, asking him to stop, but he keeps it up. Then Deborah yells, 'Stop!' and Kenny goes silent. Such disruptions have no effect on Gerald. Without a pause, he offers a pastoral prayer, speaking eloquently of the community's concerns. During the prayer, Kenny starts clapping again, and this time he is left alone. At the close of his prayer, Gerald leads us in the Lord's Prayer, and it is time for the ritual with the most movement, the sharing of the peace.

At Gerald's invitation to pass the peace, everyone rises and moves about. Many people go to the 'special needs' folks to speak to them and, sometimes, to give hugs. Gerald is the best at this. He can call most of the residents by name. Others such as Emmanuel know some names, especially Tim in the wheelchair and Lucy and Kenny. Dean, a young white man who works at a local university, contrasts Good Samaritan's passing of the peace with the thirty seconds more traditional churches allow for turning to the one beside you to shake hands. 'Ours is a virtual free-for-all', says Dean. Judging by how long they extend the ritual, it is a chaos that he and many others clearly love.

Even before we finish, the attendants begin to wheel out the Westside residents, helping others with walkers and guiding some of them to the door. The schedules of care at Westside are always at odds with the times of the Sunday service. Inevitably residents come late and leave early. Gerald expresses his regret as they pack up and leave, his voice clearly resonating with some of them.

We finally take our seats, and Gerald calls forward two volunteers to take up an offering. Standing before the altar, he faces away from us and lifts up the filled collection plates as we sing the doxology.

Following a final hymn we remain standing, and a small boy comes forward with a candlesnuffer to put out the lighted altar candles. Completing the ritual closure of formal, sacred time and space, Gerald sends us forth. His benediction commends the renewal of wider worldly space.

Assessment

Gerald's worship style has both differences and overlaps with that of Dan and Linda. His main themes contrast. While he will typically line out positions of fault and accountability for members of the community as does Dan, Gerald's vision for a place of transformation, a place of grace, is typically linked with liberation concerns. Not only does he portray God as a God who identifies with the oppressed, he will often use the relevant cultural imagery to re-imagine a marginalized community as the agent. Like his use of James Baldwin in this sermon, his illustrations are frequently drawn from communities of color. Although the history of race in his native Bahamas is quite different from that of the US, Gerald grew up in an interracial family, and a white stepmother helped habituate him into racial awareness. On occasion, Gerald even imagines the redemptive future with images of women, or other unexpected subjects, inviting the community to 'be like Mary', for example. Her 'Here am I, Lord', he says in one sermon, is a model for recognizing God's claim upon us.

Liberation themes also appear in sermons with Gerald's use of social markers of marginalization to define the brokenness in the community. The brokenness of disunity is not differences of belief. It is not heresy, nor is it definable by blurred lines between so-called secular culture and a morally pure Christian space. Rather, Gerald tells us that Pentecost addresses disunity as the socioeconomic and cultural-political effect of 'Othering'. By naming our failure to live up to the call of the Spirit, Gerald creates a subject position of culpability for us. Our denial occurs in the form of timidity, of a refusal to face reality. While these are all sins of individual agency, they are implicitly linked to involvement in patterns of social marginalization—racism, sexism, classism, able-ism. These patterns include not only the racism of the white community against the black, but of the African American against the Latino as well.

Offering relief from these judging interpellations, Gerald also invokes a subject position of change and celebration. His images combine biblical and literary possibilities: Pentecost and birthdays; movement out of racial despair; boundaries of every sort breaking down. God's spirit can melt ice blocks of denial—the racism of the white heart and the cynicism of the black heart. We are—all of us across these lines—invitees to a divine party.

The themes of Gerald's preaching are not the only meanings that circulate in worship. As with Dan and Linda's services, the residents of Wellspring are more responsive to Gerald's friendly greetings and the resonances of his powerful voice than to the content of his sermons or of biblical and liturgical readings. Their squeals and outbursts do not always coordinate with the rest of the community's, but they are often readable as indications of pleasure. Of course, incorporative practices matter to all participants, not just to the 'special needs' members. The patterns of call and response during Gerald's sermons are essential performances. In the African American worship traditions, this 'involvement of the community in the speech event' is not an extra, but a necessary element of the sermon itself. It signals the priority of the corporate identity of the congregation. Without it, the event itself is invalid.[12] In short, if there is no communal participation in this verbal performance, the preacher has not communicated the gospel. While Dan's is an appropriated style and Gerald's West Indian, something like this communal responsive pattern forms the core of their worship.

Another vital feature of the worship is the bodily movement. While the verbal responses may be more characteristic of the African and African American worshippers at Good Samaritan, the waving of arms as an indication of the Spirit is an incorporative practice common to both black and white. Movement also occurs with the singing. Indeed, worship entails the full sensorium of human experience and, as McGann says, the 'human body is...an instrument of praise and epiphany of the Spirit'.[13] The bodied display of

---

[12] Alkebulan, 'Spiritual Essence', 37–8.
[13] McGann, *Precious Fountain*, 261.

the beauty of music is nowhere more evident than in the swaying of black bodies to the beat. White members of the choir and congregation, as I said, are never quite as good at this. Jackson-Brown puts it well with the observation that 'the difference between European rhythmic conception and African is the fact that Europeans perceive rhythm by hearing, while Africans perceive rhythm by movement'.[14] And a third equally powerful set of incorporative practices happens as the greetings of friendly faces, gestures, and hugs are distributed in the passing of the peace, producing messages of welcome and concern—emerging interracial bodily habituations and beginning face-to-face encounters between the normate and participants with disabilities.

A contrast with Dan and Linda's worship style occurs in the more formal liturgical elements of Gerald's services. To be sure, these elements do not completely alter the feel of worship. There is still informal banter between Gerald and members such as William, and the contributions of the Westside residents continue to disrupt any pretense of 'sacred silence'. The call-and-response patterns are as intense, if not more so, as any produced by Dan and Linda. However, the fact that a black male body is adorned in the formal attire of clerical vestments in a mixed-race congregation invests Gerald with more than the standard authority accorded the ministerial figure. Gerald's topics and style are quite different from the self-deprecating, I'm-just-an-ordinary-sinner ethos of Dan. But even more, Gerald's leadership as incorporative ritual practice is its own communication over and above the content of his preaching. In contrast to Dan's appropriated style, his is a black performance of authoritative knowing and pronouncing with particular power in an interracial setting. His presence displays an agency and ownership of space that disrupts existent racialized body proprieties. It will no doubt communicate an ownership of space to African and African American members announcing the affirmation of black authority. For those habituated into white proprieties, that ownership will be perceived as an unsettling visceral experience. It may create an opening for a new habituation or invoke a fear of trespass that crosses the line.

14 Jackson-Brown, 'Black Hymnals', 103.

'SPECIAL NEEDS' SERVICE

Gerald welcomes his congregation in booming rich tones as they enter for the Thursday night service, calling each member by name. Some wander into the sanctuary as if by accident; some walk in haltingly, slowly. Some of the congregants are wheeled in by attendants and parked near the pulpit. Here comes Cathy, a middle-aged white woman, striding in with her arms stretched straight out. She heads right for me and I give her a hug, meeting her delighted face with a big smile of my own. Next comes Marcy, a young African American girl, screaming loudly. Two women attendants surround her in their seats, restraining her arms throughout the service. Philip, a short African American man who looks to be in his late twenties, ambles in grinning and sits next to me. About thirty people gather to worship here as the room fills with sounds of delight mixed with other, harder to identify noises.

The order of service at Thursday night worship is fairly traditional. Opening announcements, call to worship, hymns, sermon, and sharing the peace are found here, just as in most United Methodist gatherings. At these services, each element simply undergoes a twist to adapt to participants' capacities. Gerald starts the announcements by asking, 'What's new?' Bill has been to Virginia Beach, or so translates Johnny, the only one who can understand him. 'Beach' sets off a reaction; the delighted cry 'beach!' is heard from several places in the room. Gerald calls for a round of applause for Bill. As everyone claps, Bill's face is split with smiles. New people are introduced and get a hand, too. Most of the participants come from two different group homes. A couple of the worshippers live with their families. One is Daphne, whose Mennonite family brings her to the Thursday night services; the other is Bob.

An elderly white man dressed in coveralls with some dozen or so pens clipped to the front bib pocket, Bob comes in late and walks straight to the pulpit. He hands a folder to Gerald, who reads aloud the enclosed certificate of merit Bob has received for 'supporting literacy'. At Gerald's urging, we clap for Bob, who takes a bow and sits down. Gerald intones a familiar call to worship and the community echoes each line back. Some say it, some say something like it. The sound is chaotic and rich, more textured than the clear, etched noise of a group speaking in unison.

One of the highlights of the service is music. Rita, the church pianist, is there to accompany. Regulars Liana and Richard are also there and hand out musical instruments to the participants. The energy level rises visibly with the start of hymn singing. Philip, who has Down syndrome, pops up out of his seat, walks to the front, and takes the mike. Ignoring Gerald's attempt to turn him to face the community, Philip sings the entire hymn with his back to us. Some in the group shake tambourines, and a few play cymbals or clack rhythm sticks together. As we clap for Philip after the hymn, he raises his arms in a victory salute, then flexes his muscles as he strikes a bodybuilder pose. Tim sits curved and thin in his wheelchair; his body trembles a bit. His smile tells us that his guttural noises are sounds of joy.

Gerald reads the Scripture lesson about God's giving of the Ten Commandments to Moses (Exod. 20: 1–20). Engaging folks as he walks around, Gerald uses a large erase board to solicit responses to the story. He sketches a picture of lightning with clouds. 'Who is afraid of thunder? Raise your hand.' Some raise hands. 'Who's afraid of lightning?' More hands. Bob volunteers commentary, and Gerald invites him to come to the front. Bob talks in images of heaven and God and angels. Seeming to speak about his vision he says, 'and laying on your back, the clouds above roll by'. Mary, a tiny woman sitting frozen in a wheelchair, begins to squeal very loudly. An attendant wheels her around sideways and begins to rub her forehead in a soothing way. Terry sits quietly, head down, and rocks back and forth in her chair.

Gerald next draws stone tablets on the erase board to represent the commandments. He asks for the community to name the commandments, one by one. Laughing and cajoling and chiding, he gets all manner of responses. A couple of participants look at their bibles, but it is the job of enumerating the commandments that is taken most seriously. Several hands shoot up with fingers raised triumphantly in the air. 'First!' then 'Two!' 'Second', call out several of the men. Getting the 'next number' seems more important than getting the content of the commandment. Gerald writes them down, and Bob calls out, 'Love me as you love your neighbor.' Gerald chuckles and holds him off to get others to speak.

Concluding that love of God is summed up with Jesus's commandment to love our neighbor as ourselves, Gerald asks, 'Who is my neighbor?' Diane calls out, 'ME!!' Gerald roars, 'Yes, Diane!' and begins to name people to the group: 'Diane is your neighbor. Bill is your neighbor. Philip and Ralph are your neighbors.' He walks around pointing at different people. 'And we can do it because God loves us; God helps us. We couldn't do it without God.' A couple of attendants say, 'Amen!'

This cognitively participatory part of the service is followed by 'Jesus Loves Me', the most boisterous hymn of the service, which Rita accompanies on the piano. Some in the room have been gazing off into space, or sitting with heads drooping during the sermon. Roused by the sound of 'Jesus Loves Me', they respond, clapping with many of the others, sometimes waving their arms. The Lord's Prayer seems to be another familiar element. Gerald leads the group in the prayer and the resonance of voices echoing (if not repeating) his powerful voice fills the room. A call for attention, an expression of consent, or pleasure or even protest, this echoing, or *echolalia*, is itself a communication of social interaction.[15]

When it is time for the offering, three of the men and one woman, Cathy, get selected to take offering plates around. Cathy and Bob take their plates and navigate the main rows, going back again more than once and obviously enjoying the activity. Bill halts with his plate at the back and eventually has to be led by an attendant to the front with his collection. Will, an older man in suspendered trousers, stands up and, rather than passing the collection plate at all, he spends the time putting his hands in and out of his pockets trying to find change. He repeats this over and over as Rita's offering music plays out.

Philip is asked to blow out the candles. Gerald hands him the candlesnuffer, and Philip goes up to the altar. There he stops in the middle of his task, looks up, and starts talking. Waiting, Gerald lets him pray, and Philip repeats the same sound over and over. When he finally sits down, Philip gets a round of applause. After the dismissal

---

[15] Long unrecognized as communication, echolalia is a form of expression sometimes used by people with autism. Ann P. Turnbull, Rud Turnbull, Marilyn Shank, and Sean J. Smith (eds.), *Exceptional Lives: Special Education in Today's Schools*, 4th edn. (Upper Saddle River, NJ: Merrill Prentice Hall, 2003), 2.

blessing, Olive appears with Liana and Richard carrying trays of refreshments. They take cookies and punch around, making sure that everyone gets a chance to have something, finding alternatives for those whose attendants forbid the goodies. Then goodbyes and leavetaking. Some people linger. Pete is especially slow to leave, pausing a number of times along the way; attendants urge him to move along. The effect of familiarity seems vital. I say goodbye to Fred and get a minimal response. Hearing Gerald's voice, Fred lights up visibly and grins. Eventually, the room becomes silent and empty.

Assessment

As much disability literature insists, it is crucial to avoid constructing human subjects primarily through labels that define them simply as broken people.[16] All of us are persons with degrees of dis-ability, and the supposed clear line between the abled and the disabled is a social fiction. That the group home population at Good Samaritan is distinctive for members' inabilities with language and mastering of their own bodies may mark them as particularly 'different', but cannot be allowed to function as a comprehensive 'Othering' marker of what it means to be disabled, an issue for later consideration. Nevertheless the most important assumption of this worship service is that all participants are children of God. The driving question here is how effective Good Samaritan's practices are at supporting and eliciting the full humanity of these participants as children of God. So neither the service nor my descriptions can completely avoid the limiting labeling. Recognition that the persons described here are more than communication 'problems' is in some sense a reason to ask to what extent Good Samaritan's worship is a successful communicative practice for members of the group homes.

What is really distinctive about this service is its constitution by a greater variety of communicative forms than are found in a typical

---

[16] One expression of this is the choice to use 'people first' language in special education classifications. So one speaks not about 'the mentally retarded', but a student with Down syndrome, or a person with learning disabilities. There are more critical perspectives that challenge 'normal' discourse that would even characterize people this way. Turnbull et al., *Exceptional Lives*, 7–8.

Sunday morning service. It is neither the themes of Gerald's sermon nor the other practices of passing on traditional stored memories of Christian communities that stand out. Certainly it matters that messages such as God's love for each person and the theme of hymns such as 'Jesus Loves Me' are part of the service. However, most of the participants can be characterized as having some form of developmental and learning disability, and a number of them rely upon nonsymbolic communication.[17] So read or orally delivered content is inadequate as a communicative form. In large part the media *are* the message, or at least they are as important as the intended message of inclusion, and the media must be multiple. The forms of communication in the service determine what kind of subject positions are likely created for the 'special needs' worshippers by these worship practices.

Several features of the service stand out. A first is recognition. Gerald greets individuals personally as they enter. For the people who respond to verbal communication—Cathy, Bob, and Philip—being named publicly in Gerald's warm, resonant voice is an important way to be seen, to be recognized. Gerald's and my own responses to initiatives by Cathy and others—the return of direct gazes, smiles, and hugs—also communicate recognition. The clearest sign to us of successful communication is when smiles and hugs are returned. Particularly powerful forms of recognition occur when individuals are singled out not only for greetings but also for performances and applause. Bob and Philip get the space to speak and sing and receive group affirmation as well.

The ongoing conversational dynamics of the service are also important for many of the participants. For instead of constantly

[17] I interpret disability here through the categories of special education because its focus is enhancing communication. According to the US Department of Education, categories of disability include learning disabilities, speech or language impairments, mental retardation, emotional disturbance, multiple disabilities, hearing impairments, orthopedic impairments, autism, visual impairments, traumatic brain injury, developmental delay, and deaf-blindness. See ch. 1, 'Overview of Today's Special Education', in Turnbull et al., *Exceptional Lives*, 2–39. My descriptions of various conditions of the group home residents, which do not include all of those categories, are based upon my own observations plus an interview with Steve Blakeman, who was a consultant to the group homes (17 Mar. 2000). There are critics of the social power of the 'normal' who would not agree with all of these labels.

proclaiming, announcing, or telling—all typical postures of worship leaders—Gerald *asks* and *solicits* and *invites* the congregants. He asks questions of the congregants. He invites their responses. He extends the back-and-forth even to his preaching. Those with language are the most obvious partners in this conversational dynamic. As a respondent to Gerald's questions, Bill gets recognition for starting a beach discourse, as does Diane when she identifies herself as the neighbor to be loved. But even someone like Tim, who has cerebral palsy with accompanying speech disorders, is able to signal his appreciation of Gerald's style. While his speech problems make it difficult for those unfamiliar with his articulations to understand him, Tim can understand Gerald's verbal communication and respond with visible signs of enjoyment.[18]

Several other strategies help expand the sermon beyond an exercise in abstract thinking. Gerald's movement around as he talks and his pointing out different people to illustrate his questions help shift its highly cognitive register to a dynamic of visual, intersubjective relationality.[19] Being *told* one is known and loved by God gets performed as literal *face-to-face recognition*. Additional relief from the ideational character of the service comes in the physical gestures of enumerating the commandments. As congregants act out the 'meaning' of the Ten Commandments, they contribute to the sermon. No longer simply the minister's performance, it is a shared project. Equally effective is Gerald's use of pictures. His drawings on the erase board add an important visual medium to the repertoire of communication.

Given the pleasure they seem to provide for those with language and for several without it, music and movement are also important media of exchange. Unless they are obvious signs of distress, as Mary's attendant interpreted her squeals to be, increasing vocalizations often mean, 'I like this'.[20] Music always brings increasing

[18] Tim is a smart young man who can read. In other settings Gerald has listened to him read the Bible. Turnbull et al., *Exceptional Lives*, 404–5.

[19] Given the very different disabilities, this is not equally effective for all participants, but Gerald's movement around allows for more direct eye contact, which is an important part of communication.

[20] Ellin Siegel and Amy Wetherby, 'Enhancing Nonsymbolic Communication', in Martha E. Snell and Fredda Brown (eds.), *Instruction of Students with Severe Disabilities*, 5th edn. (Upper Saddle River, NJ: Prentice-Hall, 2000), 424–5. The important thing is familiarity with an individual's repertoire of communication.

vocalization, something noticeable in most Sunday services as well. Wheelchair-bound Daphne is happiest when we are singing, a response confirmed by her mother. As do many in the group, she perks up and moves her head back and forth as she sings along. The pleasure of movement and music is especially evident in Philip's seeming-pantomime of a rock star singing. Not only does he sway to the music, but his bodybuilding pose in front of the congregation brings him something resembling fan adulation. Even the more 'conventional' movements of gathering the offering and blowing out the candles provide several people with opportunities to move about and to interact, all of which enhance the sensory richness of the worship.

Explicit recognition, ongoing conversation, music, movement, pictures, and other strategies of involvement characterize the communicative repertoire of Thursday night worship. And the force of this repertoire is to produce a subject position for the participants, which at its best is a subject position of *being recognized*. With the help of Liana, Richard, and Olive, Gerald produces a space for the 'special needs' folks to appear, or at least for some of them to appear. Not simply due to the calling of individual names, this space of recognition is the creation of opportunities to speak, to perform, to interact, and to be seen as much as to be named. An important presupposition of the worship service makes this appearing possible, that is, that noise and squeals and outbursts are not problematic behavior to be challenged. Rather than disruptions to be disciplined, they are forms of communication that must be honored.[21] Hence, the creation of respectful space for this wide spectrum of communications is absolutely vital to the service.

Evidence of this space is seen in Gerald's skill at interaction. He welcomes the responses, whatever form they take, and invites them throughout the service. He often confirms that a communication has been heard—confirmations that range from words of affirmation

---

[21] This shift from treating such behavior as a discipline problem to reading it as communication is a profoundly important development in special education. Turnbull et al., *Exceptional Lives*, 239, 293, 416, 267. See Diane Baumgart, 'Treating Problem Behaviors as Communication', in Diane Baumgart, Jeanne M. Johnson, and Edwin Helmstetter (eds.), *Augmentative and Alternative Communication Systems for Persons with Moderate and Severe Disabilities* (Baltimore: Paul H. Brookes, 1990), 17–38.

to appreciative chuckles that signal his own pleasure at the inter-actions.[22] Gerald's waiting on Philip, when he paused at the altar, rather than hurrying him along, is itself a skilled response. It indicates recognition of Philip's power to communicate and likely signals as much to Philip, no small thing in a society with minimum space or patience for people like him. This repertoire of activities creates incorporative ritual practices that communicate respect for the 'special needs' community—respect that is unusual for most church services in the US. In so doing, they are fairly described as sharing the good news of welcome, and they may even enhance congregants' sense of their own worth.[23]

FORGING COMMON WORSHIP PRACTICES

I now return to my opening question. In what sense are the worship practices forging 'a common vocabulary and practices for congregational conversation' at Good Samaritan?[24] In what sense are they negotiating an identity? At this point, a number of connecting or overlapping practices of worship are worth identifying for their contributions toward the desired place for all to appear.

It goes without saying that no shared beliefs or creed can adequately describe a shared vocabulary negotiated in worship. Indeed, given some of the group home residents, the phrase 'shared vocabulary' does not offer the best image for what Good Samaritans hold in common. However, Protestant worship is the gathering where the Word, or gospel, is proclaimed. A first sign of common discourse, if not vocabulary, must be some shared good news in these worship styles. Furthermore, there are important themes in Good

[22] Siegel and Wetherby stress confirming reactions to nonsymbolic communications. It is crucial to help a person understand that they have the capacity to communicate. 'Enhancing Nonsymbolic Communication'.

[23] I do not know this, of course. Attendants do say that it is a very good thing for group home residents to go to such 'public' places and be warmly welcomed and invited to respond rather than being stared at or subjected to the rituals of degradation. Turnbull et al., *Exceptional Lives*, continually stress the importance of letting people know that they have been 'heard'.

[24] Foster, *Embracing Diversity*, 79.

Samaritan worship practices: ministry to 'those not like us', discourse about 'ordinary people', and God's work of freedom and hospitality, and so on. Indication of overlap or commonality amidst all this difference, then, is found in what I call a *logic of redemption*.

Even as they employ different images in Sunday services, both Dan and Gerald invite the community to follow a similar kind of logic. Not logic in the sense of a purely rational kind of reflection, this is rather an existential journey that moves from recognition of wrong toward recognition of wrong made right. Both interpret biblical passages so as to display a movement from conviction and judgment to redemption and grace. While their sermons depart thematically, these differences have primarily to do with specifics within this logic. Using 'ordinary us' discourse to identify the community, Dan defines sin primarily as an individual posture. His image of the Kingdom has certain liberation overtones in the sense that the church as inclusive community is his ongoing vision for Good Samaritan. However, Dan never moves to a social lens through which to understand that Kingdom. Gerald continues the interpellation of individuals as sinners, but adds liberation images of both social sin and its redemption. Despite their varying developments, however, both logics are logics of redemption, and, in different ways, they invite the non-group home congregants to fuller vocations in the world.

One might say that Dan's anti-rich (or anti-elite) discourse affirms that 'we ordinary folks' are loved by God. We may be tempted by culture, too materialistic, inauthentic, and stressed, according to several of the sermon diagnoses, but God loves us and does not require correct doctrine or any other kind of fancy church behavior to make us acceptable.[25] Instead, grace is a God who accepts imposters; grace is a God who forgives, who relieves from stress and desire for the worldly—a Savior born in 'a smelly, ordinary old barn'. However, his is not simply a logic of acceptance. While in many respects Dan's redemption logic is limited to solicitation of individual recommitment to faith every week, hardly a development of the

---

[25] Examples of Dan's descriptions of our subject positions as sinners include: holders of grudges and resentment (Luke 15: 25–32), 29 Oct. 1995; wallowers in stress and self-pity (Phil. 4: 4–7), 12 Nov. 1995; materialistic culture-followers (Is. 9: 2, 6–7; John 1), 3 Dec. 1995; superficial, inauthentic, phony (Luke 2: 1–20), 10 Dec. 1995.

complexities of a socially engaged discipleship, his vision of inclusion operates as a parallel discourse to that of 'God loves ordinary folks'. It fills out Good Samaritan's vocation in a quite distinctive way. Through the story of the Ethiopian eunuch, 'ordinary folks' became much more than a theme for invoking God's gracious acceptance. Ordinary folks are called to go to 'people not like us', which turns out to be people even more socially disadvantaged than those at Good Samaritan.

With Gerald, use of anti-rich (or anti-elite) discourse does not function to position us as ordinary, as did Dan's, but to develop claims about social oppression and God's will to liberate. His imagery is drawn from broader social, racial, and cultural sources than Dan's. But Gerald does not engage in an abstract reasoning that would fail to speak to an oral culture. His logic is regularly filled with concrete stories and images. Moreover, he offers no space for Good Samaritans to understand ourselves as privileged and free from blame as the oppressed, because he continues to position the congregation as those who are in denial, who fall short, who do not trust.[26] However, all are invited to participate in the freedom that characterizes God's Kingdom, where truly seeing is recognizing Jesus and partaking of the bread of life, where entering the Kingdom of hospitality compels us to feed the hungry and do justice.

In the ideas offered by these worship practices, there are, then, both convergences and divergences, not just divergence in ideas, but in the people who are compelled by the differently filled-in logics. Numerous congregants are attracted to Dan's theme of ordinary people. They especially appreciate his self-identification as an ordinary sinner. Dan freely shares his troubled background with the church. His family problems were only the beginning. Continuing stumbles occurred throughout his young adulthood and postconversion. There is

[26] A sampling of the way Gerald images our subject position as sinners includes: hypocrites and judgment passers (Matt. 13: 24–30, 36–43), 21 July 1996; blind, don't recognize the Kingdom, half-hearted (Matt. 13: 31–3, 44–52), 28 July 1996; too choosy (Matt. 14: 13–21), 4 Aug. 1996; easily corrupted by worldliness, like loyalty to the military, fail to fulfill commitments, like prostitutes and thieves (Matt. 21: 23–32), 29 Sept. 1996; legalists, caught up in our accomplishments, tempted to be slaves to the law, endangering the good of the community (Matt. 23: 1–12), 2 Nov. 1996; dodging our prophetic role, substitute religion for the doing of justice (1 Sam. 3: 1–20; John 1: 43–51), 19 Jan. 1997.

nothing worse than a minister who 'talks down' to the congregation, says Zelda, and Dan is always willing to share his frailties. Everybody appreciates that. Kathy speaks for many, both black and white, when she comments admiringly that, unlike most other pastors, he never acts superior.

A number of people, however, are put off by Dan's style. Originally attracted to Good Samaritan because of its multiracial make-up and the inclusion of group home residents, several white university students drop out because of Dan's sermons. Some complain about the call to recommitment that follows each Sunday. One of the more active students, Mary still complains that the call is like a 'ritual of pulling teeth'. One older white member calls them Dan's 'seeker services'. Several of the students return when Gerald becomes the new pastor and find his sermons more intellectually stimulating.

Those compelled by Gerald, however, are not only white and not only students. Several African Americans find both styles compelling. Donna admires the fact that Gerald's sermons always present the church with a challenge. 'He always tells us like, you've got to *do* something, you know, don't sit here listening to me, you know, go out and do this. Don't just sit here to listen to me talk!' After a particularly confrontive sermon, she comments admiringly about his blunt, honest speech: 'This is a money boy, he came down hard on that . . . it's a good thing.' Donna and Pam, fans of both ministers, think Dan's preaching is 'more black' than Gerald's, precisely because he does not use a written text. Kenyan Kimathi admires the substance in Gerald's preaching very much, but is one of several who also like Dan's warmth and ordinary discourse.

The different themes attract divergent loyalties; some also help create converging commitments. All non-group home participants, black and white, working class and university-connected are compelled by the discourse of diversity. Whether this discourse is articulated in Dan's vocabulary and choice of biblical imagery or in Gerald's, the members of Good Samaritan share a vision not only that the mix of races, nationalities, and abilities is their calling, but that 'this is what the church is supposed to look like', as a much-repeated phrase puts it. And of course it is more than the themes, beliefs, and ideas that constitute the worship practices and the commonalities of Good Samaritan; the practices with primarily affective resonances are equally important.

A second source key to identity negotiation comes from the practices associated with movement and music. What these offer in the forging of commonalities is a primary good of pleasure. To be sure, the subject positions offered by the ministers are positions of discomfort. Both Dan and Gerald pronounce judgment and criticism in their accounts of the community. However, no position as 'the guilty' or 'follower of worldly wisdom' is left unrelieved by a word of gospel. Parallel with the gospel as message of relief, incorporative practices of singing and ecstatic response to proclamation produce experiences of joyful exuberance. From the songs of the tradition to the echolalia that is some congregants' form of participation, they create an oral and emotional pleasure.

Furthermore, as Philip's joyful performance with the microphone exemplifies, the performance of praise is sometimes inseparable from the pleasurable display of bodies. Scholars tend to find African and African American sensibilities more advanced in the 'expressive culture of movement', and that is surely the case at Good Samaritan.[27] However, this pleasurable display is available to congregants in a number of different ways and to different degrees. And if Philip is any indication, an altered state of pleasure seems to affect almost everyone there, if only for a moment.

Worship practices also form the space where 'special needs' congregants and the rest of the congregation come together. An important third contribution to the community's identity, its success lies not only in the ministers' skills at communicating, but also in the common pleasure all members seem to share in singing and in physical welcome. Rituals of inclusion rather than rituals of degradation characterize the worship insofar as normate members come face-to-face with group home members. Several Good Samaritans are committed to the Thursday night 'special needs' services, where they help create an even wider space for the recognition of group home participants. Good Samaritan is an unusual church in its

---

[27] As Jackson-Brown puts it, movement is 'a behavior that shapes the musical event'. 'Black Hymnals', 103.

welcoming ethos of noisiness, its comfort with movement, and its encouragement of multiple forms of participation.

However, the Thursday service is a locus of missed opportunities as well, as the group home residents are far from fully recognized. The most readable communications are those where people respond with obvious pleasure, either verbally or nonverbally with smiles and laughter and participation in songs and unison responses. But several participants are not so easy to interpret. Given the prevailing assumption that 'all individuals communicate in some way', we must say that the service is not completely successful. Some of the individuals do not seem to respond. Terry, for example, rocks back and forth in her chair with her head mostly down. Nothing in this service seems to move her. Marcy has to be restrained during sections of the service. Several are responsive to music and singing, yet seem listless and nonresponsive during the verbal practices of the worship. However, these interpretations may represent a failure of comprehension rather than a failure of response. While once written off as pathological, rocking back and forth is now recognized as communication. These 'special needs' folks are very likely communicating, but no one in leadership has the skill to read and understand all of their modes of communication.[28]

As educators emphasize, while there are conventional forms of nonsymbolic communication—giving, showing, reaching, for example—a well-developed *habitus* for understanding and properly reciprocating requires practices of interaction that produce familiarity. The attendant who responds to Marcy has developed that skill. She can hear Marcy's distress and communicate with her well by soft, firm touches and moving Marcy away from the intensity of the service.

A skill for interpreting nonsymbolic communication would include the instinctive capacity to pause and allow for 'repair strategies' when a nonsymbolic communicator fails at communicating.[29] Such a *habitus* would include the capacity to change the social and physical environment when necessary, for the position of bodies is an important environmental feature affecting the ability to respond.[30]

---

[28] Turnbull et al., *Exceptional Lives*, 286.
[29] Siegel and Wetherby, 'Enhancing Nonsymbolic Communication', 427–8.
[30] Ibid. 433–4.

Along with repetitive behavior, for example, the need for predictability is vitally important for many people with autism. A well-developed *habitus* might have better understood what was being communicated by the older gentleman who kept plunging his hands into his pockets while taking up the offering. In sum, such a *habitus* would resource the best responses because it would provide us not only with a wider knowledge of the function of different communicative behaviors—the difference between behavior regulation, social interaction, and joint attention, for example—but, most importantly, with the nuance of individuals' repertoires.

It is certainly true that Good Samaritan is far more successful at welcoming difference than most churches, where much of the group home residents' communications would be disciplined as disruptive. The kind of *habitus* needed to help elicit a position of full recognition is well developed by parents such as Liana, who knows how to adjust her facial and physical responses to Esther. They know how to adjust their pace and when reinforcement is needed to signal that a communication has been understood. Judging from his sensitivity in waiting, Gerald is beginning to develop such capacities, but this is not enough. The missed opportunities to communicate suggest that an inclusion of 'special needs' folks that truly creates a space for all to appear requires more radical rethinking of the traditional structures of worship and a disruption of the normate bodily proprieties that still dominate.

If these worship practices aid in the production of a place for appearing, it is by altering the social habituations of participants into the proprieties of race and 'normal-bodiedness'. That would mean alteration of the spatial ownership characteristic of white bodily proprieties, and the double-consciousness of African American proprieties, a sensibility only just emerging for African members. Dan's regularized—ritual—way of performing worship leadership communicates identification with ordinary sinners and a safe call to inclusion. His chatty style, banter with congregants, and regular commentary on the liturgical forms create a compelling space of acceptance for many members.[31] Given that his style overlaps with

[31] Sarah says that liberation discourse doesn't quite fit because, 'we're too relational and unless you rework something like liberation discourse and put it in terms that feel relational to this place here, it doesn't work'. She explains Dan's 'ordinary

practices characteristic of much African American worship, both black and white members respond well to Dan's services. As a white man in leadership, however, his call to welcome the 'eunuch' is likely the less disruptive of the two ministerial styles, at least for the white members. His white appropriation of black styles of performance is a safe message to whites that they still 'own' the space, and a white male authority figure will not directly authorize nonwhite members' ownership of space. However, his relational, accepting, and nonauthoritarian posture may in fact be a welcome alternative to other Christian identities in their pasts, identities of control and guilt, a topic for later consideration.

In relation to racialized proprieties, Gerald's leadership offers more liberation challenges, and his performative challenges are striking as well. Insofar as his voice becomes a significant focal point in the service, it takes over the space in a powerful way. While the community still sings and responds, there is not the repartee that characterized Dan's services. The focus is forward, not diffused, and one does not have the sense of people moving around in the room. I suggest that the more formal, imposing voice, demeanor, and dress of a black man in authority produce a different experience for black and white in the congregation. Gerald's performance undoubtedly trespasses on the white propriety of ownership of space for some, even as it produces more pleasure for others.[32] At best there is some alteration of sensibilities for a variety of members.

Finally, the practices of worship have mixed effects as challenges to 'rituals of degradation' that typically characterize the socialization of many Good Samaritans who did not grow up around people designated as 'disabled'. Admittedly, the mainstreaming of relationships has not happened.[33] There is still segregation of 'normal' from 'not-normal' in the community. However, simply worshipping

discourse' in terms of the predilections of a white working-class oral culture. Things that don't touch them personally, they don't get.

[32] Distinctions need to be made for Africans' and African Americans' experiences, of course, and will be taken up in a later chapter.

[33] Quoted in Nancy L. Eiesland, *The Disabled God: Toward a Liberatory Theology of Disability* (Nashville: Abingdon, 1994), 92–3.

together and gathering in a face-to-face way makes a difference. When members of the community take time to physically welcome one another during the passing of the peace, bodily proprieties of 'normality' are breached in the regular Sunday service. Some in the congregation are learning a different way to be in relation to those marked as 'special needs' members.

In conclusion, the gathering together of differently abled and raced and gendered bodies in worship, regardless of who is leading worship, also effects a *habitus* of comfort with the other; and comfort is an important element in the larger good of welcome and inclusion. What is unique about practices of worship is that the bodily incorporative practices that bring differently racialized and abled worshippers together are paired with discourses of accountability, self-inspection, forgiveness, and transformation—hope for change. Unlike many churches in the US, at Good Samaritan a discourse of welcoming all God's children, whether simply inclusionary like Dan's or liberation-inflected like Gerald's, is being performed face-to-face with the culturally vilified 'Other'. And, however imperfectly, Good Samaritan worship is sometimes creating spaces of appearance and recognition for those 'Others'.

The meanings and the resonances that circulate through the gatherings have powerful effects on the creation of the place of Good Samaritan. While never 'doing the same thing' for all of the worshippers, these practices do produce pleasure, even an erotic sensibility of God's living presence.[34] They also solicit accountability to God and accountability to the stranger. They are productive practices, then, in ways that are quite distinctive from those not shaped by inscribed tradition. Whether the 'common conversation' they create, to use Foster's image, will be adequate to the ongoing negotiation of identity remains to be seen.

[34] This may be my white sense. For views that African American worship has not recognized the erotic adequately, see Anthony B. Pinn and Dwight N. Hopkins (eds.), *Loving the Body: Black Religious Studies and the Erotic* (New York: Palgrave MacMillan, 2004).

5

Working It Out: Homemaking Practices

> Their lives are lived out more in traditions and practices than they are in thinking and knowing the faith.
>
> Sample, *Ministry in an Oral Culture*

> Women who nurture the development of people and communities are carrying out an ancient tradition that has no name.
>
> Belenky, Bond, and Weinstock,
> *A Tradition that Has No Name*

DEFINING HOMEMAKING PRACTICES

In deciding to become a place that welcomed the outsider—those 'not like us'—the Wellspring remnant created a new vision for the community. Their Bible-generated rationale took on bodily form, first, as the all-white community sought out people of color, both Africans and African Americans, and, second, as the church moved to welcome group home residents. With this latter decision, it proved itself capable of improvisation, that is, of generating new definitions of the outsider. Having seen the importance of incorporative practices in worship, this chapter takes up activities that are typically not granted the status of ecclesial practices, primarily because activities such as cooking and cleaning and relating do not usually qualify as theological 'traditions'. Including these bodily skills will show that a variety of Good Samaritan's activities contribute not only to the heteroglossia of its identity but to its creation of places to appear as well. The activities of concern in this chapter involve the things that people do in order to maintain and sustain the community—Good Samaritan's *homemaking practices*.[1]

By 'homemaking', I mean to suggest the distinctive ways the community maintains itself as a *physical* place, for example, maintenance and upkeep, but also as a *livable* place—a real homeplace where people offer each other material, emotional, and spiritual support. This expanded notion of practices will aid proper attention to these activities. First, foregrounding the incorporative character of some activities is crucial for appreciation of their full effect. Second, understanding that the social memory of a place is not constituted simply by the explicitly interpretive activities such as Bible studies and worship helps us avoid overlooking participatory styles and skills characteristic of oral cultures. At Good Samaritan, for example, the activities of physical maintenance are as crucial to the creation of redemptive place as the Bible studies and participation in worship. For some participants, they are even more important.

Good Samaritan typifies an oral 'culture'. Alternately called 'residual' oral or 'traditional' oral, such cultures are modern—their members are literate—but their primary mode of communication is oral, not written.[2] Oral communicative engagement with the world differs markedly from the kind of thinking and communicating associated with writing. A predilection for written forms demands and produces systematic coherence, lengthy argument, and abstraction. In contrast, oral modes of expression are concrete. They take form in concrete genres, such as stories, aphorisms, and sayings rather than extensive complex arguments and theories. (Hence, filling out forms and signing checks are usually the only kinds of writing members of such cultures do.) Employing concrete genres to

---

[1] Kathleen Norris recognizes something like this in her *The Quotidian Mysteries: Laundry, Liturgy and 'Women's Work'*, Madeleva Lecture in Spirituality (Mahwah, NJ: Paulist Press, 1998).

[2] Walter Ong's term 'residual' suggests that the older tradition of orality still exists as 'residue' in literate cultures, thus distinguishing it from a primary oral culture (one that lacks a written language). Tex Sample prefers 'traditional oral' not only because the notion of residual seems demeaning to him, but '[t]here is no literate culture without this "residual" orality'. See Walter J. Ong, *Orality and Literacy: The Technologizing of the World* (London: Routledge, 1982), 20–77; and Tex Sample, *Ministry in an Oral Culture: Living with Will Rogers, Uncle Remus, and Minnie Pearl* (Louisville, KY: Westminster/John Knox, 1994), 9–10.

display lived experience, oral modes can communicate meaningful things about reality without needing to explain it. As such they have great potential to create connections between people.

Oral skills are well represented at Good Samaritan. While the small number of university students at the church is less typical of this kind of culture, three groups' practices qualify. African American religious traditions are distinctively and famously oral. The good preacher has long been the central authoritative figure in the community. One scholar of African American discourse goes so far as to say that the 'crucial difference' among Americans is the primarily written mode of communication preferred by whites and the 'spoken mode for blacks', shaped as African Americans are by African oral cultures. Franz Fanon says, to ' "talk like a book" is to "talk like a white man" '.[3]

Not all white men, however. White working-class Americans—men and women alike—argues Tex Sample, also prefer oral modes of communication.[4] Many such working-class whites make up Good Samaritan. And since some two-thirds of the people outside the US come from oral cultures, Good Samaritan's international membership includes folks whose primary way of engaging the world can be characterized as oral.[5] Indeed, although slaveowners' ban on reading and writing skills helps account for the importance of oral culture for African Americans, the centrality of oral practices in African cultures precedes as one of the historical roots of the high status of the charismatic preacher in African American church traditions.[6] While the cultural traditions of these various groups at Good Samaritan will entail different ways of being oral, we will see they share affinities for concrete and relational modes of communication.

Recognizing the importance of oral modes of expression, six activities merit particular attention as homemaking practices. That is, they contribute to making Good Samaritan a livable place. Following a review of these activities, this chapter will consider how

---

[3] Geneva Smitherman, *Talkin and Testifyin: The Language of Black America* (Boston: Houghton Mifflin, 1977), 76–7. Smitherman cites the Fanon quote.

[4] Sample, *Ministry*, and id., *Blue-Collar Ministry: Facing Economic and Social Realities of Working People* (Valley Forge, PA: Judson, 1984).

[5] Sample, *Ministry*, 9–10.

[6] C. Eric Lincoln and Lawrence H. Mamiya, *The Black Church in the African American Experience* (Durham, NC: Duke University Press, 1991).

these activities qualify as practices, looking especially for those that might be seen to contribute to an emergent *habitus*. How might they be understood as part of the traditions of Christian community? Given their conventional definition as female activities, how do these practices exceed or disrupt notions of Christian tradition? Finally, which of the practices extend the good of welcoming the outsider, that is, of 'not seeing color'?

One good 'domestic' place to start is economics. In 1995 Good Samaritan borrowed $122,000 from the Methodist Conference for purchasing land. By January of 1998, the church still owed $116,000. This considerable debt meant that several new activities were generated by financial need.[7]

MONEY-RAISING ACTIVITIES

Lack of wealth did not seem to restrict creativity at Good Samaritan. If anything, it stimulated folks. Soon after the church bought the new property, someone had the idea of creating a money-making project around the needs of the neighborhood. Olive thinks it was Beatrice, a young mother from Liberia, who first thought of the project. Beatrice got the idea from her experience at a thrift store in a nearby town selling coats on Saturdays. The loss of income suffered because of her family's move from Liberia was a constant motivator for Beatrice. She later devised a money-making craft project for herself when her housecleaning income proved insufficient for the cost of raising her two growing girls.

When the idea to sell used items circulated at Good Samaritan, Beatrice got lots of help. Everyone agreed that there was a real need for low-cost items in the area. In the church's immediate surroundings, the prominence of working-class families whose incomes were basically tied to a stagnant minimum wage meant that such needs were constant. Dan's wife, Linda, helped in the organization. Having sold her business in October of that year, Olive, a white woman in her

---

[7] Thanks to Jeanne Allen for this information from Table I, 1995, 1998, Church and Conference records.

early sixties, was free to take on a new project. Since her business had been children's clothing, both new and used, she was quite skilled at ordering, keeping track of sales, and bookkeeping. So Olive became the director. And, as Sarah pointed out, the church got two for the price of one with Olive's gifts. Her husband, Richard, a retired mailman, was always available to help. Richard soon had the dull gray shack-like edifice at the back of the property cleaned up and fixed. Thus God's Storehouse was born.

Like many of Good Samaritan's projects, God's Storehouse had a checkered history. It was certainly not difficult to get merchandise to sell. All varieties of used clothing were soon hanging from the improvised racks. Books, odd dishes, the occasional piece of furniture, and all sorts of toys were typically found there. Ivy Reese remembers with sadness that many items from Wellspring United Methodist Church were sold there—the communion tray, the baptismal font from which her children were baptized. Sometimes the small building was so full, items had to be placed on its narrow front porch. Slowly God's Storehouse began to draw folks from the area.

Participation in the project was fairly widespread, at least among the women of Good Samaritan. Besides Beatrice and Olive, regular workers included Liana (from Uganda), Grace (an African American), and (white North Carolinians) Kathy, Linda, and Martha as well. With the exception of two older white women (Minnie and Ivy, who always worked together) and Betty and May (white), volunteer sign-ups usually created pairs of workers that crossed race and nationality: Wanda (white) and Pam (African American) worked together, as did Elizabeth (Liberian) and Betty (African American), Donna (African American) and Beatrice (Liberian). These women took turns helping as clerks at the regular Saturday morning sale times. As they periodically got rid of unwanted household items, other members contributed things to sell. Richard, being retired, was there regularly to do maintenance—to fix things, mow the grass, and help with the lifting and carrying of the incoming merchandise. As with a number of Good Samaritan activities, God's Storehouse was run by a racially and globally 'ecumenical' group of folks.

Its irregular hours, however, sometimes seemed to undercut the success of God's Storehouse, or so suspected some of the women. Beatrice, the idea-woman, was known for keeping what the North

American members called 'African time'. While she was a regular worker at the store, Beatrice's work hours were not always identical with the printed information on the sign at the front of the property. Another story that circulated was that Liana found it hard to sell things at their advertised price, frequently offering to lower the price on an item so the browser could afford it. Since God's Storehouse was dependent upon volunteers from the church for its existence, however, it was hard to complain too much. The occasional 'taking stock' of the situation would lead to the inevitable vows to do better by its profit goals and an occasional adjustment to make the store more visible on the property.

If Olive as manager was frustrated with her less-than-profit-driven sisters in Christ, she did not take it out on them. She seemed to put even more energy into other money-making projects for Good Samaritan, cooking, for example. The first Sunday of every month, Olive baked and brought a station wagon full of baked goods to church to sell: rolls, sandwich rolls, pizzas, casseroles, and sometimes Brunswick stew. When they retired, Olive and Richard had given a freezer to the church. Sometimes they both fixed lunches and dinners for church events. People remember them cooking Christmas dinner for people who worked at CONTACT, a local counseling agency, at the request of Linda, who was then working at CONTACT. Olive says she did her old standby—ham, scalloped potatoes, lime Jell-O salad, string beans, dessert, coffee, and tea. With help from other women in the church, she could pull this off for meetings of local Methodist ministers as well.

COOKING AND EATING

Olive was not unusual. 'If you ask American Protestants why they go to church, they're likely to say that they go not for the doctrine or the ethics but for the community—a community usually built and sustained around food.'[8] If historian Daniel Sack's account of the

---

[8] Sack is only writing about white Protestantism, but gathering to eat is central to African American Protestantism as well. Daniel Sack, *Whitebread Protestants: Food and Religion in American Culture* (New York: St Martin's, 2000), 2.

importance of food to Protestantism is any indication, cooking and eating are an essential element of Christian community in the US. 'There's Nothing Like Church Food' in the African American tradition, say scholars Jualynne Dodson and Cheryl Townsend Gilkes. 'It is sung about. It is worried over. It is prayed over. It is the subject of church meetings.'[9] Good Samaritan is no exception.

The white-bread southern cooking of Olive and Richard was only one regular source of nourishment for the community. Getting together to eat was one of Good Samaritan's favorite things to do. While eating together in church is as old as Jesus's meals with his disciples, the function of food specifically for the creation of community has more recent Protestant origins. The earliest church meals in the US were probably the camp meetings in the early twentieth century, where revival meetings on the frontier created the need for shared meals. The more recent forerunner of Good Samaritan's activities is what Sack calls the emergence of 'the social congregation' at the turn of the century, when churches developed social events such as picnics, potlucks, camps, and baseball teams to attract people and provide community.[10] For African Americans, eating together is as old as the need to gather for respite from a hostile racist society.

In addition to its fairly regular potlucks, one of the most prized events in the life of the community was the annual International Dinner. The spectacle of food prepared for this feast was truly splendid. It is the one event that all members spoke most excitedly about.

Here Good Samaritan's distinctiveness gave a twist to the constituency of the typical white 'social congregation'. Members and their extended networks provided food from their countries of origin. Everyone came dressed up, and the most admired were those in non-Western garb, from Africans in Kente cloth to a Korean family

---

[9] See Jualynne E. Dodson and Cheryl Townsend Gilkes, '"There's Nothing Like Church Food": Food and the U.S. Afro-Christian Tradition: Re-Membering Community and Feeding the Embodied Spirit(s)', *Journal of the American Academy of Religion*, 63 (Fall, 1995), 521.

[10] Sack, *Whitebread Protestants*, 62–97. This desire to build community would likely hold across races and nationalities; however, I have no references for this particular arrangement at present. There are reasons this is distinctively Protestant, having to do with Protestantism's lack of a popular galvanizing piety like Catholicism, its need to compete in a pluralist society, among others. Ibid. 95–7.

in kimonos. Kathy even remembers a family dressed in Hawaiian garb one year—muumuus, says her daughter. There were dishes from Liberia, recipes from Uganda and Kenya. Traditional southern African American food was piled high on the tables, along with Korean dishes. There was lots of singing and performing. Dan boasted one year when almost two hundred people came to share their food, songs, stories, and native dress. So successful had the International Dinner become that tickets were sold, and once it had to be held at the national armory in nearby downtown.

Communal eating was definitely a Good Samaritan habit. Unlike many larger, wealthier white southern congregations, however, gatherings around food served double duty: they were to raise money as well as enhance community, as Olive's activities indicated. While the post-World War II period saw the rise of professional church cooks and food services in wealthier white churches of the South, Good Samaritan still needed to make money.[11] The historic black church always recognized the money-raising value of food. A number of members contributed to the occasional food sales following worship. More than once the Sunday bulletin included a flyer with pictures of food and excited graphics advertising 'Good Samaritan Home Cooking'—'Frozen Ready To Eat Goodies' available for sale after church 'on the back porch'. Hot dogs, cake, soda, and hamburgers decorated the insert along with price lists for cookies at $1.00 a bag, pizzas for $3.00 a slice, and vegetable beef soup for $3.00 a quart, among other delights. While some bought the food to take home, usually the time after church was spent standing around nibbling and chatting—'food-centered socializing', as Sack puts it.[12]

As people gathered around food at Good Samaritan, they gathered around projects. They also gathered to share life experiences. Dan claims that the only way to build a multicultural church is by developing trust. That, he says, requires three things: first, holding Jesus up above everything else, because that makes us God's family; second, making music together; and third, sharing life stories. About the third, he was absolutely right. Gathering to share stories was vital to the support and development of the community.

---

[11] Ibid. 91 ff.   [12] Ibid. 95.

STORYTELLING

For a considerable period in 1996, the regular Wednesday night Bible
study turned into an occasion to share life stories. Usually the Sunday
bulletin announced who would be 'on' the following Wednesday.
Volunteers to share their stories crossed race and nationality. For at
least some of the community, this practice was quite important, and
they are not unusual. Storytelling, along with other genres such as
aphorisms, sayings, and proverbs, is a favored form for a large
number of people who express themselves through a primarily oral
culture. As previously observed, while they are literate—can read and
write—such folks think and communicate mainly through oral
forms of expression. Oral forms are concrete and practical. As one
scholar puts it, oral communicators prefer ideas about *events* rather
than ideas about *ideas*.[13] As a discourse that charts a life through its
changes, a story is one of the primary forms of communicating
events. Two stories in particular suggest the wide range of experiences in the community.

One Wednesday night in 1996 a group of about ten people gathered at the church. Dan and Linda were there, along with Ben, a
young white man who was raised Baptist. Eventually Beatrice and
Liana came, as did Kathy, a middle-aged white woman, Miguel, her
Hispanic husband, and Kathy's daughter, Chrissie. William, an African American member, came with Letty, his Liberian wife, and their
autistic son Carl. Since Beatrice had brought her daughters, she
volunteered to take Carl and her children to another room to play.

Chrissie agreed to begin the sharing. The daughter of Kathy and
her first husband, she is a white woman in her early thirties who had
recently started coming to the church with her young son and
husband. Raised in a very conservative Christian home, Chrissie
alluded to a bad church experience and the trauma of her mother's
divorce from her father. Chrissie had married Fred upon graduation
from high school, she tells us, and alludes vaguely to problematically
different backgrounds—Fred's parents were Russian and Roman
Catholic. The detail was hard to follow, but it didn't seem important.

[13] Sample, *Ministry*, 23–44.

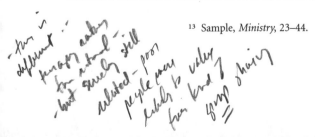

The meat of her story was the birth of her son Ricky—or rather, the birth and the many medical travails and miracles of Ricky's young life. While living in Ohio, a normal procedure to have Ricky's tonsils removed turned into a story about disaster and miraculous recovery. Chrissie tells of the days after what they thought was a successful surgery. Suddenly Ricky's spiking fever sent her to a doctor with him. But the doctor proved indifferent and apparently overlooked Ricky's infected and gangrenous adenoids. Chrissie's voice trembles as she talks. At the point of death, she says, he had to have an emergency operation. To the doctor's surprise, Ricky survived. Chrissie's story took an even more dramatic turn as she recounted several years of heartbreaking physical tragedies.

Her story of tumultuous parenting was also a story of unusual healings and visions. Chrissie tells the group proudly that Ricky remembers his first surgery as an experience of going to heaven. Describing heaven in great detail, he told of meeting Jesus adorned with the crown of heaven. Assuring him, Jesus told Ricky that he would undergo more tribulations and that he would survive. Sure enough, Chrissie continues, Ricky had a prolonged period of deafness. He later developed a brain tumor. As she filled in the story about his surgeries, Chrissie recounted these years through a litany of divinely sent messages. Ricky received the vision of God's assurances of his future, she says, noting proudly that his faith is a source of real courage. Chrissie herself had a vision of an angel. There is conviction in her voice as she tells of a great peace that settled upon her during these difficult times—a peace that her husband saw in the form of a visibly glowing light surrounding her.

The response to Chrissie is strong as people attempt to support her, particularly when she breaks down in the telling. Many nod in agreement when she confesses that her faith was also fractured by anger during these difficult times. The strongest reaction, however, comes from William, an African American. Parenting Carl, he admits sometimes creates difficult times for his own faith. Twelve-year-old Carl has severe autism and is unable to speak. He appreciates her story, William says, because 'I want to believe that our children can be healed and their suffering ended—that Carl will respond. Everyday', he says, 'I look at Carl and only hope that someday he will look at me and say, "Hi, Dad, here I am." I just have to hold out hope that there might be a possibility of a miracle for us.'

The gathering ends soon, but only after Dan remembers the prayer network that had been in place for Chrissie, Fred, and Ricky when they were living in Ohio. A momentary almost palpable sense of closeness filled the room. It seemed possible that, even with their vastly different social and cultural backgrounds, there could be a sharing of such experiences. Whether or not there would be miracles ahead, the group agreed that stories mattered.

On a Wednesday night in late February, Elizabeth tells a very different story. A slim Liberian woman in her late thirties, Elizabeth had been drawn to Good Samaritan through her friendships with the other African families. A group of nine Good Samaritans gathered that night to hear her tell of her experiences in Liberia as a refugee of the civil war of 1989. With an affect of self-conscious laughter that belies the horror of her tale, Elizabeth speaks of being raised in a home that was half Muslim and half Christian. Sent to a Christian school at an early age meant her eventual identification with the faith, but Elizabeth also tells us of living with Muslim grandparents. The first real test of her faith, she says, came with the Liberian civil war. Samuel Doe led the 1980 coup and became military ruler and president in 1986, leading a regime with much economic corruption and abuse of civil rights.[14] Sometime in 1990 when she was on holiday visiting her mother in the capital, Monrovia, an attack led by the rebels under Charles Taylor overran the small town in which she lived. If she had gone home, Elizabeth reports, she feared she would be murdered.[15]

However, Monrovia proved no safer. While Elizabeth was there, Doe's men invaded. She and her mother fled, she tells us, moving from house to house to avoid being captured. They found a temporary refuge when a Catholic priest helped them hide in a convent. There, along with many other women and children,

[14] The oldest republic of Africa, Liberia was first founded/colonized in 1821–2 as a home for freed American slaves, who were sent by the American Colonization Society. Liberian independence was proclaimed in 1847 by its first nonwhite governor, Joseph Roberts.

[15] Her father's tribe was Mandingo, assumed to be supporters of President Samuel Doe, and her mother's the Mano, thought to support the rebels led by Charles Taylor. Both associations put her in danger.

they stayed for over a month. The sound of sporadic shooting frequently made them afraid to go outside. One night while listening to the BBC, they heard of a nearby Lutheran church where twenty-four hours earlier several hundred people had been massacred by the rebels. A Red Cross flag flying over the church proved to be no protection.

Elizabeth talks about her fear in the convent. They were without water, save for the rainfall, and they had very little food. She speaks of the feeling of having no power at all—no power to control anything. The refugees were caught there—only the nuns could go outside— and all they could do was pray. Elizabeth remembers praying during periods when the gunfire was so loud they could not hear anything else. One night soldiers invaded the convent. Elizabeth remembers hiding upstairs in terrified silence as she and the others waited for the horror they were sure would soon come. Again, all they could do, she said, was to pray silently in their hideout above. Inexplicably, the soldiers left without coming upstairs. As time went on, Elizabeth says, their prayers gave them an eerie sense of calmness and peace, a sense of accepting the inevitability of death.

When she and her mother were finally able to escape from the convent, they became refugees again. Life on the move meant never having enough food, a constantly empty stomach. However, something always came through, some small rescue. Always, she tells us, she was enabled to go on. Breaking her grim story with an occasional remark about rescue, Elizabeth tells of being on the run, of walking over bodies, of having people fall dead around her as snipers' bullets came out of nowhere. Refugees for almost a year, Elizabeth and her mother struggled to leave Liberia, discovering when they finally found a rescue boat that their names were on the lists of the 'Missing'.

As she tells the story, Elizabeth speaks often of her faith, alternating between convictions that God was intervening in her rescues and observations of the evil of the killing around her. When it was all over, she says, she saw that God was protecting her. Her favorite verse was John 3: 16, 'For God so loved the world that he gave his only begotten Son, whosoever loves him should not perish, but shall have eternal life.' Offering no rationalizations, Elizabeth does not try to make sense of her own survival in the face of 'good people dying for no reason'. The one thing she does know is that God has some purpose for her.

As with Chrissie, the response of the group to Elizabeth's story is strong and supportive. Liana, whose Ugandan experiences gave her a special empathy with Elizabeth, leans over and touches her, as does Kathy on her other side. Dan and Linda express their respect and appreciation of her faith. But Beatrice is the most animated, talking about Liberia and her very different experience of having lived there in a period of peace. She marvels at how hard it had been for her to imagine Monrovia—a place she had loved to visit—as a place of devastation, of slaughtered women and children. Ben, the young white man of Baptist background, speaks of how 'insulated' his life has been. In almost embarrassed tones, he marvels at how protected he has been from these kinds of horrors.

When Elizabeth leaves, Liana and Beatrice share some of the differences between their African homelands and the US, from the very different, more respectful African attitudes toward the elderly to the problems Africans have in the US. Remarking on how little understanding there is in this country of the complex and some-times brutal situations elsewhere in the world, they lament North Americans' suspicion of foreigners and their inability to imagine that Africans come with accomplishments and credentials.

Such storytelling is effective as the shared experiences evoke new levels of understanding from people of widely different backgrounds. Chrissie's struggles with her son's health and Elizabeth's time of horror as a refugee displayed very different journeys, unlike those of many in the room. But these stories resonated with something in the lives of their sympathetic hearers. As Dan had hoped, organizing gatherings for such sharing of life experiences did seem to bring people together in ways that other activities did not. Stories some-how opened up not just their differences—and they did do that—but also the resonances of common fear and anger and hope that shape all human lives.

Even more intense forms of mutual support at Good Samaritan happen as people find out about one another's lives in the interacting and gossip of ordinary life.

MUTUAL SUPPORT

Pam, an African American woman, says that Good Samaritan is a 'hands-on' church. 'You can call anyone when you're in need.' Grace, also African American, agrees, saying that at Good Samaritan she's 'never heard people share a need when someone didn't respond to meet it'. Christians have long been in the business of providing mutual support for one another. From ancient traditions of caring for the widow and the orphan, and sharing possessions in the earliest churches (Acts 2: 43–7), down through the centuries a wide variety of ministries has emerged to define and meet members' needs.

Stories of help overheard and shared with me in interviews are telling. Donna, an African American mother who has struggled on and off welfare, tells of the church's support during one of her worst years. Remarking that in the same year her mother died, she lost her job, and her best friend died, Donna relates the disasters with a tale of Good Samaritan help. Working three part-time jobs, she was trying to make enough to pay $400 rent plus her power bill. 'I was trying to keep lights on,' she says, 'the car from breaking down, to keep from getting put out,' and 'Dan would give me money and say, "I can't tell who gave you this."' Once when the car broke down and her husband Johnny was working the third shift from midnight to 7.00 a.m., she said, 'People actually got out of their beds to come get him and take him to work!' Comparing Good Samaritan to the first church in Acts where people would sell everything they had and share it with their brothers and sisters in the church, Donna's gratitude to the church took an eloquent theological turn as she thanked the community one Sunday morning. 'This is what Jesus would do if he was here. We're supposed to be his arms and his legs, eyes, and his hands, you know.... Don't stop.... Keep on doing what Jesus would do.'

The church's generosity also supported Chrissie. Her account of her son's illnesses was only part of a story of family hard times. When Chrissie's husband, Fred, heard of an opportunity for a better-paying job in Ohio, this white working-class family suddenly decided to move. Within a year, however, the opportunity failed to pan out, and the family moved back to Durham, virtually penniless. Their

The Practices that make Place

embarrassment and sense of failure was acute. Immediately the women from United Methodist Women organized a 'shower' to help give Chrissie and Fred a new start. Black and white women filled the room in the sanctuary, which doubled as a room for meetings and social events. Zelda, an African American woman, had taken the lead, planning the shower so that it would be a surprise for Chrissie. Kathy was let in on the secret so she could bring Chrissie to church for a 'special Bible study'. The joy in the room was palpable as Chrissie realized the gathering was for her. When she opened her first package and saw the dish towels and salt and pepper shakers, tears came fast. Nothing fancy—a mixed rather than a matched set of dishes, some of the gifts were used. But there were no questions about the rumored foolishness of the move. The women were there to help her get her home back together.

Then there is Liana. Liana is a central figure in the community. Raised in a Ugandan version of the missionary Church of England, she was sent away from her home country by her parents during Idi Amin's brutal rule. After schooling in England, she found herself in the US, a single mother. Learning about Good Samaritan through a local flyer, Liana became one of its most active members. A regular at God's Storehouse, Liana does janitorial duty. She comes to Bible studies and is always at Sunday worship. Liana's own vulnerabilities surfaced when she traveled to Uganda in 1996 to spend several weeks with her family when a sister died from AIDS. When returning to the US, Liana got as far as England, where her visa was rejected. She was stunned to discover it might take a year to reapply for a new visa—a year in which her daughter Esther would be left alone in a residential treatment center in North Carolina.

Severely autistic, Esther is Liana's 'mission' in life, as she put it. Although she does not live at home, Esther sometimes comes to Bible study with Liana, who visits her regularly. Heartbroken at the thought of her daughter's inevitable feeling of abandonment, Liana had no choice but to find a job in London, working as a home care assistant with the elderly. But it was Liana's worry about Esther that made the months so painful. She sent an occasional check back to the States, checks that paid her Durham rent and were a small thank-you for her Good Samaritan 'sisters', as she calls them. These sisters organized prayer chains for Liana and Esther. Pam and Donna took care of her apartment and made regular visits to Esther, carrying her mother's messages of concern.

There are many other instances of support at Good Samaritan, much of it informal and undramatic. There is care across racial lines. Donna, as already noted, has been on welfare recently. Her husband, Johnny, is in and out of work and their daughter, Jeanine, is in her early adolescence. Wanda is an older white woman. She and her husband, Barry, are recently retired, coming to North Carolina from lay mission work in the Midwest. Since moving to Durham, Barry has had a stroke. While not completely debilitated, his life and his family's are greatly affected. Despite her own worries, Donna is quite concerned about Wanda and the effect of Barry's stroke, which has precipitated loss of mental capacity, on their lives. As his condition deteriorates, Wanda cannot go anywhere without him. Donna worries that she feels trapped, because she has to watch him all the time. *why not ?*

There are other members who are <u>not likely to</u> tell their stories in Good Samaritan's intentional gatherings. Their forms of caring are more indirect. While these members are fans of both stories and mutual support, their mode of participation in a community is better described by other habits characteristic of members of oral cultures.

MAINTENANCE/JANITORIAL PRACTICES

Lacking ritual or other explicitly 'religious' symbolisms, janitorial and maintenance practices are not typically considered ecclesial practices. I take them up along with the more conventionally recognized church practices of mutual support to question that conventional wisdom. For most middle- and upper-middle-class white churches, a nonmember is hired to do the work of cleaning, emptying trash cans, and general maintenance. In such churches, if not anonymous to most of the members, janitors are at best treated in the kindly patronizing way in which relatively comfortable Christians tend to treat the lower classes. At Good Samaritan, maintenance activities are done by members, however, and not simply because the finances are stretched too thin to hire anyone else, although that is the case. I focus on these activities because there is reason to consider them as the kind of practices that best display the skills of many working-class persons.

The financial straits of Good Samaritan made it absolutely necessary to minimize expenses. Living on the financial edge was not unfamiliar to numerous members of the church. While it was the rare family that was on welfare, not a few had more than one job. For some members living on the financial edge has been the occasion for expanding their skills. Zelda, an African American woman whose husband is a truck driver, insists, 'You must have a back-up skill in case your main source of income disappears.' She supplements her job at a local pharmaceutical company by baking wedding cakes to sell out of her home, painfully aware that the recent merger at her company has put many hundreds of jobs at risk.

Some church members have jobs that make them particularly skilled for the church's maintenance needs. Having left a decent-paying bank job in Liberia, Beatrice now cleans houses to supplement family income. Liana also falls back on domestic work for extra cash when her teaching salary fails to cover her family expenses, as does Dina, whose former life in the Bahamas was defined by staying at home with her children. Having done some of this work himself, African American William had recently started his own cleaning service. Along with a number of white members unable to boast this extensive cleaning experience, many of these Good Samaritans take turns committing to the weekly job of cleaning the church buildings. Molly, the white professor, and May, a white computer worker at a local hospital, along with Beatrice and Liana, regularly volunteered. Having signed up myself, I discovered that there are better and worse ways to vacuum three buildings. Aligning oneself with one of the pros is the first good choice. A second is working with a member who enjoys the opportunity to share stories and gossip.

A few of the men stand out as exemplary. Take Richard. After a career in the US Army and a number of years as a mailman, the 60-year-old white man is retired and seems to spend the majority of his time enhancing the ministry of Good Samaritan. Richard does this ministry in ways best described as resoundingly practical and operational, as Tex Sample puts it, rather than introspective or abstract.[16] Indeed Richard is not likely to display his faith either by telling his story or by attending discussion groups or Bible studies. Rather, his faith is communicated by a consistent presence in the upbuilding and sustaining of the community, in its most literal material and constitutive social sense.

Despite the loss of two fingers on one hand, Richard is agile with tools. He is there to fix things, to mow the grass, to fix the mower when it breaks. While he does come to worship, Richard is much more likely to appear when the 'special needs' services need helpers, the food made by Olive needs carrying, and the community gathers to work or to eat. In that sense he fits a group quite common in oral cultures—those 'who come to church when there's something to do (paint a room, rebuild a wall, cook a supper, volunteer time for community service)', as Sample says, 'and don't come to Sunday school class or even to worship'.[17] In contrast to practices that foreground interpretive activities, his way of gaining wisdom is by apprenticeship rather than intellectual inquiry.[18] Richard is one of Good Samaritan's best practitioners of homemaking as maintenance of the physical facility. A 'Martha' rather than a 'Mary', he thereby helps sustain the community.

If much of the activity at the church described thus far has been informal and conventionally gendered female, there are also activities that are officially gendered. While the United Methodist Men get together occasionally for breakfast, by far the most prominent organization is the women's—a group that is multiracial and multinational, demanding considerable work along with fellowship.

UNITED METHODIST WOMEN'S PRACTICES

The official name of the group is United Methodist Women. Typical of many Protestant women's organizations that originated

---

[16] Richard fits Sample's description of traditional oral people particularly well. *Ministry*, 16–19.

[17] Ibid. 16.   [18] Ibid. 30.

in nineteenth-century mission organizations, UMW has as its ante-cedent Methodist mission societies of the early 1800s. These societies were first concerned with helping women and girls overseas. Later in the century, home mission societies focused on educating girls and women in the US.[19] Historically, such organizations constituted women's free space in the many denominations where males dom-inated official leadership. With varying degrees of autonomy, such organizations gave women the opportunity to define their own discipleship and create projects that displayed their faith in the world. Often they were typically 'domestic' kinds of missions—collecting clothes for missions and the poor, education programs for Native American, Mexican, and immigrant girls and women, serving meals, wrapping bandages to send overseas.

As the twentieth century advanced, women's organizations in Methodism took different shapes, and in 1972, the current United Methodist Women came into being.[20] Defining its purpose as 'to know God and to experience freedom as whole persons through Jesus Christ', United Methodist Women focuses on fellowship and an expanded understanding of mission that not only includes support of foreign missionaries, but advocates for social change such as antiracism programs, pro-environmentalist activities, and work to end child labor.

Good Samaritan women put their own stamp on the national Methodist women's vision. Their activities at the church range from regular monthly meetings, where a devotional and current mission projects officially dominate the program, to beach retreats where the women gather for fun and relaxation. During Dan's min-istry, the beach retreat was annual. Linda tells of the first one, where choices of motel roommates divided along racial lines. Never one to mince words, Linda pointed it out to the group, and all agreed that they needed to take seriously the community's commitment to

---

[19] Patricia R. Hill, *The World Their Household: The American Woman's Foreign Mission Movement and Cultural Transformation, 1870–1920* (Ann Arbor: University of Michigan Press, 1985). See the United Methodist Women's web page at http://gbgm-umc.org/umw/history.

[20] See also, *To a Higher Glory: The Growth and Development of Black Women Organized for Mission in the Methodist Church, 1940–1968*. Available online at http://gbgm-umc.org/umw/history/books_index.cfm.

diversity. Never again, or so Linda hoped, would they split along these lines. The trips continued to be a favorite activity.

A UMW meeting at Zelda Ramirez's house in January of 1997 is typical of the group and shows the imprint of the national organization's vision on it. A stylishly dressed African American woman married to Stephan, a Hispanic man, Zelda's home reflects her striking decorative skills. In a new interracial development rather far from the church, the Ramirezes' small brightly colored house is impeccably neat and filled with pictures of Zelda in glamorous poses. She provides a hot meal of roast chicken and mashed potatoes for the group, and members arrive at various times in typical Good Samaritan fashion. By the end of the meal, six of the most active United Methodist Women have gathered. That number includes Donna, her daughter Jeanine, Beatrice (and her two daughters), Della (a middle-aged African American on welfare), Pam, and Mary (a white graduate student from the local university). Zelda leads the meeting in a very business-like fashion. Responding to her request for committee reports, Mary, the mission chair, hands out a list of mission options in Durham, asking the women to pick out a favorite and make commitments. Reminding everyone of their habit of getting excited about something 'and then only two people show up', Mary pleads, 'this time we need to decide on something we'll *really do*'. Following more checking of calendars, there is some discussion of Mary's challenge, but the talk soon turns to the beach retreat, clearly a topic about which people can get enthusiastic.

Dina, wife of the new minister, Gerald, leads the devotional, meditating on the beatitudes and what it means to be 'poor in spirit'. Conversation turns to the ironies of this biblical state of being. What if you are not metaphorically ('spiritually') poor, someone observes, but *really* poor—either way you need to be absolutely dependent upon Christ. As she tells of the fall in her family's income, Dina notes wryly that such reliance upon Christ is never an escape from troubles. Usually, in fact, troubles increase. A conversation version of call and response emerges from the African American women in the room. Clearly, everyone in the group agrees with the notion that a Christ-centered life is still a life full of struggle.

A white graduate student at the local social work school, Mary has told me of her great fondness for the women of Good Samaritan's

UMW. As an opportunity to get to know women from very different social locations, she finds it wonderful for friendship and bonding. As a mission chair with high goals for the women, however, Mary thinks that the group needs more focus. She complains about the familiar Good Samaritan style—the meetings tend to start and end a half-hour late.

Nevertheless, once they are under way, meetings are full of plans and projects. In September 1996, Laura, a white nutritionist at a regional hospital and one of the few professionals in the church, hosts a fall kick-off meeting with refreshments, a devotional, a movie about mission in Bolivia, and a talk from Mary about her summer involvement working with orphans in that mission. Planning proceeds for the surprise housewarming for Kathy's daughter, Chrissie. Laura takes up collections for a rehabilitation program in town, and hands out lists of the items needed for the Durham Women's Shelter. Filtering throughout the meeting and all its enthusiasm, the women connect around children and husbands, or the lack thereof, and other current gossip items in the church.

Mary is right that these plans and projects do not always come to orderly fruition. What drives Mary crazy, though, seems for others to be a style that gestures toward the right way women exist in the world. Furthermore, the value of the group to some of the other women goes much deeper, and the events of a meeting at Pam's house are illustrative.

A spring meeting occurred at the very small apartment of Pam, an African American single mother who works as a secretary at a local drug company. The living room is crowded; a couple of card tables take up all the space. But Pam has decorated with great flair. The napkins are carefully folded and tied with colorful ribbons to complement the colored paper plates. Matching colored cups hold our drinks. Zelda comes with Della and Betty. Donna again brings her daughter, Jeanine. Laura brings Dina. Beatrice and Liana are there as well. This group of women has two white women—Laura and me—five African American women, and three African and Bahamian women of color. We sit in a friendly circle around the tables with the usual laughing and kidding that accompany these meetings.

Dina leads us in a devotional from the Gospel of John. She talks about the nature of the abundant life, a life offered through following

Jesus. The burdens of the community—financial distress, in particular—are mentioned for prayer, but Dina stresses that 'God doesn't take burdens away, but allows them to be borne. Give it over to God and give it up', as she says, getting murmurs of appreciation from the other women. As a follow-up to the devotion, Pam presents a surprise gift to Dina. Dina's continuing struggle with cancer of the lymph nodes and subsequent damage to her right arm goes unmentioned. They were burdens of which everyone was aware. Pam proudly presents Dina with a check for $250; collected from UMW, it is to go toward the $700 needed to buy a brace for her arm. Her surprise and appreciation for the gift fill the room for some moments, as does the language of thanks and trust in God.

A few moments later, planning resumes for the many projects that might or might not get done in the coming months. The women voted on which books to read for the United Methodist Women study sessions. There is discussion of the need to get more advertising for God's Storehouse. Its location at the back of the property makes it hard to see, just as its housing in a gray shed-like edifice makes it hard to recognize. Eventually, the women name more personal concerns, and Zelda shares her worry about her Puerto Rican husband's inability to get adequate health care. His job driving trucks does not include health care benefits.

Other than moving God's Storehouse to the house on the front of the property, few of these projects will actually be completed. What are most striking, however, are the lasting supportive relationships that are sustained here. Pam puts it just right when she observes that her Baptist grandmother always said that if anyone needs anything, just come to the church. 'Especially to the women', someone adds.

HOMEMAKING ACTIVITIES AS PRACTICES

So with all this activity—eating and cleaning, planning projects and listening to one another's stories and supporting each other—what do we make of the community's homemaking activities? How do they qualify as practices? These are essential ecclesiological questions if these activities can be considered part of a tradition that is normatively to shape the place Good Samaritan.

Cooking and cleaning are two likely candidates for practices in Bourdieu's sense of *habitus*. While neither is explicitly ecclesial, they may at least be considered for their status as skills. Even so considered, there may be a question about the latter. Having been called an 'art' and given professional status when done by males, cooking is the more highly prized of the two. Cleaning well has little visibility as a valued skill, much less as an art. Further, it may not seem to qualify as a *habitus* compared to examples like piano playing or the art of fencing.

However, the analogous example of gendered body carriage suggests that janitorial activity most certainly qualifies as a bodily skill. If knowing where to place your body, how to arrange your legs when you sit, and when to avert your eyes as a woman in a patriarchal society is a bodily *habitus*, so is knowing where to plant your feet, when to kneel, how to crouch, and how to wield a cloth. The skill of cooking is likewise a bodily wisdom. An analysis of the 'gesture sequences' of cooking by Luce Giard grants it a ritualistic quality that mobilizes body knowledge 'and all the resources of intelligence and memory'.[21] A good cook has such 'knowledges' as the feel of adequately kneaded dough, the taste of just-enough spice, the hand's sense of how to wield a chopping knife, and the visual sense of a 'done' cake or pie. Both cooking and cleaning require some sense of what to do in a situation, as a *habitus* requires, a sense that is neither automatic nor innate. They require experience. When done well, they have real status as bodily knowledges; they are skills of 'ordinary culture'.

As befitting Bourdieu's notion of practice, the skills of cleaning and cooking are learned and expanded over time. Domestic workers know in their bones how the skill to clean swiftly and well is improved by experience. As Olive's practice clearly demonstrates, the skills of cooking can only advance with trial and error. More

---

[21] Luce Giard, 'The Nourishing Arts', in Michel de Certeau, Luce Giard, and Pierre Mayol (eds.), *The Practice of Everyday Life*, ii. *Living and Cooking*, trans. Timothy J. Tomasik (Minneapolis: University of Minnesota Press, 1998), 151–69. Id., 'Gesture Sequences', in de Certeau et al. (eds.), *Practice of Everyday Life*, ii. 200.

years create the possibility of more culinary wisdom. It thus makes sense to locate the continuity of these practices in the capacity to improvise.[22] The ideal way to reproduce a practice improvisation is illustrated when the best cooks typically transcend recipes, using their developed sense of taste to cook for a particular meal, adding a little more of this ingredient or subtracting a little of that. Giard describes this improvisation well: 'To the extent that experience is acquired, style affirms itself, taste distinguishes itself, imagination frees itself, and the recipe itself loses significance, becoming little more than an occasion for a free invention by analysis or association of ideas, through a subtle game of substitutions, abandonments, additions, and borrowings.'[23]

The significance of these practices for the community's identity is found in their ends. Do they have ends of their own in the sense of MacIntyrean practices, which have ends and generate internal goods when done well? By producing nutritious and good-tasting food, cooking has the ends of satisfying human need—bringing health— and providing pleasure. In addition to being a productive practice (generating external goods), cooking generates internal goods for its practitioners—'happiness, pleasure, and discovery', as one writer puts it.[24] Insofar as good cooking is defined by standards developed in as many different cultures and historical periods as there are people, cooking is a socially established practice. Just as the white-bread tastes of Olive and Richard developed out of social preferences, so the African American culinary standards and the different African tastes and preferences come from shared social values. Good cooking emerges out of traditions, and traditions have their own standards of evaluation.

---

[22] 'One has to know how to improvise with panache, know what to do when fresh milk "turns" on the stove, when meat, taken out of the package and trimmed of fat, reveals itself to be not enough to feed four guests, or when Mathieu brings a little friend to dinner unannounced and one has to make the leftover stew "go a little farther"'. Giard, 'Gesture Sequences', 200.

[23] Ibid. 201.

[24] Ibid. 151. There is an Aristotelian distinction between action that is poesis— produces something or has an end external to itself—and praxis, which is a doing whose end is internal to it. All of these practices contribute to a kind of homemaking that is not simply the producing of something external. However, MacIntyre might quarrel with my assigning internal ends to cooking and cleaning.

With respect to cleaning and janitorial skills, Bourdieu's terms are also helpful. Honoring the capacity to adapt and improvise basic body awareness to deal with space is a likely way to grant cleaning the status of a *habitus*—a skill with bodily knowledges. The notion of ends can be judged according to the desirable end product of these skills—a cleaned and livable space.[25] Simply because the populations who typically have done cleaning are those with the skills of 'ordinary culture' does not negate its value or mean that the practice has no unwritten social conventions that reach back into history. Martin Luther King Jr honored janitorial practices when he urged the street sweeper to think of her/his work as an art: 'Go on out and sweep streets like Michelangelo painted pictures; sweep streets like Handel and Beethoven composed music; sweep streets like Shakespeare wrote poetry.'[26]

Storytelling and mutual support are also intelligible as practices. While the foregrounded skill of storytelling is verbal communication, good storytelling also requires prereflective bodily wisdom. Telling a story well requires a sensibility to the listener. Excellence is not defined by mere repetition. The really good storyteller is capable of improvising on the basis of a competence to 'read' each situation. The teller correlates her narration to the audience, all the while making subtle readings of facial and bodily cues. What I have described as mutual support includes some of the same sensibilities. To provide support one must be able to listen, to interpret with sensitivity, and to adjust one's responses according to the perceived needs of the other. While this capacity is one of conscious interpretation, when done well, mutual support requires the accumulated wisdom of a bodily *habitus*, as well, one capable of 'reading' the other and being appropriately improvisatory in responding.

Activities of raising money and participation by United Methodist Women are best thought of as an overarching collection of practices.

---

[25] MacIntyre would see it as an example of a lesser activity like bricklaying, tic-tac-toe, and planting turnips. Alasdair MacIntyre, *After Virtue: A Study in Moral Theory*, 2nd edn. (Notre Dame, IN: Notre Dame University Press, 1984), 187.

[26] Martin Luther King Jr, 'The Three Dimensions of a Complete Life', in Clayborne Carson and Peter Holloran (eds.), *A Knock at Midnight: Inspiration from the Great Sermons of Reverend Martin Luther King, Jr.* (New York: Warner Books, 1998), 126. Thanks to Maurice Wallace for this.

They involve skills and bodily dimensions, but are less obviously discrete bodily skills like cooking and cleaning. As the activities of UMW and God's Storehouse overlap with the activities of storytelling and mutual support, they nevertheless qualify as practices of care and nurture and mission necessary to the whole community.

In sum, all of these activities in some way qualify as practices. They differ in the degree to which the bodily skills are primary, but all require learned wisdoms that transcend the accumulation of information. Indeed, the best way to understand these homemaking activities as practices is Bourdieu's: a *habitus* is a bodily knowledge, not 'caused' by principles but done in a way that responds appropriately to a situation; it draws from 'the past' but in an improvisatory way. The next question is how these homemaking practices are crucial to the faithful formation of Good Samaritan.

HOMEMAKING ACTIVITIES AS TRADITION

For homemaking activities to count in the faithful formation of the community they must qualify as 'tradition', that is, those memories that carry forward social identity. First, we consider *homemaking practices as part of inscribed tradition*.

Homemaking activities are in large part not recognizable as historic traditions in the sense typically understood by theological discourse, that is, inscribed memories granted authorization by official ecclesiastical judgments. While groups such as United Methodist Women have historic precedents in the church, along with cooking and cleaning they are not specifically designated as crucial in the sense of biblical stories, beliefs, and doctrines.[27] It is hard to imagine, of course, that any Christian community could have come into being or lasted for any amount of time without people willing to

---

[27] It is important that recent theological work on practices has included the meeting of human needs as part of Christian practice. Thus, in addition to such traditional practices as keeping Sabbath, household economics, along with hospitality and honoring the body are included. See Dorothy C. Bass (ed.), *Practicing Our Faith: A Way of Life for a Searching People* (San Francisco: Jossey-Bass, 1998).

do these things. Not only are the practices of food preparation and maintenance necessary to the well-being of a community, but they have ends with standards of excellence.

These do seem to be activities that merit more status than they have traditionally received. However, historically they have been gendered female and carried out by lower-income populations; thus cooking and maintenance practices have not qualified in the MacIntyrean sense of tradition, that is, the authoritative source for normative evaluations of a community's activities. As such, homemaking practices are well described as what feminists call 'traditions that do not have a name'.[28] Women's activities, regardless of race or class, have long been invisible to many classificatory systems.[29] Because money is not exchanged, women's domestic and childrearing activities, for example, are not counted as productive work. Other 'nameless' social practices are found in the work of women's groups that have long-standing traditions of support and mentoring for the voiceless. Women leaders able to see the potential in others, to nurture and encourage, and to lift up society's excluded have formed groups such as Mothers Centers movements and African American culture workers, among many others, where they share their significant skills for nurturing leadership abilities.[30] While not typically known by the dominant society, practitioners of these skills have names internal to communities, such as 'community othermothers' and

[28] Mary Field Belenky, Lynne A. Bond, and Jacqueline S. Weinstock, *A Tradition that Has No Name: Nurturing the Development of People, Families, and Communities* (New York: Basic Books, 1997). Interestingly, National Public Radio has recently started a series to recognize cooking traditions in the US. Called 'Hidden Kitchens', it has a precursor in the 'America Eats' project of the Works Project Administration (WPA) in the 1930s. The oral history done on these practices did not, unfortunately, result in a book. NPR broadcast, 19 Nov. 2003.

[29] The authors of *Tradition that Has No Name* cite Marilyn Waring's analysis of economic accounting systems that render women invisible in the way they chart census and national resources. Belenky et al., *Tradition that Has No Name*, 22–3. See Marilyn Waring, *If Women Counted: A New Feminist Economics* (San Francisco: Harper & Row, 1988).

[30] In addition these feminists studied the National Congress of Neighborhood Women and the Center for Cultural and Community Development. What these groups share is that they are founded and led by women with strong knowledge of and commitment to women's public agency and have as their aim the enabling of marginalized people to gain voice. Belenky et al., *Tradition that Has No Name*, 156.

'Sisters'.[31] Their skills are passed on and, as such, they constitute a *habitus that develops and enculturates others over time.*

That such practices have not been officially part of what counts as tradition is not a disqualifier. As Mary Helen Washington puts it, 'The creation of [a] tradition is a matter of power, not justice, and that power has always been in the hands of men—mostly white but some black.'[32] Not only is skill displayed in white women's mentoring groups or African American 'othermothers' learned via apprenticeship, but historically these kinds of practices are ordered by ends—to gain voice and agency in a world that has denied these. They not only deserve to be counted as tradition, but have accumulated stories and icons that sustain them.

One could say that Good Samaritan's homemaking practices would not typically be considered a normative inscribed tradition in part because of who has had the power to create Christian tradition.[33] But this does not mean that they have no potential to matter as inscribed tradition, and the question is how these practices, when done well, contribute to the ends of the faith community. As with the women's mentoring communities, their ends and contribution will be connected to the larger power relations in which they occur. To surface that connection, I turn to the second meaning of tradition, *homemaking practices as part of incorporative tradition.*

Incorporative practices matter because in the performance of bodies that are present to one another, distinctive communications occur that cannot be reduced to the inscribed commitments of a community. Gestures, facial expressions, and bodily postures send their own messages, and they are not reducible to the verbal and written commitments of Good Samaritans. The shared convictions of a community to be welcoming and inclusive may or may not be matched by the communications of bodily practices. To get a sense of the contribution of homemaking activities to the larger ends of the

---

[31] Ibid. 12 ff.   [32] Cited ibid. 293.

[33] MacIntyre excludes some activities because they don't have a tradition with standards. His failure to adequately treat power issues may make him overlook the possibility that having a publicly visible tradition is connected to power and status in a society. An activity such as cleaning could have such traditions, at least oral traditions, its 'invisibility' being related to the social status of its practitioners. *After Virtue*, 187–91.

community requires connecting them to the most significant bodily practices at Good Samaritan.

The incorporative 'traditions' that matter most for assessing these activities are the deeply embedded bodily proprieties around race. (Members from group homes were not mainstreamed enough to participate in homemaking practices; thus associated normate bodily proprieties around their 'difference' cannot be explored.) Some Good Samaritans have been habituated into white bodily proprieties and the inextricably connected African American proprieties. African members come from habituations where 'race' has little salience to a country where their bodies are most immediately 'read' as black. The question is what difference the bodily dimensions of homemaking practices in such a setting might make in relation to the ends of welcoming 'those not like us'.

Most of what have been called homemaking practices are the everyday, lived world activities of average people. They do not require special theological knowledge, nor are they necessarily identifiable with Christianity. Everyone's property must be maintained one way or another; everyone must eat and pay her rent. Most of us engage in some kind of empathetic behavior, even if only with our families. Nothing extraordinary here. What would qualify these activities as practices that potentially sustain a distinctive place has to do with the skills they display and their effects on the different cultural and racial habituations of participants. I contend that at Good Samaritan some kinds of alterations are likely of both the propriety of white ownership of space and the African American propriety of heightened vigilance. While there are signs of continued obliviousness on the part of whites, some advancement of the ends of welcoming outsiders occurs as well.

First, these practices brought people together in a variety of settings that contravened many of their inherited racialized enculturations. Whites were often in the minority in these activities; they were mostly working with African Americans and Africans as equals. Complete obliviousness to the marked 'Other' was not an option. For the African Americans, I can only guess that these white postures created at least a potential space to experience more safety with whites. Working together may have contributed to the diminishing of Africans' and African Americans' mutual prejudices as well.

An example of such beginnings is church members' sharing of stories. This activity is striking because it offered more than simply the opportunity to learn about one another. This sharing entailed something more than the opportunity for individuals without a lot of power to be 'on stage', to have a group's attention focused solely on their own lives. While all of these things are true, there is more at stake. As Sample describes it, the prominence of storytelling in oral cultures has the potential effect of enhancing relationships— relationships across race and nationality. A good descriptive story 'expands the range of the empathic core'. It engages the other and involves listeners in relational thinking, a form of thinking that stretches their care for the other. Indeed, what he calls 'scenario thinking' is involved with this communicating through stories. 'One story triggers a story in the listener, and the listener thinks through her own story, the communal relations it entails, and the empathic associations connected with it.'[34]

Ethical thinking is also displayed here, most specifically in the instances of storytelling. It is not an ethical thinking that theorizes or abstracts, assessing the good in terms of universals. Rather, it is characterized by 'empathy, communal knowing, relational thinking and stories', as Sample puts it. This thinking is seen especially in responses to others' troubles, as in the stories told by Chrissie and Elizabeth, which evoked from the listener an empathetic response by which s/he finds connections to her/his own story.[35] This relational thinking is, again, particularly powerful in the instances where people from different races and nationalities are involved: a white Euro-American's response to the dilemmas of Africans—such as Ben's to Elizabeth's—and of whites' to African Americans'. Or the response of one Liberian, Beatrice, who had escaped the civil war, to the suffering of another, Elizabeth, who had not.

Particularly noteworthy is the scenario thinking of an African American man, William, to the suffering of a white woman, Chrissie. While Chrissie's story related events that would have invited critical disbelief in some other setting—namely, her descriptions of divine intervention that were not even typical of Good Samaritan testimonies—her recounting elicited neither skepticism

---

[34] Sample, *Ministry*, 39, 38–44.   [35] Ibid. 37–8.

nor patronization from the group. Instead, listeners responded with sympathy for her struggles, and an African American man whose primary concern was his child offered her appreciation. William translated Chrissie's story of miraculous healing into a testimony of hope for his own young autistic son. Such activities are conducive to a place not only where people learn things *about* one another, but also where there are real possibilities of coming to understand and have sympathy for the dilemmas and tragedies of others.

Homemaking activities brought people together in decision-making, as well. That most of the practitioners were women suggests that such activities may well enhance the gendered sense of agency, although clearly to different degrees for different 'races'.

Offering opportunities for learning about different cultural habits and negotiating ways of working together, however, decision-making displays some important residuals of obliviousness on the part of white members. For example, God's Storehouse brought to focus members' different 'temporalities'. The decision to make Olive the director of God's Storehouse, even though it was Beatrice's idea, signals the inscrutability or unintelligibility of the African body for sensibilities defined by the white ownership of space. What may well have been wisdom accumulated through Beatrice's experience in her own Liberian community and working with lower-income folks in the US was read by white members as her untrustworthy and undependable habits of 'African time'. Likewise, judgments that Ugandan Liana was too lenient in her sales or Mary's criticism that the UMW's work was too undisciplined may signal an inability to recognize a gifted form of negotiation in the former example, and what Teresa Fry Brown calls the 'commitment to time as a social phenomenon', in the latter.[36] Habituation into white professional class proprieties of orderly, businesslike, and efficient modes of meeting is not a bad thing, of course; however, it may well occlude the different 'goods' of styles forged out of marginalized histories.

Overall, however, practices of mutual care were vital and made a difference in people's lives. Even if sometimes the care was only

[36] See section 'Money-Raising Activities' and Mary's criticism in the section 'United Methodist Women's Practices' in this chapter. Teresa L. Fry Brown, *God Don't Like Ugly: African American Women Handing on Spiritual Values* (Nashville: Abingdon, 2000), 51–2.

expressed verbally or when differences were not always bridged, the activities displayed 'operational and situational thinking', as Tex Sample puts it. Such thinking is constitutive of the moral reasoning of oral culture. Not only is this a kind of reasoning that needs to shape a normative Christian community, these practices served ends that resonated with a primary identity of the community, the desire to be a place where outsiders are welcome and where 'we don't see color'. These homemaking practices contributed to that end insofar as they enhanced empathy between people who had been shaped and defined racially and nationally in very different sociopolitical ways. Some people who were largely invisible to one another began to 'appear' for one another, as the responses to stories illustrate.

Members not only began to 'appear' for one another by learning to listen empathically and reason morally, 'appearing' for one another also required a bodily comfort with the 'Other', the second reason for their contribution. As the continuing obliviousness of the white women illustrates, good intentions about inclusion are never enough. As 'meaning well' will not always be enough, having full agency and presence for one another will equally depend upon the incorporative character of these homemaking practices. This is to say that these practices may have contributed to transforming racialized proprieties, even if incompletely, as much because of altering incorporative proprieties as the content of the discourse. The empathetic body postures of telling stories (and listening) enacted respectful alternatives to these inherited proprieties of 'Othering'. All such bodily performances and interactions might, with some time, help diminish/destabilize the obliviousness of whites and the hypervigilance of people called black. Such changes are minimal but necessary features toward forming a place for all to appear.

If homemaking practices deserve normative status in Christian communities then, it is because they mark the need for face-to-face activities of mutual care and sustenance, support for every kind of need, from emotional to physical, and contribute to altering social forms of 'Othering' by their incorporative and inscribed nature. To be sure, Good Samaritan reproduces a stereotypical association of such activities with women; this is in part because the majority of church members in the US have been and continue to be female.[37] Signs of the disruption of this stereotype, however, are at least nascent in their practices insofar as they hint at the expansion of homemaking to a *human* vocation. Not only does Richard, the retired mailman, symbolize this disruption by being one of the best practitioners, an underdeveloped resonance haunts these homemaking practices. Women of color's practices problematize the long-standing identification of homemaking with the romanticized domestic sphere of the privileged white woman. While not unproblematic, given their low-wage compensation, the association of domestic work for African American women and the African women of Good Samaritan is the 'real world'. As work, it confounds the boundaries of private and public space, and 'homemaking' need not have the privatized, escapist connotations of the privileged white domain. With failures of recognition still operative at Good Samaritan and society at large, new valorizations of mutual sustenance as a human work are nevertheless a necessary and worthy symbolic gesture. Importantly, homemaking practices are distinctive insofar as they bring people together to attend to the *everyday* in an *egalitarian* and *sustained* way. They signal future normative work for all Christian communities.

Fully answering the larger normative question of the effects of these homemaking practices, however, requires assessment of the combined force of all the practices of the community.

[37] Ann Braude, 'Women's History *Is* Church History', in Thomas A. Tweed (ed.), *Retelling American Religious History* (Berkeley and Los Angeles: University of California Press, 1997), 87–107.

6

Being Biblical: Interpretive Practices

The real test for God's voice is whether it conforms with the Word. We must stay in the Word, know the Word, memorize the Word.

Wanda

The whole Bible boils down to this—this is my favorite—love your neighbor as Jesus loves you.

Beatrice

We shouldn't read literally. Words can mean something different in the Bible than they mean today.

Donna

Christianity and the Bible can be control tools.

Diane

DEFINING BIBLICAL PRACTICES

It is a bit misleading to confine the treatment of Christian Scripture to one chapter as if the use of the Bible is limited to one kind of practice. Signs from this authoritative text circulate throughout a faith community—in worship, ordinary conversation—and in the national culture as well. 'Since biblical references constitute a cultural resource,' as one scholar puts it, 'they can occur wherever and however participants make sense of their situations.'[1]

[1] Grey Gundaker, 'The Bible *as* and *at* a Threshold: Reading, Performance, and Blessed Space', in Vincent L. Wimbush (ed.), *African Americans and the Bible: Sacred Texts and Social Textures* (New York: Continuum, 2001), 754.

However, these multiple biblical appearances are not all 'doing' the same thing; nor are Christians 'doing' the same thing in their different *uses* of the text. In this chapter I take up biblical practices that are defined by a particular use and a particular end—communal interpretation of the biblical text as Holy Scripture. Such practices occur as people gather together to read the Bible to discover its meaning for their lives. While there are always other topics in these gatherings, the biblical text itself is taken to be the common subject matter. What is more, this subject matter is understood in a very particular way, that is, to provide access to 'God's will for our lives', as one member says. Not aimed at historical recovery, understanding the ancient world, or aesthetic appreciation, these practices are about how to live faithfully. As such they are in a long line of Christian activities that center around the text's significance for Christian discipleship.

As traditional as Bible study may be, it has always taken very different forms and does so at Good Samaritan. In this chapter I examine three kinds of Bible study at the church. All are concerned with the power of the text to shape faithful lives, but they are distinguished by different approaches to the text and ways of thinking about its authority. Evaluating these activities as practices in relation to the goods of the community requires consideration of their distinctive characteristics.

All Bible reading, whether done by Good Samaritans or anyone else, is constituted by framing devices.[2] These African American, African, and white readers are not just shaped by different cultural forces of racialization, gender, and class; their approaches to texts are a result of habituation as well. What we might call 'biblical habituation' is partly a function of the religious tradition that formed them, but it is also a result of the many other 'places' that produce them. All readers of texts order or *construe* the text in a particular way.[3] While frequently unacknowledged, this construal or 'pre-text' is a way to make sense of the heterogeneity of Scripture and displays the very different things that matter to variously shaped readers.

---

[2] Stanley Fish, *Is There a Text in This Class? The Authority of Interpretive Communities* (Cambridge, MA: Harvard University Press, 1980), 1–17, 322–55.

[3] David Kelsey develops this idea in *Proving Doctrine: The Uses of Scripture in Modern Theology* (Harrisburg, PA: Trinity Press International, 1999).

One feature of this pre-text involves the way participants understand the *nature of Scripture* as a text that makes claims upon their lives. Not always explicit as a theory of inspiration or authority, this understanding will be evident in the way the Bible is characterized and the use that results from that characterization. Since these practices are undertaken to enhance Christian life, a second feature of this pre-text is accounts of that life. How do participants conceive of the shape of faithful response to God, and how might that shape be connected to their view of the nature of Scripture?

A third feature concerns the kind of discourse or 'logic' that constitutes these biblical practices. For example, while they are 'studies', these biblical practices are not carried out as a discourse of scholarly analysis. Answers to questions about the nature of Scripture or the shape of Christian life will not evolve from careful investigation of historical, archeological, or theological sources. Rather, the questions, assignments, and 'answers' all proceed in forms of discourse with a kind of nonlinear logic of their own, a logic characterized by the connecting communications, the resonances that help form community. This is not to say that such discursive logics *invalidate* the insights generated. Indeed, my point is the opposite: respecting this kind of logic is necessary to proper recognition of a 'biblically formed' place.

Following consideration of these hermeneutic pre-texts and their assumptions about the authority of Scripture and the shape of Christian life, I will consider the logics of these different activities, concluding with evaluation of their status as practices and their effects in the community.

READING THE GOSPEL OF JOHN FOR GOD'S WILL

A first kind of Bible study was initiated by Dan.[4] Under his leadership, a group of Good Samaritans gathered every Wednesday evening for the express purpose of studying Scripture. On the face, it would appear to be study characterized by direct contact with Scripture, distinctive because it does *not* employ a mediator such as a study guide. No

---

[4] These two Bible studies were typical of a number I attended from 1995 to 1996.

readings are assigned other than the biblical text. A specific biblical passage or set of passages is identified in every Sunday bulletin as the reading for the following Wednesday night. Following two of the sessions, however, reveals that questions provided by the pastor and the interpretive assumptions brought by the participants frame the text in quite distinctive ways, exposing some of their assumptions about the nature of Scripture and the shape of Christian life as well.

One Wednesday night in mid-March a group of ten, including me, gathered in the house that doubled as the church office to discuss the tenth chapter of John. A mix of Caucasians, Africans, and African Americans, we sat in the living room in wooden folding chairs gathered in a circle. Dan and Linda were there. An older white couple from the Church of the Brethren tradition, Wanda and her husband, Barry, brought one of their daughters who went to a nondenominational 'Bible church' nearby. Suffering the effects of a stroke, Barry sat with his head down through the entire discussion while Wanda was an enthusiastic participant. Letty was a regular. Raised in a Liberian Muslim tradition, she had more recently converted to an evangelical nondenominational church since her marriage to William, an African American. William came in a bit late from his cleaning service job. Also arriving after the others was Beatrice from Liberia and Emmanuel from Kenya.

John 10 is part of the 'book of signs' (chs. 1: 19–12: 50), where Jesus's public ministry takes place as a display of God's revelation in sign and word.[5] Following chapter 9, centered on the theme of light, the tenth introduces Jesus's teaching and sheep imagery. The chapter begins with a parable—'a figurative attack on the Pharisees', as Raymond Brown puts it—that bridges two Jewish feasts.[6] It then moves from Jesus's parable of the shepherd, sheepfold, and sheep (vv. 1–5) and explanations of the parable (vv. 6–18) to the crucial reactions by those who see and understand and those who do not (vv. 19–21). The second half moves from Jesus's pronouncements that he is Messiah and Son of God (vv. 22–39) to a conclusion (vv. 40–2), which signals the end of his

---

[5] I am drawing largely from *The Anchor Bible: The Gospel according to John I–XII*, Raymond E. Brown, SS (introd., trans., notes) (Garden City, NY: Doubleday, 1966), pp. cxxxviii–cxliv, 383–415.

[6] Ibid. 383.

public ministry. The key themes of the chapter are thus shepherding, challenging religious authority, and recognition/nonrecognition of Jesus's true identity.[7]

The Good Samaritan inquiry began with a handout from Dan with a series of questions. But first, offering the only historical reference of the evening, Dan talked about what it meant to be a shepherd back in ancient Palestine. Details about the profession were followed by his description of how a shepherd cared passionately for each sheep and put his own body on the line to protect the flock, lying down at the door of a sheepfold to ensure their safety. He then opened up discussion of chapter 10.

In the conversation that followed, Dan stressed the analogy between the care of the shepherd for his sheep and the caring love of Jesus the Good Shepherd for his flock. This comforting read of the parable drew assent from everyone. Save for a few brief mentions of Christ as personal savior, they passed over the extensive Christological possibilities of the text. Instead, Dan brought up the topic of God's mode of communication. Volunteering that his daughter takes literally the biblical stories in which God speaks to people, he said that 10-year-old Patty was distressed that God did not speak to her. What did people think about that? he asked.

Wanda offered a clear method for determining God's message to her—reading the Bible. Her ideas are tested and confirmed, she said, insofar as they do not contradict the Word. She went on: the real test for what counts as God's voice is whether in fact something conforms to the Word. 'We must', Wanda said, '*know* the Word, *stay* in the Word, and the best way to do that is to *memorize* the Word.' Her Church of the Brethren tradition, she continued, taught her the important practice of stating the citation of a biblical verse before reading it, then repeating it again as a way to help remember where the verse is. But no, she acknowledged, she had never literally *heard* God speak.

Wanda's account prompted a story from Letty, who described what it meant for her to hear from God through Scripture. She told of a time in their marriage when William worked all night. She could never sleep, she said, being constantly worried until she heard his car pull in during

---

[7] Note my own pre-text, of which the most obvious elements come from scholarly commentaries.

the wee hours of the morning. One night Letty opened her Bible, she continued, and found herself reading from 2 Timothy. With prompting from William, Letty quoted a passage from Timothy that said that God gives a man his work to do and protects him. Everyone laughed and commented upon what a perfect verse this was for her situation. Letty told us that she got peace from this Scripture and understood that God called William to work to support his family, that God would protect him in that, and that she needed to quit worrying.

Letty's testimony elicited sympathetic responses. Emmanuel spoke about how good it was to get that feeling from reading Scripture. Unfortunately, he added, usually a few days later God's message does not feel as real, and we get pulled in by the ways of man. Several nodded agreement; worry about the negative 'pull' of the world was shared by many concerned that their relationship with God remain primary. Beatrice joined in with observations about what it meant to her to hear from God. It is a sense of being confirmed in a decision, she said; of knowing that it is right. It is reading Scripture for sure, but, more importantly, it is having that feeling of *doing* that right thing, the thing God wills that indicates God is communicating.

While these discussions about God's mode of communication are consonant with fairly literalist views of the status of the biblical text, inviting a close reading of the text, Dan's next move provoked looser ways of thinking. Directing our attention back to the Gospel of John, we focused on verses 12–13. In contrast with the Good Shepherd Jesus, who will give his life for the sheep, Dan lifted up the reference to the hired man who deserts the sheep when trouble comes. Taking the text as a warning about contemporary forms of bad shepherding, Dan said, 'This convicts those of us who are Methodist ministers, because it is easy for us to leave a flock.' With examples, he referred to his own errors. He had great difficulties with his first church, Dan continued, and was tempted to ask the Conference to move him—to abandon his flock.

The hireling then became the central figure of the discussion, and participants took up the problems of failed leadership. The failed shepherd linked with Dan's confession reminded some of the difficulties churches have in the contemporary world—particularly the difficulties of Good Samaritan. Beatrice spoke of Dan's reappointment at Good Samaritan for another term and expressed appreciation for his gifts. A kind of associative thinking began. Beatrice imagined that other ministers might wish to be assigned to the church because of its stellar reputation as multicultural. Someone observed that 'other ministers' would have no idea of the difficulty of ministry at Good Samaritan and how much blood and tears and pain had gone into making the church. There were nods of agreement, and Dan appealed to the real shepherd, who is Jesus. Jesus, he reminded us, will lay down his life for the flock. The connection of good shepherding with troubles got Linda reminiscing about the real danger that has faced them at Good Samaritan. Voices combined to tell of the time a member of the Ku Klux Klan made threats and left a Confederate flag in the church.

Eventually memories of the church's early experiences offered a segue back to Dan's handout. The conversation turned to verses 37–8: 'If I am not doing the works of my Father, then do not believe me; but if I do them, even though you do not believe me, believe the works that you may know and understand that the Father is in me and I am in the Father.' The complexities of the verses were quickly abandoned along with the fact that they are primarily about Jesus's claim to be from God. What captured the group's imagination was thinking about whether *our* works are signs of Jesus. Dan remembered the public hearing where their request for city permission to build the church was contested. At the hearing, he reminded everyone, people were calling us crazy; even worse, words like 'nigger' and 'retard' and 'refugees' were used, he said. 'But look at the works that we are doing! That's a sign of who we are.' His comments elicited enthusiastic agreement. Eagerly claiming the Good Samaritan's multiracial ministry as a sign of Jesus, Beatrice said, 'That's us!' Emmanuel added, 'Outsiders!'

Linda continued. To be a Christian, she pointed out, is to be persecuted. The topic of Jesus's works as signs that he is from God (vv. 37–8) was again transposed into the question of whether *our* works were adequate signs. Dan invited us to hear this as a call to make our works faithful. Being faithful is attractive, everyone agreed. However, not all felt that they measured up. Letty commented on her own inadequacies. Beatrice spoke of a recent incident when she worried about whether to pick up an elderly woman swaying back and forth under a load of groceries on the side of the road as she drove by. She confessed, 'I just might be the only help, the only chance that person has all day... and yet sometimes I'm afraid.'

Wanda assured us with a Bible verse that it is God who will give us the discernment to make these decisions; if we are trusting in God, then God will give us the wisdom 'to know when to offer and when to protect ourselves'.

With closing comments from William, assuring us that the Bible contains eternal facts—it is reality and should be our source for all decisions—the group concluded, and we broke up after closing prayer.

Similar dynamics characterized an early April Wednesday night Bible study with Dan. Present were Dan, Wanda and Barry, Ben (a young white man of Baptist background), and Pam (a single African American woman, mother of Billy). Letty and William were back, and Beatrice came in a bit late. Continuing to read the Gospel of John, the group met this night to discuss chapter 14 and its wealth of promises.

The chapter occurs as part of the long 'last discourse' of John 13: 31–17: 26, which follows Jesus's celebration of the Last Supper.[8] After announcing Jesus's departure in 13: 31–8, chapter 14 speaks of problems created for his disciples. With intricate invokings of Jesus's relationships with the Father and the Paraclete, it is a chapter of reassurances. Jesus promises to prepare a place for them in his Father's house and to return (vv. 1–5); he identifies himself as the way to the Father (vv. 6–11): promises that belief in him will bring power to the disciples, the sending of the Paraclete, and his own return (vv. 12–19). Announcing that keeping his commandments and loving him are the way to the Father and the Father's love (vv. 21–4), Jesus ends by promising his Father's coming and the gift of peace (vv. 25–31).

The most obvious pre-text for this chapter was itself a text that we were assigned. Dan handed out a sheet of questions entitled 'The Chapter of Promises', and we divided into groups to answer them. The first five questions asked us to identify the promises and other specifics about the passage. The last three were focused on our own lives, asking about the significance of the promises to us and to rate ourselves on our peace and 'at homeness' with God, Jesus, and the Holy Spirit.

Paired with Wanda, I deferred to this very close reader of texts. She expressed delight to discover even more promises than she ever imagined in this text. Writing before we even started to discuss the

---

8 *The Anchor Bible: John*, 545–7.

passage, Wanda was identifying and listing every possible comment that could be identified as a promise. Breezing in late, Beatrice joined us and summarized the entire hermeneutical exercise. With a response to a verse about Jesus's new law, she said, 'The whole Bible boils down to this—this is my favorite—love your neighbor as Jesus loved you.'

When we gathered back as a group, Dan asked for reports. What were the promises in the chapter? And what evidence does Jesus give for these claims? I told on Wanda, saying she knew the verses so well that she had started writing the promises down before we even began our discussion. Comedian William complained that she was a cheat, which got a lot of laughs and became a ritual teasing throughout the evening. When asked to name the promises, Wanda agreeably did so, after asking with a laugh if she would be challenged. With her zeal and biblical memory bank, that was not likely. Along with the enumerated promises, she identified Jesus's evidence for his claims with verse 6: the evidence is who he is, she said with conviction; 'He is "the way, the truth and the life"!'

Dan next paired verses about loving Jesus and keeping his commandments, which gave the conversation another burst of intensity and sharing. Ben was adamant that the right kind of love calls us to risk. Jesus always risks, he said, and so should we. In the wake of numerous murmurs of assent, Dan remembered doing a workshop for multicultural churches in which he told the story of Good Samaritan. Following his account of the area around the church, some of the men in the group said it was wrong to put women in places such as housing projects or neighborhoods where they might not be safe. Dan reported recoiling at such thoughts. Nowhere in Scripture does Jesus tell us to be concerned about our safety, he insisted. We must go out in love, do things, and risk!

Wanda connected Jesus's risking love with one of her favorite themes. It is important to know the difference between doing good and doing good in such a way that we depend upon God, she said. Good that is our own thing is not good that is God's will. Wanda is right, Dan said, because people can get into 'do-gooding' all the time and not actually be doing God's good works. 'It is pride that makes this happen,' said Wanda—a comment that got strong agreement from Pam.

Ben brought us back to the theme of risk. He worried about the fine line between different kinds of risk, the challenge to tell the difference between being foolish, just caught up in yourself, and the kind of risk entailed in truly following Jesus's call. Reiterating her conviction that God keeps you safe when you stay in God's will, Wanda added a new twist on the meaning of 'safe'. Telling a story of five men she knew who had given their lives in Ecuador as martyrs, she insisted that they had not been foolish. Preparing for this for years, she said, they had gone out into the jungle and been killed for the good. Being 'safe' in God's will clearly did not mean coming to no harm.

We turned next to Dan's second set of questions, which asked us to rate ourselves on our peace and spirituality. To chart our current 'peace quotient', the options ranged from 'smooth sailing' to 'furious storm' on a continuum from one to ten. Similarly we were to rate how 'at home' the Trinity was in our current life situation, with one indicating 'owners' and ten, 'temporary guests'. Ben confessed himself a seven on the peace quotient; he was going through some hard times, he said. Letty responded with confessions of painful self-scrutiny and got the conversation going in a slightly different direction. In the past she felt like she could not call herself a Christian, said Letty, because she was never able to live a totally Christian life, never able to follow God's will any single day. She once told William that she didn't think God ever listened directly to her. The best she could hope for when she prayed was that God might hear little pieces of her prayer that 'came up through the floorboards'. William's response had been a virtual command: 'You are a child of the King. Act like that. God hears you, God always listens to you,' he said. 'Jesus died for you and you should act as if you are worthy of that.'

A discussion began to give Letty more space—permission to be less than perfect. She acknowledged Pam and Beatrice as important supportive friends. They helped her understand that Christians were something quite other than perfect. Offering testimony about their own experience helped in her reeducation, she said. Beatrice had talked with Letty about how angry she had been at God—ranting and raving at him. Pam shared with her friend her own difficulties walking with the Lord. All of this was moving her along, admitted Letty, as she came to believe that God can truly hear her even as she is.

The Bible study closed with a topic that had shaped much of Beatrice's life, her reasons for anger at God: Liberia, where rebel violence still endangered church members' families. A prayer chain was started for family, for friends, for all the people of Liberia.

IF WOMEN HAD WRITTEN THE BIBLE...

A different set of biblical practices formed a women's Bible study. A weekly gathering of Good Samaritan women was initiated when Dina, the wife of the church's second pastor, asked me to lead a Bible discussion for women.[9] Accustomed to getting together as the United Methodist Women, some of the women were pleased to have a chance to focus on the Bible with each other. Although the group stayed small, it was faithful in its efforts and met for a little over a year. Scheduling the Bible study immediately after choir rehearsal meant that the membership tended to coincide with the primarily female membership of the choir. As the women of the choir were overwhelmingly African and African American, so, it turned out, were participants in the Bible study.

Renita Weems's *Just a Sister Away: A Womanist Vision of Women's Relationships in the Bible* was a study guide used in our meetings. Written especially for African American women who, as Weems puts it, are 'hungry for stories of women they can recognize', it attempts to redress the invisibility of women of color in church literature in general and in feminist theological writing in particular. The book combines feminist biblical criticism's directive for recovery of women's stories with 'the best of the Afro-American oral tradition, with its gift for story-telling and its love of drama'.[10] Each chapter takes up a biblical story in which women are central characters or illustrates the dilemmas of women in the biblical stories that often render them invisible or worse. Ranging from the story of Hagar and Sarah to the sacrificed daughter of Jephthah and the women who mourn her to Jesus's women followers, Weems's chapters creatively reconstruct the lives, passions, and struggles of these women.

This study guide is explicitly aimed at *recreating* the text, not discovering its 'real meaning'. Given how little information the biblical text provides about women's lives, Weems acknowledges

---

[9] My leadership amounted to starting up each session and asking an occasional question. The impact of my whiteness and perceived status as an academic is more important, but harder for me to gauge.

[10] Renita J. Weems, *Just a Sister Away: A Womanist Vision of Women's Relationships in the Bible* (Philadelphia: Innisfree, 1988), pp. viii–ix.

that hers is necessarily creative fiction. But it is just this kind of imaginative portrayal that can show how life struggles of biblical women and women of today are analogous. The stories create a 'common thread of sacred female experiences' between ancient and contemporary women.[11] As such, *Just a Sister Away* was to meet with much success in the Good Samaritan gathering. Participants would find many commonalities with the biblical women.

However, Weems's text also provoked a response from the group that contested as well as confirmed her guidelines—a response that itself suggests an important feature of biblical practice. In a word, *a reading of a reading* of Scripture in these meetings helped expose a biblical practice. Guiding hermeneutical assumptions for the group appeared in the conversations of the very first meeting of the Bible study—assumptions that would continue to shape the gatherings. Armed with our bibles and *Just a Sister Away*, seven women, including myself, met in early January 1999 to discuss the story of Sarah and Hagar. African Americans Pam and Donna, and Beatrice and Liana from Liberia and Uganda were there and remained consistent participants. Occasional participants included African Americans Elaine, present that first night, and Betty and Delores, who came to later sessions. First, Weems's text.

The narrative of Sarah and Hagar pits two women against one another. Weems draws from Genesis 16: 1–16; 21: 1–21 to recount and elaborate on this drama of an Egyptian slave and her mistress. The story begins with Sarah's barrenness. This 'problem', according to the ancient patriarchal system, was addressed by allowing her husband to impregnate her slave, Hagar, to ensure the family line. With her newfound 'status', Hagar becomes contemptuous of her mistress, and Sarah demands that she be punished. Escaping to the desert, Hagar is met by an angel of the Lord who empowers her to return for the birth of her son, Ishmael. Sarah then conceives and bears a child, Isaac, who will bear God's promise to Abraham. But this time Sarah's jealousy causes her to banish Hagar. Preparing to die with her son in the desert, Hagar is again visited by God's angel, who provides water and the promise of a future nation through her son, Ishmael.

---

[11] While not 'factual', hers are 'responsible and realistic testimonies of the ways in which women sometimes perfectly, other times imperfectly, love themselves and one another'. Ibid., p. x.

Following an opening prayer the group shared their reasons for interest in such a gathering. Beatrice noted that 'even though it was biblical times, it seems like there were lots of struggles for women'. She needs to find out how these women went through struggles, she continued, particularly how they were able to trust God. Liana added that she knew little about the women of the Bible and wanted help in dealing with her own life problems. Dina agreed that she needed to be fed more by the Bible and to be fed in conversation with other women.

Expressing a similar need, Elaine went in a different direction. Weems was too negative, Elaine complained. She wanted something fresh, a new perspective. Donna chimed in with her usual bluntness: 'All [the book] was talking about is class differences and money differences and how Sarah had power over Hagar because she had money and status and didn't have respect because she couldn't have any children and she used Hagar to get what she wanted and it didn't work out,' said Donna. 'I'm like, yeah, I *know* all that. I *know* all that . . . she was a bully, she was petty and she was irate. And Abraham was a wimp and he let his wife push him around so he had to take this woman and have a son.' Everyone laughed, and Donna concluded: '[I]t's just like yeah, where is the good part?'

Concerned to connect the ethnic differences between Hagar and Sarah to those of modern women, Weems's primary focus is the power-fraught history of relationships between African American women and white women. Moving artfully between the situation of ancient times and analogous economic, sexist, and racist oppressions in the history and present of African American women in the US, Weems opens to view the dynamics of ancient and recent histories of power and abuse in women's relationships. Great-granddaughter of a slave, daughter and granddaughter of domestics, Weems acknowledges her own privilege as an educated African American woman. However, the story is a stark display of the enormous cost to women through the ages resulting from powerful forces of economic and racist injustice.

While Donna and Elaine found this too negative, it is unlikely that their judgments come from privileged ignorance of the harsh realities of racism and economic disadvantage. Neither are strangers to the race dynamics of southern culture. Both women are African American; Donna grew up on welfare. Later discussions will return to the problems and struggles Weems wants to highlight. The real point is not that the realities of human oppression should be denied—as we will see they cannot be—but that dealing with them requires another kind of discourse, one with some kind of good, a reason for hope. As Donna says, she has desire for a 'good part'.

To address this need, Pam lays out a hermeneutic for the group. An African American divorced woman with an autistic child, Pam has her own stories about financial and racial struggle. However, here she offered the important interpretive principle that would dominate the Bible studies. Agreeing that the material is too negative, Pam announces that the 'fresh perspective is going to come from this group'. Confident that there are life-giving ideas here, she insists it is this group that will help her deal with whatever strife the coming year has in store. Echoing Donna's wish for a 'good part', Pam invokes the wisdom of the group as the primary interpretive grid.

With this hermeneutical choice, the conversation leaves Weems to range over a number of topics, beginning with empathetic readings of the two main characters. Beatrice imagines Sarah's embarrassment and humiliation. However wrong in her dealings with Hagar, she was forced to suffer the culture's low esteem for barren women—a prejudice Beatrice says she still finds in her home country of Liberia. More than once the conversation returns to the social realities that mark women with the responsibility for reproduction. 'Men are never at fault in Liberia,' says Beatrice. 'It is always the women who are blamed for a childless marriage.' The pressure is heightened, she explains, by the 'macho thing', a cultural account of masculinity demanding that men always have to produce.

Next Donna and Elaine discuss the urge for power in Sarah and the almost irresistible temptation to use that power against the weaker woman. Several offer sympathetic readings of Sarah's dilemma, admitting that they, too, feel the urge to overuse power when they get some. Even Hagar is not free from this urge, Liana points out, for when she gains status with her pregnancy, she lords it over Sarah. Power is a multilevel reality in this story.

Donna makes her regular sarcastic comment about the male role in the mess. 'We women always get secondhand news,' she complains, pointing out that God told Abraham first about the fathering of a nation; Sarah was the last to know; and Abraham's use of a concubine is not a thing of the past. That reminds Beatrice of the practice of polygamy in Liberia and the power of the man who can pick a third wife any time he wants. She returns to the way Liberian women, never men, are held responsible when a couple does not have children.

The conversation moves back and forth between the figures of Sarah and Hagar, offering critical judgment and sympathy for both. Elaine and Beatrice interpret Sarah's overreaching as the doomed human propensity to try and get ahead of God. Dina can totally identify with the story, indeed with Sarah's 'uppity air that I am the wife. . . . All power resides in me' and with her vindictiveness, observing that this is human nature: 'I can understand Sarah wanting to throw Hagar out—I would, too,' she continues. Then when Hagar has a son, *she* becomes the 'uppity one'. Beatrice agrees, pointing out that from then on Hagar would always be able to 'put it over your head that she was the first to produce an heir'. Dina empathizes with both: in this story God is showing 'that all of us can be Sarah and all of us can be Hagar, put in their positions'.

Laughter and agreement follow this identification. Talk of the limited possibilities available for each woman returns Beatrice and Liana to the subject of multiple wives in their countries, a practice found in their own families—Beatrice's grandfather had five wives. There are hierarchies in these arrangements, Liana admits, and the husband dominates. But the head wife has more power than the other wives; she gets consulted first. An exchange ensues comparing these patriarchal cultures with the situation of women in the US. Beatrice extols the benefits of the US for women: 'I tell my mother that *here* we have some power.' Liana agrees, pointing out that in the US women can leave their husbands, can have economic power, and have much more freedom.

When I ask about the possible benefits of the African arrangements, Beatrice admits that there *is* security for women in such families; 'everyone had their place' and things ran well with everyone knowing what to do. Indeed, she continues, there are often good relationships between wives, a lot of respect; she saw it in her own relatives. Jealousy was rather pointless. 'How can you be jealous when you're one of six?' She concludes that once you are married into a family, you are taken care of.

'Maybe in *your* context,' comments Pam dryly, 'but that would not work well here.' Donna's 'they keep trying, though', brought appreciative laughs and a discussion of the American version of polygamy as we are entertained with a bit of signifying on the male species.[12] Donna observes that male propensities for affairs and mistresses here in the States are virtual replicas of the Liberian and Ugandan polygamous families. Laughter all around again signals our sense of sharing something—dilemmas of sisterhood despite wide differences in race and cultures. Pam points out an additional negative in our American arrangements—at least the African patriarchy includes the honor of marriage.

I turn the discussion to the presence of God in the story, asking the others how they understand God's appearances to Hagar in the desert through an angel. Beatrice identifies with Hagar: after what she had done, Hagar was feeling left, abandoned, but God still came, she says: 'I get that feeling sometimes, that I don't measure up, and I'm not doing what I'm supposed to be doing.' But you're not supposed to give up, she continues; you don't deserve it, but 'sometimes God still finds you in all your rotten places'. Pam picks up immediately, identifying with feeling at a complete loss with no place else to go. Even when you know better, she says, there's still some small part of you that wants to control things, and that tiny piece is what's going to 'mess you up'.

Associations take over. You need to pray, to be in humble submission, Pam goes on. But you still mess up, she continues: humble submission, failure, God comes in, observing 'I think that's when something gets done'. Looking at Liana, she adds, 'Ain't nobody else brought you back from Africa!'

With groans all around, the group remembers Liana's recent year-long exile in Uganda and, finally, England. 'Nobody—nothing else makes sense,' agrees Liana, about the cause of her return. Referring to the disaster when her trip to visit family in Uganda turned into a nightmare separation from her daughter, Esther, Liana says she is only back because of the 'grace of God'. Difficulties with an immigration

---

[12] 'Signifyin' is 'ritualized verbal art in which the speaker puts down, needles, talks about (*signifies on*), someone, to make a point or sometimes just for fun. *Signifyin* depends on double meaning and irony, exploits the unexpected, and uses quick verbal surprises and humor.' See Geneva Smitherman, *Black Talk: Words and Phrases from the Hood to the Amen Corner*, rev. edn. (Boston: Houghton Mifflin, 2000), 260. I suspect my own racial experience meant that much of this went unnoticed by me. See ead., *Talkin that Talk: Language, Culture and Education in African America* (New York: Routledge, 2000), 223–30, 251–68.

office that delayed a new visa for over nine months when her wallet and visa were stolen gave Liana more than the usual inconvenience of displacement. Her pain at separation from Esther back in the States was heightened because of her daughter's autism: 'I don't ever know what she's thinking,' says Liana, remembering how her forced absence could not even be explained to Esther.

Someone mentions the despair Hagar must have felt as she waited in the desert for her child and herself to die, which evokes more sharing of feeling abandoned by God. Dina speaks of the difficult negotiation of God's promises. Easy claims about a happy Christianity or a God who rescues believers are at great odds with her own protracted struggle with cancer. Yet, along with the honest litany of struggles, the women continually return to claims about God's inevitable arrival: 'God will pick you up,' says Dina; 'Even in turmoil, if you can stay calm with your faith, it will subside. We don't know when, but just to have that, you know, mind of the Lord, all of this is because of the Lord in the end . . .'. Liana: 'Just wait for him.'

'But it doesn't take away the pain,' admits Beatrice. Another thread is woven into this emergent lived theodicy when Dina reminds us of the Christ of the Bible, a Christ who feels pain, who came to the poor and the sick. A direct contradiction, laughs Beatrice, of the 'name it and claim it' gospel of prosperity.

The remainder of the discussion circles back to Weems's claims. I ask, 'What about her discussion of racism and race relations between white women and black women?' Donna says again, 'This story is about money and power'. Pam thinks the domestic-employer relation in the story is, here, mostly about black women; it's about race. Dina connects the money-power issue with her own experience as a domestic in the US. With passion in her voice, she says her experience cleaning houses proves again and again that having money does not bring you 'proper breeding' or 'class or compassion'. Describing behaviors of people who define worth by how much money you make, Dina tells of a white lady she works for who refers to her as 'the maid', instead of by her name, even in her presence. In contrast with another employer who offers her food, this woman will 'sit right in front of me, eat her sandwich, drink her juice!' Money gives you power, says Dina; it is no indication of worth.

The Bible study closes out with a shared rip on men. Pam takes us back to Weems. The tragedy of this story, she says, is that it is not

Sarah or Hagar's story. It is *Abraham*'s story. If anybody messed up, it was him, says Donna: 'He had so many choices being a man, and the guy with the power, and he let his wife do what?!?', she snorted, 'you know!' Agreement all around. 'Makes you wonder', she continues, 'why God gave them the power over us, because they don't have the sense that he gave the dog running around the tree.' With a laugh we come to a close, agreeing that the wisdom of the group will give us plenty to talk about in the weeks to come.

Later texts on Mary, Martha, and the women around Jesus brought rich ruminations about the female character and women's special gifts. All agreed upon the importance of mutual support, and each Bible study included some reference to women's community. In the first gathering, Liana spoke movingly of the lifeline she had in friends like Pam and Donna, who visited Esther and paid her rent while she was caught in Uganda. The models of Mary and Martha evoked much identification with their felt compulsion to be Martha. Betty shared her dilemmas with being 'caught in female habits' of endless care of children and husband and never taking time for herself, dilemmas that were shared in some form all around. Vowing to take time for themselves, to 'prioritize', and 'strike a balance', all agreed with Dina's diagnosis that we're 'stuck in the Martha mode', while men get the benefits of that and can themselves be free like Mary.

The support of women who mourned the death of Jephthah's daughter brought strong analogies for women's community and women's gifts for caring. As Dina summed up the story: 'Whenever there's trouble, go to a woman for support.' With an occasional reminder that women can be 'our own worst enemies' and that men can quickly divide us, most of the talk was of our gifts. Explaining the women at the tomb, Pam spoke of women's sensibilities: women are 'more receptive to new and different things'; having children means that 'we have to be ready for the unexplained and unexpected'.

Jesus was clearly aware of these gifts; all agreed that is why he connected with women and why Mary Magdalene and the other Mary were the first witnesses to his resurrection. Pam: 'He was no fool.' 'He knew where his backup was at,' added Donna. 'Women took care of his needs; they did his laundry,' says Pam; 'made sure that he ate, went to sleep, and wasn't starved', says Donna. And not just Jesus, says Liana, but his disciples too: 'Big, grumpy, smelly disciples who walked those dusty deserts and then they come into your house.' The endless, everyday care—all done by the women. No wonder Jesus valued them.

One discussion itself had women's gifts (and limits) on display. An additional participant in the discussion of the story of Vashti was Liana's daughter. Visiting her mother from the nearby residence program for children with disabilities, Esther had a particularly severe case of autism. A developmental disability that affects verbal and nonverbal communication as well as social interaction, it left her unable to talk or live at home but clearly able to communicate with her mother.[13] From their long friendship with Liana and familiarity with Esther, the other women also seemed to know how to create a welcoming atmosphere for the young girl. Repetitive behavior, a broad repertoire of squeals, and variously pitched noises were her primary forms of communication.

The hour-long discussion of the adventures of Queen Vashti and King Xerxes was punctuated by Esther's squeals, loud yips, and bangs in addition to the usual enthusiasm. With an occasional bang on the table, she rocked back and forth and shook a rattle periodically through the evening. As caring as the group was, of course, it was Liana who really 'spoke her language'. Seeming to know just how to respond to each, Liana sat alternately cradling Esther and replying to her squeals and loud yips with loving noises of agreement.

As the Bible studies continued, the talk did not stick to one kind of woman. As muted as discussions about race appeared to be in light of my presence, more distinctions emerged than the differences between African and US cultures on gender. 'Black women have always worked.' Made more than once, this comment was a typical racialization of gender and reminded us all that 'woman' is not a universal category. 'Black women are independent; they have to be,' says Donna. When sexual objectifications of women came up, talk turned to the different ways that women comply. We have to stand up to these problematic images, someone said, and Delores and the other African American women spoke of the dilemma of black women's hair. Pam remembered when she felt shame about her 'nappy hair',

[13] See 'Autism', in Ann P. Turnbull, Rud Turnbull, Marilyn Shank, and Sean J. Smith (eds.), *Exceptional Lives: Special Education in Today's Schools*, 4th edn. (Upper Saddle River, NJ: Merrill Prentice Hall, 2003), 282–307.

and black women straightened their hair in a desperate attempt to meet white standards of beauty. In light of those dilemmas, 'standing up' came to mean being Afrocentric for some, and several discussed their need to accept 'authentic' blackness.

Acknowledging the ways nation, economics, and race complicate gender does not mean that self-identifying labels are easily found for these Good Samaritan women. It is more accurate to say that a kind of negotiating of identities went on in the Bible studies. That was clearest when participants were refusing labels. Mention of equal rights in a riff comparing African attitudes and American got Donna going about the women's movement in the 1960s, with all the marches for equal pay and equal rights. But 'black women have always worked.... Why are white women hollering about this stuff?' Donna wondered. Why were they so anxious to work? 'We've been doing it for four hundred years!' she laughed. 'And it's not so great.'

This negative reaction to feminism came up again in a discussion of the creativity of the group, which Donna claimed is preferable to the womanism of the study guide. A 'Womanist' is 'a black feminist: a courageous woman who is committed to *whole* people, both men and women.'[14] Echoing a majority of black churchwomen in her discussion of Walker's definition, Pam rejected the label of black feminist as well as white. It's negative, said Liana. Feminist means marching and lesbians, it means anger and meanness, said Pam; hollering and screaming, added Donna. It's not that we don't want to criticize what men do, she explained, when I asked, it's just that we don't want to be labeled, or to think in absolutes—that all males are bad, that all blacks' problems are due to racism. 'Courage? I'm that anyway. I'm a woman,' Pam repeated for emphasis. 'I know I'm a woman and I know I'm black,' she said, summing up. 'That's enough right there. I love the Lord, I'm a woman, and I'm black.'[15]

When it came to the authority of Scripture, hints of their views emerged in a conversation that began with comments on the maleness

---

[14] Weems, *Just a Sister Away*, p. ix.

[15] Sociologist Cheryl Townsend Gilkes says, 'Most black churchwomen would eschew the label feminist and consider themselves simply to be black women who are or are trying to be "good Christians." ' Cheryl Townsend Gilkes, '*If It Wasn't for the Women...*': *Black Women's Experience and Womanist Culture in Church and Community* (Maryknoll, NY: Orbis, 2000), 10.

of biblical authors. They hardly tell us anything *interesting* about Jesus, someone complained. The group began to reimagine stories of Jesus as if a woman disciple had written the New Testament. 'She would have been more descriptive, that's for sure,' said Pam, 'like telling us what he looked like. Good looking brother, 6'2', olive complexion,' Pam continued. 'Broad shoulders,' added Donna, commenting that men's inability to tell what is interesting is obvious from what is not in the biblical text. Liana went on, 'At the wedding at Cana miracle—we drank wine, had a good time.' Donna picked the story up, 'We danced till dawn. Then the Lord said, "That's enough now, break this thing up. Y'all go home, you know."' Donna turned to the story of the Nativity: 'The child was born in the middle of the night. Joseph was losing his mind. Sweat from all over. . . .' Everyone was laughing. If women wrote the Bible, Pam said, 'it would probably be twenty-six volumes—fifty-five volumes!' 'If I saw Jesus,' Liana intoned. 'Right! *that* would be a volume,' laughed Pam. 'Revelation would be fifty volumes right there.'

PRACTICES OF BIBLICAL CONTROVERSY

A third and very different kind of biblical practice surfaced at Good Samaritan with a controversy around 'homosexuality'. It began at a meeting to plan vacation Bible school. Carol, a white professor at a local university, asked if her daughter's friends, whose parents were lesbians, would be welcomed at these church events. Raised southern Methodist, like many of the university students, Carol had a liberal activist streak that had drawn her to the interracial church. Her question initiated a debate over whether Good Samaritan's mission of 'inclusiveness' applied to homosexuals. The debate was further intensified when Gerald, Dan's successor, told the Pastor/Parish Relations Committee that he wished to hire a new music director who was an out gay white man. Arguments in these meetings quickly spilled over into a Sunday school class led by Gerald, who then decided to lead several sessions on the *Book of Discipline of the United Methodist Church*.

Present at one of the Sunday school sessions were Carol, Dina, Kathy, her Portuguese husband, Miguel, William and Letty, and several others.[16] Following a discussion of the Social Principles in the Methodist *Discipline*, the latter part of the lesson concerned issues of community, including abortion and homosexuality. Two things stood out, said Gerald. The United Methodist Church's position is that homosexuality is 'incompatible with Christian teaching'. The *Discipline* claims, however, that homosexuals are of 'sacred worth'.[17]

The response in the group was intense. Raised in a variety of Bible-centered denominations, Kathy was quite active in the church and had a lot to say. After quoting Leviticus 20: 13, which condemned homosexuality, she said quite matter of factly, 'If the Bible says that, that's the end of it. It is an abomination.' Carol was not satisfied with this and inquired of Gerald about the limits of the church's exclusion of lesbian, gay, bisexual, and transgendered persons. No ordination, he reported, but they can certainly be members. 'How about holding church office?' Kathy asked, and expressed disapproval when Gerald said that they could. But homosexuality is wrong in the eyes of God, she insisted: 'When He created human beings it was not man and man, it was man and woman.' At that point Carol said very calmly, 'I could not disagree with you more strongly.'

Remembering the class later, Gerald notes that he had hoped to simply study United Methodist positions in order to understand them, not to make participants agree or disagree with them—certainly not to divide members. But his hoped-for outcome was not to be. Both Kathy and Miguel were very upset, he said. The class ended that Sunday morning, as Gerald remembered, 'pretty much with the lines drawn'.

At the next Wednesday night Bible study the debate continued. Innocent of the previous dispute, Beatrice expressed her curiosity about homosexuality. Grace, Liana, Pam, and Dina seemed truly interested in exploring the issue, or so thought Gerald. However,

[16] I was not present for the session and recreate its general themes on the basis of interviews with Gerald, Carol, and Diana. Kathy would not return my phone call.

[17] The 1996 version of the *Discipline* reads, 'While persons set apart by the Church for ordained ministry are subject to all the frailties of the human condition and the pressures of society, they are required to maintain the highest standards of holy living in the world. Since the practice of homosexuality is incompatible with Christian teaching, self-avowed practicing homosexuals are not to be accepted as candidates, ordained as ministers, or appointed to serve in The United Methodist Church.' *The Book of Discipline of the United Methodist Church* (Nashville: United Methodist Publishing House, 1996), 65G, p. 89; 301.4, p. 172.

Miguel, Kathy, and Chrissie were also there and remained adamant that Scripture condemns homosexuality. Several themes emerged in the session; few themes—or participants—really connected. Gerald admitted that Scripture has much opposition to homosexuality, but stated that the important thing is God's love for all people. The Methodist *Discipline* affirms homosexuals as persons of 'sacred worth'. Liana and Beatrice wondered if people are 'just "hard-wired" that way'. Pam remembered when her race kept her out of many churches.

Miguel observed that it is their *sin* that rightly keeps homosexuals out of the church. When Dina mentioned the many sinners named in Scripture whom we don't exclude—like gossipers and fornicators—Kathy responded with an appeal to the story of Sodom and Gomorrah in Genesis 19: 1–29. God's wrath against homosexuality is so great, she argued, that he destroyed the city. Gerald then spoke of the complexities of Old Testament laws: some continue to be followed and some, such as dietary restrictions, no longer have force. But appeals to contextualize prohibitions did not faze Kathy's family. Chrissie continued to insist, 'The Bible says it, so that's the end of the argument.'

Two other families were equally clear in their opposition. William and Letty had already expressed their disapproval—or at least William had—at the Pastor/Parish meeting. There William appealed to Scripture to challenge the hiring of the gay choir director. Wanda heard about the disputes and came to talk with Gerald to indicate her concern. Wanda was most distressed by the idea that Methodists were to welcome homosexuals into the church. Sadly, she confessed that she really loved Good Samaritan and its people, but that her sense of biblical morality and the high standards a church should have, made it impossible for her to reconcile staying. Homosexuals are sinners, she maintained, and they would destroy themselves because of their lifestyles.

This debate constituted an important moment in the church's life. Kathy, Miguel and family, William and Letty, and Wanda and Barry and their families soon left Good Samaritan for other non-Methodist churches. Not only did this debate precipitate departures, these events continued to have impact as other forms of inquiry emerged, a topic to be taken up in the next chapter. What is distinctive about the debates as a biblical practice, however, is that the claimed transparency of biblical meaning is front and center in the discourse against homosexuality.

Scripture is clear on a matter, according to this view, and that constitutes sole and sufficient warrant for a judgment.

For a fuller account of this biblical practice, I turn to a comparative
look at all three.

INTERPRETING INTERPRETIVE PRACTICES

These three different kinds of biblical practices are not utterly discrete
activities; they share some features. Several Good Samaritans partici-
pated in more than one of these discussions and engaged in more than
one of the practices. There are, however, distinctive identifiable patterns
in the three gatherings—patterns that do not always correlate with
individual readers, but that are produced in the gatherings.

All three types of practice assume that Scripture makes a claim
upon peoples' lives, that is, the Bible is authoritative. However, that
can mean very different things. In the first practice, described in the
section 'Reading the Gospel of John for God's Will', a fairly clear
account of that authority is offered. Participants in the two Bible
studies on the Gospel of John assume some version of the notion that
the Bible is the revealed will of God. According to this view (sometimes called evangelical biblicism), 'All problems of faith, life and
theology were to be solved simply by use and exegesis of the Bible,
and ... no other consideration need be taken into account than the
knowledge furnished by the Bible.'[18] Participants approach the biblical text as the sole *source* for inquiries on how to live, a source that
can also double as an adequate *field of evidence*. Neither psychology
nor sociological handbooks—not even Bible commentaries full of
contextual information—must be consulted or invoked. The Bible
alone (prompted by Dan's questions) is considered sufficient for
these discussions about how to live.

---

[18] James Barr calls this 'biblicism', which he distinguishes from fundamentalism. Unlike
fundamentalism, such biblicism can admit of errors, just not errors on the important
issues of how to live according to God's will. James Barr, *Fundamentalism* (Philadelphia:
Fortress, 1978), 6. Cf. Nancy Tatom Ammerman, *Bible Believers: Fundamentalists in the
Modern World* (New Brunswick, NJ: Rutgers University Press, 2002), 1–16.

William's appeal to the text for life decisions is congruent with this view; as he put it, full of eternal facts, the Bible *is* reality. To Dan's question about how God communicates, Wanda assumed this position when commenting that the way one tells if something is from God is by checking it in the Word; one memorizes the Word and should know verse and chapter as well as words. Letty's story also exemplifies this view. Getting a message from God by letting the Bible fall open to a random text assumes that any passage in the text is identical with the divine will. These views of biblical authority also underlie the third practice of Bible citing, where members use biblical texts as sufficient source for evidence to authorize condemnation of homosexuality.

Distinctions emerge, however. The assumption of the first practices— that the biblical text can authorize life decisions directly—does not necessarily amount to the view that any and all texts, the 'leveled' text, can be equally authoritative. Even Kathy's use of texts to condemn homosexuality, implicitly valued those passages over texts about gossip or other sexual behavior. Recognition of the inevitably *selective* use of texts virtually compels us to look for the additional elements used to construct these texts, that is, to identify the views of Christian disciple-ship that help define shared pre-texts. Here the first and third practices diverge.

The practices of reading John's Gospel take the Bible to be most fundamentally *about believers' lives.* Not a particular issue or moral problem, but about the *shape* of their ongoing lives. Of course not all parts of that text are taken as relevant to that task. A pre-text selects what is relevant. Some of John's main themes were not taken to directly address their version of that life. Nor did challenging religious author-ities, Christological nuance, or recognition/no recognition themes catch their interest; neither did the potentially Trinitarian possibilities of John 14. Indeed, these themes never even appeared in the discussions. To fill out the operative pre-text we turn to what *did* capture their interest: the shape of ideal Christian life as they constructed it from John.

Being Christian for these believers is not simply about attendance at Sunday worship. Discipleship is demanding and full-time. Little attention was paid to Dan's opening remarks on the shepherd-like love the Savior has for them as they focused on the challenges of faithful life. To be sure, a reassuring sense of being loved and guided undergirds their confident claims about God's communication through Scripture. However, there was more concern about the contrary pull of the world that tempts them to abandon that God and about the many possibilities for bad shepherding. Being faithful for these believers is about vigilance in a world full of danger and bad alternatives.

Even as God's abundant promises were celebrated, the conversation did not linger there either. Discussion quickly turned to the risks that come with experiencing God's love, and two ways of thinking emerged. First, risks and difficulties have to do with the temptations of individual souls. The lure of 'the world' can cause individual struggles as believers try to trust the God of promises and compassion, but the very attempt to do good, as Wanda insisted, is another way to fail in the journey. Proper dependence upon God requires heightened self-scrutiny. 'Are our works signs of Jesus?' was of primary interest in the first session. If the insecurities of well-meaning discipleship were not enough, Letty confessed to a guilty self-doubt that added even more torture to this piety of risk and difficulty. Her self-abrogating fears that God cannot even see or hear her add a particularly female-gendered dimension to the sense of worthlessness so often attached to Christian repentance. Christian life—dependent upon a covenanting loving God, say these believers—is an ongoing struggle within the self.

The difficulties and risks of discipleship are understood here in a second way that potentially counters the paralyzing, quietist potential in this first kind of piety, preventing its collapse into world-avoidance or the endlessly guilty conscience. For numerous participants, the struggle of faithful discipleship has a social character. The nature of Jesus's love, as Ben said, compels you to risk; and risking is doing. As Beatrice put it, love your neighbor as Jesus has loved you. And for this community, the neighbor turned out to be the social 'Other', not simply an individual needing a lift, but those caught in complex sinful structures, from racially divided Durham to war-torn Liberia. The difficulties of faithful shepherding, as they acknowledged, came from being a racially diverse church in a hostile racist culture.[19]

---

[19] Even Wanda's intense self-scrutiny is attached to a piety of a historic peace church—Church of the Brethren—which made serving others, from the poor in Ecuador to the populations of soup kitchens and homeless shelters, central to its definition of faith. Joan Deeter and David Radcliff, 'How Do We Live Out Our Faith?' <http://www.brethren.org/anotherway/belief/liveout.html>.

The second practices—'women rewriting Scripture'—display more freedom than the others, which puts them at farthest remove from the 'practices of Bible citing'. To be sure, the women come from traditions with high views of Scripture.[20] Several, particularly Donna and Pam, were quite good at quoting Scripture. However, their understandings of the authority of Scripture were completely compatible with recognition of its human and fallible character. As Dina said, 'The Bible is divinely inspired, but written through men's prejudices.' Not only was there continual comment in every session on historical context—'you have to read a passage in context' someone would say—there was also recognition that the 'biases' in the text were not simply a result of quaint history. Delores was blunt: the Bible can be 'a control tool for the masses—a great tool for keeping people in line'.[21] In short, the women's practices recognize the authority of the biblical text, but not according to the pattern of 'evangelical biblicism', where the text is sufficient to authorize any decision. While the Bible *claims* them, its status is not defined by identification of its content with God's will.

What did claim them was neither sayings nor speeches, not laws or prohibitions. What claimed these readers were *stories*—stories about their agency and stories that mirror their exclusions and oppressions, stories that beg for imaginative recreation. Even a Bible 'divinely revealed', as Dina put it, does not require a God who is a literalist without a sense of humor. In some senses these practices exemplify what Vincent Wimbush calls the best of the 'Afro-Christian' tradition, a construction of Scripture to counter the oppressive text of the slavemaster.[22] Unlike

[20] Pam and Betty from black Baptist traditions; Donna, a black Pentecostal; Beatrice, a Liberian Methodist; and Dina, shaped by a British Caribbean Baptist tradition. Liana grew up in a missionary Anglican church in Uganda, but learned most about the Bible in her boarding school. I do not know Elaine's and Delores's formative church traditions.

[21] Discussing the story of the woman and the unjust judge (Luke 11: 27–8), Dina asks, 'Why all the negatives about the woman?' Donna replies, 'Because men wrote the Bible.'

[22] For different ways of framing Scripture in the Afro-Christian tradition beginning with Africa, see Vincent L. Wimbush, 'The Bible and African Americans: An Outline of an Interpretative History', in Cain Hope Felder (ed.), *Stony the Road We Trod: African American Biblical Interpretation* (Minneapolis: Fortress, 1991), 81–97; Vincent L. Wimbush, 'Introduction: Reading Darkness, Reading Scriptures', in Wimbush (ed.), *African Americans and the Bible*, 1–43. Despite their differences, many African practices provide ways to freely navigate and correct the text. Recent work by African women employs what Dube calls an 'oral-Spirit framework' to create such liberative freedom. Musa Dube, 'Scripture, Feminism, and Post-Colonial Contexts', *Concilium*, 3 (1998), 52–3.

modern biblical criticism, such practices do not 'stay always focused upon the [details of the] text and the past that the texts ... are claimed to represent' in order to dig out the correct meaning.[23] Nor are they confined (hypothetically) to everything in the text, like evangelical biblicism.[24] A tradition forged out of survival, Afro-Christian biblical practices *had* to be creative; they could *never* agree to be limited to what the text said. And they effected a 'shift of focus from the past to the modern to the present', as Wimbush puts it, 'from preoccupation with interpretation of texts to interpretation of religious life as the creation of social-cultural life'.[25]

The presence of African women—Liberian Beatrice and Ugandan Liana—and Caribbean Dina forbids a complete collapse of these practices with African American traditions. African women come from traditions marked by patriarchy and colonialism, shaped by Christianities that have alternatively repressed African religions and (sometimes) attempted to reappropriate them. Their various cultures use other sources than Scripture, other methods, such as divinization, and, as Beatrice and Liana illustrate, have other forms of patriarchy.[26] However, important overlaps exist for they represent a freedom necessary to marginalized or subaltern groups. And storytelling is a primary practice found in communities that, however different, are about resisting oppression.[27]

While the traditions of these Good Samaritan women are not coincident with any one hermeneutical approach, in their redoing of Weems's womanism and trust in their own experience the women's practices resonate with all these cultures of resistance. Just as Weems reads African American women's lives through the lives of

---

23 Wimbush, 'Introduction', in *African Americans and the Bible*, 10.

24 Albert G. Miller, 'The Construction of a Black Fundamentalist Worldview', in Wimbush (ed.), *African Americans and the Bible*, 717.

25 Wimbush, 'Introduction', in Wimbush (ed.), *African Americans and the Bible*, 13.

26 For divinization, see Musa Dube, 'Divining Ruth for International Relations', in Musa Dube (ed.), *Other Ways of Reading: African Women and the Bible* (Atlanta: Society of Biblical Literature, 2001), 179–95. Indirect communication is part of the signifying of many African oral traditions. Oyeronke Olajubu, 'Scriptures among the Yoruba: Signifying Meaning from a Woman's Perspective', Paper given at the American Academy of Religion, Nov. 2005.

27 Storytelling is women's role in many African cultures. Dube, *Other Ways of Reading*, 1–6.

imaginatively reconstructed biblical women, so the Good Samaritan women read their own lives through these fictions. Their 'readings' were artful practices that moved effortlessly between the stories of the biblical text and contemporary storied lives with a freedom that recreated the text in ways reminiscent of oral traditions of 'telling and retelling' of African American and African cultures. It is a freedom that allows for alternative forms of communication—viz. Esther—as part of the changing forms of historical struggle. The women do not worry about chronological distance, but operate with sacred time, allowing 'an immediate intimacy with biblical characters as faith relatives', as Katie Cannon puts it.[28] Such retellings, exemplified in the women's rewriting the stories of Jesus, constitute a very different practice than Bible citing or the tightly controlled readings of biblicism.

This version of biblical authority has a view of faithful discipleship found intertwined with the stories that claim these Good Samaritan women. As compelled by stories of oppression and liberation, of waiting on a God who does not rescue and a Savior who identifies with pain and suffering, the shape of faithful discipleship looks like courage, like waiting and trusting, like hoping and solidarity with other women. It has an element of the piety of the first practices, with its care to depend upon God and not get ahead of him, along with a touch of self-scrutiny. It resonates with the piety that can define risk as becoming interracial. But it rules out the piety of the third practices, where the historicity and fallibility of biblical texts cannot be acknowledged. What is striking about this picture of life is its flexibility and openness to changing circumstances, features that fit well with its creative approach to sacred texts. Its criteria cannot be simply whether something is biblical or not, but *whether it provides one with hope that can deal honestly with the sufferings of life.* It effected a linking of lives that might be called women's solidarity.

In contrast to these women's biblical practices, the 'practices of Bible citing' present as very rigid. If the pre-texts of Christian life help make sense of these first and second biblical practices, they are absent

---

[28] Katie G. Cannon, 'The Wounds of Jesus: Justification of Goodness in the Face of Manifold Evil', in Emilie M. Townes (ed.), *A Troubling in My Soul: Womanist Perspectives on Evil and Suffering* (Maryknoll, NY: Orbis, 1993), 224.

with the third. It is not that these 'Bible citers' lack accounts of Christian discipleship. Indeed the members who argued against homosexuality with Bible verses have strong commitments to faithful living and plenty to say about it in other settings. Unlike the others, however, these biblical practices do not present with criteria that fill out Christian faithfulness. The opponents of homosexuality did not appeal to other features of Christian life to make their arguments. If there is sense to be made of these as distinctive biblical practices, then, it comes from attention to *conflict*, the context that gives them a particular shape. Here the important issue is the final feature of biblical practices, what I have called their 'logics'.

The practices of Bible citing best fit the logic of 'authoritative religious judgment', or so suggests sociologist Penny Becker. By 'logics', Becker refers to patterns of thinking that Christian communities typically use in situations, in this case in conflicts. Comparing what are basically moral (as opposed to political or secular) logics in church debates, she finds an oft-used logic to be an appeal to a mandated, unquestionable authority. In contrast to a 'logic of compassion or caring', which involves dialogue and compromise, this 'authoritative religious judgment' or 'what is right' logic functions to identify 'some positions as true (or right, or authoritative) and others as false (or wrong, or illegitimate)'. In Protestant communities such as Good Samaritan, a 'what is right' logic is carried out by 'proof-texting and the congregational rhetoric of "following what the Bible says"'.[29] Thus, this third biblical practice has no need to articulate the shape of Christian life to display its criteria. The function of the Bible *in these practices* is simply to stop conversation.

In contrast, the logics of Good Samaritans' other biblical practices are distinctive precisely as conversations characterized by mutual sharing and disclosure. The discussion of John's Gospel followed a logic of association. Making a reference relevant to one's own life was more important than following the text in great detail or mapping the chapters in relation to their larger contexts in the book of John. While not surprising, given Dan's guiding questions, such a logic is a

[29] Penny Edgell Becker, 'What is Right? What is Caring? Moral Logics in Local Religious Life', in Penny Edgell Becker and Nancy L. Eiesland (eds.), *Contemporary American Religion* (Walnut Creek, CA: AltaMira Press, 1997), 130–1.

fundamental ingredient of this kind of biblical practice. It bypasses much that would concern scholars, from the significance of these discourses in relation to the Last Supper and the Passion Story that follows, to the abundant references to what could fund a discussion of Trinitarian relations. Nor did any conversation emerge from a close reading of the text, or from what is commonly called 'proof-texting'.[30] Rather, a view of Christian faithfulness and the way in which Good Samaritans' own lives match up to that directed the conversation (i.e., provided its *logic*).

Similarly, the logic of the women's group developed around places for mutual sharing and disclosure. Due to the narrative structures of the readings and the oral traditions of African and African American traditions, it was funnier and explicitly freer, offering open-ended possibilities for identification and elaboration as Dan's specific questions did not. Although here provoked by *biblical* stories, the logic is akin to what was earlier called 'scenario thinking' in Good Samaritan's homemaking practices. There members gathered to share their own faith stories, 'trigger[ing] a story in the listener' and thus creating 'empathic associations'.[31] Connections were made, for example, when the story of women's support for Jephthah's daughter (Judges 11) triggered stories of Donna and Pam's support when Liana was trapped in Uganda. But it is not just stories that make the women's biblical practices stand out from the others. Skills at elaborating and signifying on regular 'talk' did a lot to enhance the relational effects of scenario thinking, as their testimony about male behavior attests. The laughs shared, the mutual understandings assumed and expanded are as constitutive to the practices as the biblical text itself.

In sum, Good Samaritans engaged in biblical practices of citation that avoid sharing wisdom about the nature of Christian life in order to perform what is 'right'. Two other types of biblical practices were

---

[30] One possible exception is Wanda's citation of Jesus as the way to the Father. 'The name [proof text] comes from the idea of supporting an argument by finding the "texts" that are the "proof" of God's Answer. Any portion of scripture, no matter how small, can be used. In fact, small portions (verses or parts of verses) are most often cited.' Ammerman, *Bible Believers*, 53.

[31] Tex Sample, *Ministry in an Oral Culture: Living with Will Rogers, Uncle Remus, and Minnie Pearl* (Louisville, KY: Westminster/John Knox, 1994), 39, 38–44.

defined by sharing life wisdom—one more tightly bound to the supposed 'real meaning of the text', the other bound chiefly to the raggedly redeemed and sometimes funny shape of fallible lives.

EVALUATING BIBLICAL PRACTICES

In what sense, then, do these practices contribute to the ends of the community? When it comes to assessing these biblical practices as part of a tradition, their diversity is not a problem. There is no continuous, fixed practice of Bible study in the history of the church.[32] Differences abound—from different biblical texts, different hermeneutical pre-texts, to different forms of accessibility.[33]

Residual strands of tradition, however, do help account for them. Study of Scripture is natural for a denomination that sees Bible reading as necessary to engender a Christ-like holiness.[34] Even with Methodism's quadrilateral of sources for faithful decision-making, the granting of priority to Scripture easily makes the gathered Bible study a Methodist thing to do.[35] Ironically, what we see in the biblical controversy at Good Samaritan and, analogously, in the Wednesday night studies is more like the *modernized* attention to Scripture than the more rigorous form of Christian discipline that it replaced, the Methodist class meeting. The latter required regular meetings for believers where Bible reading and exhortation occurred for the purposes of inquiry, scrutiny, reproof, and advisement on members' spiritual states.[36] Like the class meeting, Good Samaritan's practices of 'Bible study' are primarily about shaping piety,

[32] See Catherine Gunsalus Gonzalez, 'Reading the Bible in the First Sixteen Centuries', in Gayle C. Felton (ed.), *How United Methodists Study Scripture* (Nashville: Abingdon, 1999), 13–37. R. S. Sugirtharajah, *Voices from the Margin: Interpreting the Bible in the Third World*, rev. edn. (Maryknoll, NY: Orbis, 1995).

[33] Robert M. Grant with David Tracy, *A Short History of the Interpretation of the Bible*, 2nd edn. (Minneapolis: Fortress, 1984).

[34] Ben Witherington III, 'The Study of Scripture in Early Methodism', in Gayle C. Felton (ed.), *How United Methodists Study Scripture* (Nashville: Abingdon, 1999), 39–65.

[35] See Ted A. Campbell, 'The "Wesleyan Quadrilateral": The Story of a Modern Methodist Myth', *Methodist History*, 29/2 (Jan. 1991), 87–95.

[36] See David Lowes Watson, *Class Leaders: Recovering a Tradition* (Nashville: Discipleship Resources, 1991), 44–53.

but they do not share their rigor and in some ways have more connection to the practices of the wider contemporary Protestant church in the US. Given the diversity of the community, it is more likely that these Protestant traditions, especially the evangelical rather than explicit Wesleyan pieties, shaped two of these Bible practices.[37]

Mentioned earlier, a third shaping influence for Good Samaritan's biblical practices comes from the traditions of the black church and other subaltern habits of reading, which appear so strikingly in the women's Bible study. While there is no one 'black church' in North American history or in the backgrounds of Good Samaritan congregants, the unique legacy of the African American experience of slavery still shapes black churches.[38] Stories of suffering, liberation, perseverance and hope, aphorisms and sayings, unforgettable images and characters equal virtual sustenance from Afro-Christian constructions of Scripture—all of which signal the freedom of a living oral tradition. Something in their pasts gave Beatrice, Liana, and Dina a similar liberative license with the text. This freedom and creativity characterizes the women's practices at Good Samaritan. Raised in these traditions and provoked by Weems, they refused to be bound by the written text, retelling stories and putting them to use for much-needed attention to the sufferings and agency of black women.

How is it then that these biblical practices were effective? As practices of inscription, what is gained from these Bible studies other than the biblical content that is gleaned from careful readings? How to evaluate them and how do these practices relate to the larger ends of Good Samaritan?

From attending to the pre-texts or prior commitments that come with biblical practices I am arguing that these are defined by the general good of discernment for changing lives. Whether the explicit end is identified as 'God's will' in the text (shaped by traditions of Protestant evangelicalism), or safe places for women (shaped by subaltern traditions), or as 'what the Bible condemns' (shaped by

---

[37] See Ammerman, *Bible Believers*; J. D. Hunter, *American Evangelicalism: Conservative Religion and the Quandary of Modernity* (New Brunswick, NJ: Rutgers University Press, 1983).

[38] The impact of black fundamentalism cannot be completely ruled out in these practices. Miller, 'Construction of a Black Fundamentalist Worldview', 712–27.

intersecting forms of biblicism), these practices were driven by some version of the faithful Christian life—the first two explicitly, the last only indirectly. Evaluation, then, is determined by how one judges the different notions of the faithful life and practices' effectiveness at enhancing it.

The logics of these practices indicate that more than content is at stake. The practices of reading for God's will and the women's rewriting of Scripture not only had the extension of faithful living as their ends, both occurred as discourses that enhanced mutual understandings. The first did this through a shared piety that involved risk and self-scrutiny and constantly renegotiated dependence upon God; the second through a freer storytelling that produced a sense of female solidarity. These effects are laudable as enhancements of community and are not likely to have resulted from a scholarly information-gathering logic. Terms for evaluation are not rightly defined by sophistication of exegesis.

The least compelling of the three is the practice of biblical citation. While its end was to do the right thing, its manner of achieving that 'good' was a logic tied to conflict. As 'authoritative religious judgment', it was an appeal to a mandated, unquestionable authority. Its manner of achieving its end involved no obvious negotiation, no attempt at mutual listening or understanding. It ultimately involved departures from the community. To judge its contribution to the larger ends of Good Samaritan, however, is more complicated than this breaking of community. For the controversy precipitated an ongoing crisis that allowed Good Samaritan to explore more deeply its commitments to its vision. As we move to the larger questions of what kind of place(s) constitute Good Samaritan in Chapter 7, the later effect of these Bible-citing practices will prove to be more gracious than its adherents ever imagined.

PART III

What Kind of Place?

7

Good Samaritan Church:
The Unity of the Place

Uniformity isn't necessarily unity.

Ben

Good Samaritan is a learning tree.... Being able to confront your
own biases and uncomfortableness is the litmus for those who stay.

Betty

Far from threatening the stability of a Christian way of life, the
fact that Christians do not agree in their interpretation of
matters of common concern is the very thing that enables social
solidarity among them.

Tanner, *Theories of Culture*

So do these practices of formation, homemaking, worship, and Bible
study produce a place—a unified entity? If so, what kind? At one level,
this is a question about the ways in which practices overlap. What one
thing, or things, do they produce? It is also a question about how the
vision articulated in the community's formation practices continued to
order its life. How successful has Good Samaritan been at becoming a
'place for all to appear'—a place that welcomes the overlooked or 'those
who are not like us', as Dan put it?

The simple answers are in the affirmative. Clearly there is something
there. The converted garage sanctuary, brick-house office, lean-to
structures, and their accompanying relationalities make a place. And
certainly this 'gathering' is constituted by strong impulses of welcome.
Given the divergences already evident in the practices of the community,
however, the unity of this place or even its way of following a vision

cannot be monolithic or simple. What unity exists will be the result of converging and overlapping sensibilities about being a welcoming community that are produced by its practices. These sensibilities will have differently connected resonances that pull people in more than one direction. Indeed, a multiple set of factors pulling people in contrary directions eventually led to the closing down of the place called Good Samaritan United Methodist Church. In 1998 the Methodist Conference decided that chronic economic shortfalls in the church budget necessitated that it be joined with another Methodist church that, though financially strapped, had a sanctuary and building with historic value. From 1998 to 2000 Gerald had a linked charge. However, the numbers at Good Samaritan continued to shrink. The community finally came to a major transition, when Good Samaritan UMC was officially absorbed into Wesley Avenue Methodist, a predominantly African American church.[1]

Good Samaritan UMC existed for a decade trying to become a place for all to appear, and it is that set of practices with which this chapter is concerned. Having reviewed the prominent practices that made this place, the question now is what they have in common and how they diverge. First, a synchronic look at three dominant images articulated in the practices and wider conversations in the community, always attending to the contributions of bodily habituations.[2] Then, for a diachronic sense of communal identity the chapter turns to the role of conflict in the community, asking how divergence over time helped define both identity and faithfulness to identity. Finally, the chapter explores the role of the larger social formation in producing this place.

DISCOURSE OF WELCOME: INCLUSION, NONJUDGMENTALISM, AND LOVE

If there is an image of the church shared by practically everyone, it is that of welcome. Welcome is a message found on church brochures:

[1] An important topic, neglected here, is the question of the adequacy of Methodist Conference support for these fragile interracial communities.

[2] I have expanded the themes somewhat by drawing upon interviews with members. The limitation of these discursive domains comes from the fact that I was not able to interview everyone in the church. Thus these represent my sense of prominent meanings in the community.

'There is Room for You at Good Samaritan!' exclaims a typical adver-
tisement with pictures of people of multiple hues. 'We are ... African
American, White American, Asian, Native American, Latino, Mentally
and Physically Challenged. ... Come & Share God's Love!' When I first
asked permission from the personnel committee to write about the
church, the primary boast of a white member regarding the radical
nature of its welcome was the claim that 'we don't see color here, just
Christians'.

And this was not just a formal claim. The feeling of being welcome
was the most frequent reason given by members for their attraction
to Good Samaritan. Across race, nationality, class, and gender, people
attested to the warmth of the community and contrasted it with their
experiences at other larger, more formal churches. Liberian Beatrice
had experienced prejudice in other churches and raved about how
welcome she feels at Good Samaritan. Elizabeth found the community a marvelous haven after her desperate flight from the violence of
Samuel Doe. Speaking admiringly of the Martin Luther King Jr
service, Marxist/liberationist scholar Carol finds the community 'so
welcoming and nonjudgmental' that she believes Good Samaritan is
'what Christianity is *supposed* to be'. Others speak movingly of its
warmth in connection with their experiences of rejection in other
churches: Zelda and Stephan, whose interracial marriage had been an
issue in both black and white churches; Pam, who found that her
autistic son, Billy, was unwelcome in most churches.

Like symbols anywhere, those of welcome resonated differently—
had varying associations for members.[3] The meaning of a welcoming
community most compelling for the university-related population
at Good Samaritan had to do with *who* was welcome—persons of
different races, cultures, and abilities. Mary, a white social-work
student, says she 'fell in love' with the church when she saw its
interracial make-up and group home residents. A student involved
in activism for persons with disabilities was attracted to the inclusion
of group home participants. African American student Dwayne lauds

---

[3] Anthony Cohen argues that the symbolic meanings that create communities'
boundaries will always be interpreted differently by its members. See Anthony
P. Cohen, *The Symbolic Construction of Community* (London: Ellis Horwood Limited,
Tavistock Publications, 1985), 13.

the church, pointing out that homogeneous churches are a result of classism and racism. Other students from the local university were also drawn primarily by the diversity of the community. 'It's a family', they said over and over, the kind of family that 'the church is supposed to be'.

The strongest resonances produced by the image of welcome for these members were connected to the actual racial and 'able-ness' diversity of the community. Just being there and experiencing this rare mix of people confirmed the rightness of the community for these Good Samaritans. The discourses that best developed the image's social justice resonances came from the liberation-inflected preaching of Gerald. While Dan's commitment to 'ministry to the eunuch' was foundational to these associations, the extrapolations of Gerald's sermons were more compelling to the members with more liberal, progressive religious backgrounds.[4] 'Welcome' was associated for them with addressing forms of social oppression and with the antiracist implications of the phrase 'not seeing color'. Thus, Gerald's use of the biblical imagery of justice appealed as did his identification of sins of denial with blindness to social oppressions. From the Hispanic migrant worker, the unemployed African American, and the Native American to the single white woman on welfare, he imagined a version of 'those left out and overlooked' that broadened what a welcoming community might look like.

A different sense of welcome compelled other Good Samaritans. While this group shared pride in the 'color-blindness' of the church, their favorite way of describing welcome was the church as an alternative to the strict, 'loveless legalism' of other churches, as Beatrice put it. There is a nonjudgmental feel in Good Samaritan's hospitality that Kathy and Miguel loved. Coming from churches where ministers were remembered as high and mighty, constantly posturing as 'holier than thou', many of these members deeply appreciated Dan's very different style. 'He's not pretentious', says Ben, who came from a conservative

---

[4] What seems the clearest divide was between the working-class white members who came from very conservative traditions (Baptist, Nazarene, Church of the Brethren, and Pentecostal) and the whites (mostly students) from United Methodist and other mainline denominational backgrounds. The latter were more attracted to Gerald's 'social justice' preaching. African American and African members seemed to resonate with both.

white Baptist background. Dan is 'so available' and 'authentic', Ben went on; he wears no masks. Linda and Edgar, a white couple from conservative backgrounds, saw Dan's warmth as the most important draw of the church. With a Church of the Nazarene background, which she remembers as highly moralistic and controlling in its piety, Kathy glows when she speaks of how Dan accepts people just as they are. Grace, an African American woman raised Baptist, left a local church for its inflexible view of Christianity. It was 'their way or nothing' when it came to interpreting Scripture and doctrine, she says, a rigidity completely foreign to Good Samaritan.

As with Linda and Edgar, most of this group account for the welcoming character of the church with the friendliness and attention of Dan and Linda, who made good on the promise of community and support in their everyday ministry. The themes that resonate most strongly for this sense of welcome are found in Dan's worship practices, which conveyed not just a sunny 'glad you're here', but a deep sense of forgiveness and acceptance. The continual reiteration of 'ordinary folks' discourse in his preaching created subject positions of acceptance that were particularly compelling for congregants from strict, moralistic church backgrounds and with more working-class backgrounds. Dan regularly identified a subject position in worship for the 'we' who are ordinary, not rich, not powerful, not intellectual; it is this ordinary 'we' whom God loves and accepts. While Dan interpellated listeners into a space of unworthiness, as well, he regularly identified himself with this 'we', acknowledging his own mistakes. His style as an imploring, scolding, and intensely caring father/older brother, drove some members crazy. But for those from conservative pieties, he produced a space of acceptance, not simply guilt. God loves ordinary sinners, and that is what welcome is about.

What appear to be two different sets of resonances associated with the welcome of Good Samaritan—one of social diversity, the other of acceptance/forgiveness—do not correlate neatly with discrete groups. There are always overlaps. Whether they are inclined toward categories of oppression and liberation, as were Carol and some of the students, or shaped by the black church and 'theologically conservative and socially liberal', for many the image of a welcoming place is connected to the kind of love displayed by Jesus.[5] In discussions including more conservative members, not infrequently appeal was made to the interracial mix of the church as the display of Jesus's kind of love. Pam says about their diversity, 'We're demonstrating the love that Jesus wants us to have. The people in this church live Jesus.' The John Bible study affirmed Dan's interpretation of the church's diverse make-up as the work that was its sign of Jesus. People who would not have initiated such a 'social diversity Christology' seemed happy to accede to it.

Practices that nurture and develop this discourse of welcome include worship, where some form of the *message* of welcoming and loving the neighbor could be heard. Such cognitive directives were not necessarily the most powerful inducements, however. For communicating welcome to group home members, the aesthetic and physical arrangements and communications mattered most. For Liana's daughter, Esther, as we saw, the ideas of the Bible study were the least important in her engagements with mother and friends. Given racialized proprieties, the power of the Word, whether preached or read in Scripture, was likely not the most important in producing welcome anywhere in the community. Given the lack of correlation between beliefs about equality of the races and persons with disabilities and successfully diverse churches, it was the practices that brought people *physically* together in settings of equality that provided the crucial minimal conditions for altering bodily proprieties toward comfort with the other.

The second and third images emerging from Good Samaritans' practices articulate logics for negotiating change and difference in the community.

---

[5] This is a categorization of many nonwhites, especially blacks and Latinos, that accounts for the higher percentage of interracial attendance in evangelical churches, but also the limitations of conservative theology for dealing with needed social change around such issues as race and class. Many African American members at Good Samaritan are socially liberal, while theologically conservative. E-mail exchange with sociologist Michael Emerson, Rice University. See Michael O. Emerson and Christian Smith, *Divided by Faith: Evangelical Religion and the Problem of Race in America* (Oxford: Oxford University Press, 2000).

DISCOURSE OF CONVICTION: SELF-SCRUTINY, DISCOMFORT, AND A CALL TO ATTEND TO DIFFERENCE

An important constellation of images for church members develops the notion of conviction, that is, the sense of being wrong and needing to change. Like those of welcome, the images of conviction do not correlate exactly with conservative or liberationist pieties, nor are they identifiable with any particular tradition. Indeed, given that the end of Christian faith is salvation, requiring *some* kind of alteration, images of conviction are fundamental to Christian discourse of any sort. However, Good Samaritan's logics are distinctive.

First, examples of conviction discourse are found in confessions and self-scrutiny. While Beatrice's confession of her own hesitance about picking up a stranger was a mild form of self-criticism, Letty's concern about her inadequacy before God in the Bible study conversation is a prime example of conviction discourse. Her worry that she was never able to follow God's will for even a single day exemplified conviction in the form of marked guilt and a *need* for change. Wanda's insistence that even good deeds need to be investigated for false self-dependence illustrates a hypervigilance about this guilt-*cum*-need-for-change. Even when doing God's will one should worry. Less intense markers of this need are found in the women's Bible study. There the identification with biblical women's stories produced critical judgment and sympathy that often led to fairly compassionate self-incriminations; indeed, a feel of female solidarity seemed to offset debilitating effects of guilty verdicts. As Dina put it, 'All of us can be Sarah and all of us can be Hagar.'

Another form of conviction discourse intersects with the focus on the individual and with the larger issues of social injustice. What makes it distinctive is the display of a willingness—even a call—to be challenged by difference. Betty and Pam insisted that it is crucial for Christians to be made to feel 'uncomfortable'. Pam spoke often of the need to be challenged by the faith. It was important, she told Gerald, that he make them feel uncomfortable. Discomfort, as Pam understood it, was the necessary first step in a challenge to attend to those who are different from us. A similar discourse of change came from one of the first black members regarding her interracial experience at Good Samaritan.

Speaking of her accumulated fear and distrust of white people, Betty told of what a challenge it had been to trust Dan when she first came to the church. In the first group of African American children in her southern hometown to integrate grade school, she 'began to stereotype all white people the same. They hate us', she said, 'and they were even dumb.' Having internalized white standards of beauty, Betty also saw how her own self-image had been damaged by racism. However, her gradual habituation in the community of Good Samaritan gave her a different sense of whites. Her distrust of Dan's whiteness gradually went the way of her stereotypes of Africans and people with disabilities later in the church's life.

Betty's discourse of conviction and change was forged from these experiences. Being faithful, she insisted, requires being made to feel uncomfortable. But discomfort, as with Pam, is not a reason to run away. It is a call 'to confront my own biases and prejudices'. Being uncomfortable is a sign that she must face them, Betty insisted. The ability to *confront* these biases and to learn something new about the stranger, she said, is a 'litmus for those who stay at Good Samaritan'.

Although rarely as well articulated as Betty's, this logic of discomfort as a call to attend to difference helps make sense of quite a few Good Samaritans' testimonies about the effects of relationships with those of different races and nationalities. A number of white Good Samaritans spoke of their changed sense of race as they came to share their faith lives with African Americans and African members. Earlier examples were Rita's admission of 'superficial judgment' about blacks and the more public confession of Dora about her prejudice in the presence of Africans and African Americans. Ben said that people come to the church with stereotypes and prejudices—'they can hardly help it' as he alluded to the racist culture. However, 'to stay in this church', he continued, 'you have to abandon them'. Only people who can do that stay, he concluded.

As Betty admitted her preconceptions of Africans as 'wild and uncivilized—savages with bones in their noses', so Beatrice was typical of African members who acknowledged their preconceptions and prejudices about African Americans. Unaware of the history of racism in the US and frequently inexperienced with racism in their own countries, these members believed the white myths of the 'welfare mother' and the shiftless, complaining African American.[6] But it was just these recognitions that emerged in their discourses of conviction, of being called to face such prejudices.

Discourses of change have been noted in Good Samaritan's worship practices. The logic of transformation in sermons was fundamentally a summons to change, from a diagnosis of the community to a call for response that was calibrated to the problem. Along with his 'ordinary folks' discourse, Dan talked about giving over trust in worldly wisdom to trust in God. Saying 'Yes, Lord,' as Dan commanded, meant giving God rather than ourselves the credit for our accomplishments. In his sermon on Pentecost, Gerald identified the problem in social as well as individual terms. The boundaries of racism, classism, and sexism needed overturning, he insisted, if we are to fully celebrate God's party. However different, conviction as call to change was as fervent in Gerald's discourse as it was in Dan's calls to the altar.

The contribution of bodily practices to the function of conviction as self-criticism is likely. A good example comes from gendered sensibilities. It is one thing to engage in self-criticism in the physical presence of other women, as did the members of the women's Bible study, where a sense of solidarity could mitigate the female proclivity to self-denigrate. The dynamics of Letty's self-scrutiny were undoubtedly gendered in quite another way, however, when performed in the presence of male figures, not only her own husband, but the authoritative figure of the white male minister. The mark of guilt is clear, but the dynamics for change are less likely, because, with the exception of all-women conversations, the community did not identify gendered difference as a gap needing to be addressed. Similarly even *with* Richard's disruption of conventional categories, the conventionally female-defined homemaking practices so essential to the church's well-being were not recognized in such a way as to raise gender consciousness.

Of the incorporative practices that did help produce a change around racial and ability difference, certainly such homemaking practices as the gatherings for sharing life stories were key. The

---

[6] Gerald thinks that internationals of color 'don't understand the systematic evil' that racism is in the US. Likewise, African Americans besides Betty had stereotyped the Africans and confessed to some resentments of Africans' obliviousness of the oppressive function of race in the US.

opportunities for persons of different races and nations to share space equally and to experience empathy with one another's narratives, the 'yeast' for realizing the need for change, were necessary ingredients for bodily habituation into comfort with the stranger. The homemaking practices around sharing narratives were especially conducive toward this possibility, but support for changing views of the 'Other' could come through any number of the other practices where one's stereotypes could be challenged, both intellectually and viscerally. Working together for God's Storehouse, the projects of the United Methodist Women, even sharing different foods at the International Dinner, would not *guarantee* the insight into guilt—that one had 'misrecognized' the 'Other'. Various already-oblivious choices of white leadership show how difficult such changes are. These practices might, however, contribute toward this possibility.

DISCOURSE OF GOD-DEPENDENCE: WHO WE'RE CALLED TO BE, SELF-AUTHORIZATION, AND FLEXIBILITY

A third constellation of images focused on depending upon God. Like conviction talk, such discourse is fundamental to Christian faith. Of particular interest are three ways Good Samaritans' assertions of dependence upon God functioned—to name how to be in the world, to authorize one's own behavior, and as a discourse of flexibility.

By and large Good Samaritans' discourses about God came from traditional worship and doctrinal heritages. Language about God in services ranged from the traditional Father, Son, and Holy Spirit, and attributions of God's redeeming love and providential agency to more culturally provocative images such as 'He's an on-time God', or 'God is like a good housewife seeking her lost coin'.[7] The interest here is in how invoking God as that which ultimately matters correlates to a particular

---

[7] In surveys asking about favorite ways to define Jesus, a few Good Samaritans espoused Trinitarian language about God, but I did not hear explicitly Trinitarian language outside of worship.

posture toward the self and world.[8] Claiming God's activity in one's life as a performance of God-dependence language, whether orthodox or innovative, comes with a wide variety of such postures—from compassionate and caring to dogmatic and judgmental. Dan's merciful all-wise God, for example, positioned folks as ordinary, guilty-but-forgiven believers who rightly gather as a multicultural community. Gerald's God of justice positioned them to repent and broaden their social world.

For most members, an appeal to God functioned to identify the nature of the good and, correspondingly, how to be in the world. Linda is representative when she said about racial divisions, 'God doesn't want things that way' or 'everybody was the same in the sight of God'. Much of the God discourse involves this kind of reference— an account of the kind of life God wants us to be living. Whether as a claim about God's will for our lives (e.g., God wants people of different races to be together), or a deduction from God's character as love for the proper shape of human relationships, many claims invoking God as ultimate reality are claims about the nature of Christian community.

A different kind of appeal to God characteristic of some Good Samaritans occurs as a piety that understands God to intervene in personal life, from the smallest events to the providential guiding of nations and history. An example is Letty's belief that God led her to a particular biblical passage that spoke to her fear about her husband's work life. Citing instances of God's direct work in his life, Miguel spoke of God using him when he preached a sermon at Good Samaritan. His assertion that 'God never lets the church fall on its face' was God's intended message for the community.

Appeal to God's presence can easily function for both purposes, illustrating the character of God's ends for human life *and at the same time* referring to a direct intervention of divine agency. However, simply to do the latter—invoke an intervention without displaying the desired ends—can function only to authorize one's behavior. Letty's invocation of God selecting a Bible passage tells us little about a desired posture toward the world; it simply authorizes that

---

[8] This claim has a long theological tradition going back in its more explicit form to Friedrich Schleiermacher. His work, *The Christian Faith* (Edinburgh: T & T Clark, 1928), was structured by the view that a claim about God entails a claim about the self and the world.

passage as the correct one. Miguel's claim that God used him functions to authorize what he said. Many Good Samaritans, in contrast,
refer to God's active presence in a way that communicates a valued
way of living. They say that the feeling of being forgiven and accepted
is evidence of God's Spirit in one's life, or that the joy experienced in
the worship service with the movement and music is a sign of God's
presence. By attesting to the communal feeling of love and welcome
in the community as a sign of God's Spirit, they not only tell us that
God acts in the world, but describe its lived effects.

Another discourse of God-dependence stands out as a distinctive
way to navigate everyday life. While it intersects with the others—it
is a claim about the way to live and a claim about God's presence in
the world—this discourse is a way of invoking God-dependence
that produces flexibility for the believer. Its distinctiveness is clarified
by a contrast with versions of God-dependence that require a
worldly posture of self-abnegation/criticism. A favorite theme of
Dan's preaching was the admonition to rely only upon God, that
nothing is our doing—a worldly posture of self-denial. Similar worry
about proper dependence was voiced by Wanda, who warned the
Bible study group against good works that are not truly dependent
upon God. The claim to rely only upon God could have a very
different function, however, when it *dislodged and freed* the believer
from a paralyzing discourse of self-scrutiny.

Such possibilities appeared in the women's Bible study conversations. Identification with Sarah and Hagar, for example, brought
with it identification with their mistakes. Referring to her unjust
treatment of Hagar, someone commented that we often charge
ahead like Sarah, failing to wait upon God. But the point was not
simply to confess sin. Waiting—dependence upon God—is vital, the
group agreed. God always comes, even to the despairing. To Hagar,
seemingly abandoned in the desert, God finally came. Such appeal to
God is a discourse that provides assurance, but not the assurance of
rescue. Speaking of her chronic illness, Dina said, God always comes.
Dependence upon this God, they insisted, is not what allows you to
escape life, it is what *gets you through.*

What distinguishes this dependence from a posture of constant self-
scrutiny is its openness to the unexpected and complex character of daily
life. Resonating with the faith traditions of survival communities—the

African American traditions of the 'on-time God'—the elasticity of this God-dependence is its ability to believe, to trust the self, and to hold on regardless of what the world delivers. Liana's exile in Uganda was not met with passivity, but much activity on her part and her friends; these activities occurred simultaneously with prayers that eventually gave God's grace the credit for her return.[9] While such a discourse of God-dependence can certainly be combined with self-blame and a self-recrimination that paralyzes action, what the women in the Bible study invoke is a way of doing what you can do and trusting that God will act, however unpredictably.

Waiting on this God is reflected in Gerald's vision of that 'on-time God', invoking a kind of courageous patience that refuses to expect easy rewards, but knows that God is trustworthy. As Gerald said, 'He may not come when you want Him, but He'll be there right on time.'[10] The response to such a God, for both ministers, was never inaction. As the debates over homosexuality broke open, for some of the community this patience took the form of a willingness to change one's mind about what God wanted—to be open to the possibility that God was doing a new thing, and that one was called to 'wait on Him', to 'depend upon Him' as this new thing unfolded.

A variety of messages from practices of inscription would enhance this discourse of God-dependence. We could also say that empathy and agency, ends particularly relevant in homemaking practices, support the capacity to 'go on', to be flexible for an 'on-time God'. But a particularly powerful contribution to this ability to wait, to not know and yet to trust, is in worship's incorporative effects. Practices of worship were noteworthy not only for providing insight, but also for the pleasure attached to music and movement among a delightful mix of people. Pleasure was experienced in many of those other practices, such as the dinners and gatherings, but a pleasure associated with aesthetics, desire, and the physical joy of movement were distinctive of worship's *habitus*. Pleasure would no doubt help

---

[9] Liana was quite active. After failing to get a new visa quickly, she went to England where she had family and got a job as a home health-care worker until she could finally qualify for another visa. Her Good Samaritan friends took great care of Esther and Liana's apartment.

[10] Sermon preached on 29 June 1997.

sustain this logic of transformation, risk/self-scrutiny, and freedom
for solidarity in the struggle.[11]

In the terms of postmodern place theory, these shared or overlapping
discourses indicate that a 'place' came into being—a place of welcome.
Not created simply by shared views, the production of this place
required practices of formation, worship, homemaking, and biblical
study as well, all of which had incorporative dimensions. Its unity was
not based upon experiencing these symbols in the same way; they had
alternative resonances for different groups, resonances refracted by the
different bodily proprieties of various members.

Welcome meant a way of feeling included, accepted, and that others
were interested in you. Welcome also meant a response to the inherited
exclusions of history and society, the inclusion of people from different
classes, races, nationalities, and abilities. From the confession and self-
scrutiny that marked the need for change in individuals to the performed call for transformation in worship, to the logic of discomfort as a
first moment in attention to social difference, conviction for change
resonated in several directions. Invocations of God also functioned in a
variety of ways—to attest to a desired form of life, to authorize one's
activity, and to claim a source of assurance that created flexibility for
how to respond to the world.

Thus the convergences were discursive and more. Whether it is the
mutual pleasure of food and shared stories, the sense of mutual
support in times of difficulty, or the erotic and aesthetic joy of
music and movement in worship, commonalities were shared. They
included the experience of receiving gifts when Billy, Carl, and Esther
were welcomed along with their fellow exceptional learners from the
group homes—gifts on both sides. This 'gathering' that was place
included the pleasure some got from chores and maintenance, that
some got from organizing and meeting, and that some got from
learning with the children. To be sure, there were continuing forms of
obliviousness in the place, to the dominance of whiteness and the still
marginal role of group home members. But there was also depth to
this place, a transformational sense, however transitory, when deeply

---

[11] 'Joy, like the breath of God's Spirit, creates a sense of élan, a security in one's self,
a readiness to encounter the other.' Mary E. McGann, *A Precious Fountain: Music in
the Worship of an African American Catholic Community* (Collegeville, MN: Liturgical
Press, 2004), 15.

embedded fears and prejudices began to dislodge for many and be replaced by openness to new possibilities.

With these convergences, also came divergences. Places do not exist without the instabilities that come with its 'gatherings'. The resonances around each primary set of symbols—welcome, conviction, and God— that brought people together also pulled people in varying directions, potentially providing elements for different places. Indeed, diverging resonances drew some away. Four families left Good Samaritan over the issue of homosexuality. To view the further complexity of the place the analysis turns to a diachronic view, which will be suggested by tracing out this crisis. There the possibility to rethink commitments reveals more about the connections, the differences, and the varying logics of gospel shown thus far.

WHO ARE WE—REALLY?

While there were differences among Good Samaritans over such matters as worship, music, and organization that shaped the texture of the place, even creating proclivities for other places, they did not generate any serious divisions. What did divide matters not only for the centrifugal forces it illustrates, but also for the unique opportunity the conflict offers to see the effects of Good Samaritan's practices. Unlike the inevitable instability of a place, certain 'critical events' in the making of a community, says anthropologist Veena Das, provide a privileged occasion for the congealing of its processes and practices. Critical events issue in 'new modes of action . . . which redefine traditional categories' in a particular culture. They surface what is valued and sometimes 'unsaid' in a community. In them we recognize the temporal and unstable nature of communities, but also glimpse something distinctive that congeals, even if only temporarily, as a display of character.[12] The response to a crisis offers the opportunity to see if a community can *improvise*, that is, enact a vision in response to new and unexpected situations. As argued earlier, such abilities are

[12] Veena Das, *Critical Events: An Anthropological Perspective on Contemporary India* (New York: Oxford University Press, 1995).

crucial not simply to the ongoing life of a community but to the enhancement of its character.

The controversy provoked over the United Methodist position on homosexuality was just such a 'critical event' for Good Samaritan. Discussions that followed prove instructive about the kind of place Good Samaritan is, or wanted to be. What the community valued most was surfaced, as well as some of its unacknowledged realities— the 'unsaid'. Having seen how particular practices enhanced these welcoming capacities, in this critical event a larger version of such enhancement can be seen. The conflict unfolded as follows.

Word spread quickly that Kathy and Miguel were leaving Good Samaritan. A middle-aged white woman who worked in a wireless phone store in town, Kathy was quite active in the church. She had been president of the United Methodist Women for the previous two years as well as a member of the Pastor/Parish Relations Committee. Miguel was of Portuguese background. Even though his work managing a local car wash frequently kept him from Sunday services, he, too, was an enthusiastic fan of the church and a member of several committees. The first group conversations about their departure occurred at the UMW's regular meeting, where people expressed shock and disappointment. The conversations were difficult; some tried to figure out how they could understand Kathy and her family—still care for her—and affirm the welcoming character of the church as well. Referring to the rumor that they had left over the possibility of homosexual members, Zelda expressed her sadness, but defended Good Samaritan's inclusivity: 'We have different beliefs here. That's OK. Jesus never turned anyone away.' Beatrice chimed in, saying that we should all stick together; being at Good Samaritan is 'a commitment for the long haul'. Zelda agreed and called for a united front. 'That's what this church does,' someone else summed it up: 'Accept people for who they are and where they are and what they are.'

Having lost their president, the UMW responded with shared dismay. A scheduled retreat to discuss Good Samaritan's mission also turned to the topic of the departures.

Gathering at the church one Saturday morning soon after the departures, a group of about fifteen church members came for a visioning retreat. Among those present were Ray and his wife Olive, two white graduate students—one of whom, Mary, was quite active in the life of the church; the other, Eddie, a divinity student, had started coming recently. Two of the Liberian members came (Tarley, Beatrice), Liana from Uganda, a Kenyan member—Emmanuel, and Betty and her husband, Ronnie, the first African American couple in the church. Also present were Donna and Gerald's wife, Dina. Gerald opened the retreat with a meditation on Acts 1: 1–8, the story of the commissioning of disciples. The mission of a Christian community, he said, is like throwing pebbles into a pond—the ripples image the purpose of the church to go out to the world. Good Samaritan's particular call, Gerald reminded the group, is to those considered 'not like us', the different, the 'least lovely'. Following his introduction, he asked the group to define Good Samaritan's mission.

In response a couple of folks ventured hesitantly, 'Yes, we had a mission statement . . .'. 'But if you don't know it, then it isn't doing anything,' remarked Gerald. 'How about this?' He read from a brochure: 'We are diverse yet united disciples of Jesus Christ, who are called to be faithful *NOW* (through *N*urture, *O*utreach and *W*itness).' Betty remarked that a really important word for her in their previous mission statement had always been 'inclusive'. 'It suggests that we are different from other churches,' she continued. 'In other churches you get together because you're the same economic level and for being comfortable, but I'm not *to be* comfortable in the church. I don't *want* this church to be like other churches!' Others nodded in agreement.

Pam picked right up with Betty's thought. 'Yes,' she said, 'the church has got to be where our comfort zone is challenged.' A lively discussion followed and several people, black and white, crafted the definition of Good Samaritan's mission to say 'inclusive' and 'faithful'. All agreed: just being 'inclusive' was not enough. The point, as Mary put it, 'is being faithful to God'. Inclusivity, they concurred, comes inevitably with that kind of faithfulness.

This clarity of definition set off a bit of reminiscing about the church's beginnings. Betty began. 'I remember when we started out with Dan. First there were white people. Then some black people came, and that was fine . . .'. Emmanuel interrupted her. 'Fine??!!' he exclaimed, incredulously. Everyone laughed. 'And a lot of white people left,' someone else chimed in. Murmurs of agreement were heard all around. This set Tarley off. 'We always *said* that we were inclusive,' he exclaimed with passion, 'but I want to know what that *means*!! Some things have been happening here . . .', he went on, not finishing his sentence. It was as if a damn burst. Pent-up feelings came tumbling out from everyone, but mostly from the people of color. The discussion turned to the departure of Kathy's family.

Betty had strong feelings about the departures. Taking issue with what they did, she said, 'I am supposed to accept other people for who they are, sexual orientation or whatever. We are all the same and I'm not supposed to judge. If a homosexual person comes, I accept them. Only later, in the community, I may show Scripture to them or they might come to know that something isn't God's will for their life; but we all have sins and it's not true that one is greater than the other.' Her husband, Ronnie, agreed and interjected passionately, 'People—just as they are off the street are supposed to be included. The bottom line is that Jesus never turned anyone away.' As people nodded, he added, 'Only God can judge.'

From these initial ecclesiological insights the conversation deepened further as people returned to the meaning of 'inclusive'. What, asked Gerald, does inclusive mean? 'What is the common denominator to "being included"? Is it being human?' Beatrice volunteered that it was about just being willing to work on your spiritual life. Since we are all sinners, she continued, and we all need further work on our relationship with God, willingness to work on yourself is the common denominator. It's 'all you have to have to be here'.

Ever the pragmatist, Tarley threw out some hypotheticals. 'What about the Liberian minister who has two wives? What if he comes here? How will people react? Will they be included?' he asked. Reminding us that polygamy is an accepted custom in Liberia, he pressed the group to continue to think through this complicated word, 'inclusive'. Betty responded that the test for a behavior is 'whether it is of God'. Eddie, a gay man who was not 'out' at the church, pointed to further complexities. It is difficult to interpret what it means to be 'of God', he insisted. Scripture, the usual authority for this, he went on, is 'interpreted differently by different people'. When he enjoined them to struggle together to understand and respect our different biblical interpretations, the group agreed. Beatrice commented that simply citing Scripture was never adequate; in fact, she was beginning to be especially suspicious of people who did it.

From recognizing inevitable differences in a Christian community, the discussion turned to the kind of accountability that should accompany disagreements. Gerald invoked Matthew 17, which calls for Christians to speak honestly with a brother who sins. Expressing feelings of anger at the families who left without taking their grievances to the rest of the community, Emmanuel spoke passionately about Christians' accountability. They must commit to honesty in their corporateness, he insisted, and not be satisfied with superficial claims to community. Betty's comments spoke eloquently of such ecclesial communion: 'Regardless of who comes, I'm supposed to see that person with hope. There is hope that God will change them. The church is the place we all start. You come in just as you are, but you may not leave the same.'

The retreat went on to other matters, but proved an important conversation that clarified for its participants a complex notion of inclusiveness as a central commitment. Their mission, as they said in the statement, was to be 'faithful and inclusive'. Faithful inclusivity, at least for this group of active members, included the following crucial elements: faithful inclusivity is a form of life patterned after Jesus; it is enabled by God; it involves loving acceptance of people for who they are; anyone off the street should feel welcome—regardless of their race, culture, or sexuality; it requires continual reassessment; it is not being without standards; it is not continuing to be who you are; it should unsettle your comfort zone; it involves transformation of sin, but no sin in particular; and it will attract people.

With this conversation comes not only a clarification of their current vision of mission, but an articulation of that vision in light of their past—the original notion of welcome to 'those not like us'. The concern for the recent departures prompted at least the beginning of a look at elements of faithful inclusivity that had been missing. From acknowledgement of the racism of the past to regret about the failure to have honest conversations over the issue of homosexuality, the conversation provided a critical sense of ways the vision had been inadequately fulfilled. And some 'unsaid' surfaced. Several people commented that a lesbian couple had been a part of the church for several years and, although it was widely known, their sexuality had never been publically resisted or even acknowledged. (Notably, Eddie did not feel safe enough to 'come out'.) Others spoke of their suspicion that the real reason people had left the church was not homosexuality, but the race of the new minister.

These shared confidences were not simply indulgence in gossip. As members recognized the gap between talk about welcome and its profound and difficult conditions, the retreat allowed a kind of honest accounting that began to perform what it claimed to want. For the gathering did not serve simply to lament the past. The retreat displayed a process of accountability that suggested an improvisatory capacity already developed and relevant for the future. The practices of being together over the years had habituated some of these Good Samaritans into new ways of being faithful, new ways that not only included intellectual flexibility, but affective and visceral openness to those who are 'Other' as well.

Several of those at the retreat remember that first extension of welcome by (some) white members to people designated as 'black'. A few, such as Liana and Pam, who have children with disabilities are particularly grateful for the extension of that capacity to welcome the outsiders the church calls people with 'special needs'. Others, such as Richard, Olive, Gerald, and Mary, are part of the group that itself began developing the skills—incorporative practices—to communicate with this new set of congregants. With the recognition of 'homosexuals' as another problematically excluded group, signs of newly developing modes of action or improvisation begin to appear.

The capacities to imaginatively develop practices of welcome for those who are racially and ably 'Other' from the dominant population of whites and normates involved changed bodily habituations as well as justifying appeals to the gospel. These capacities were slow to develop when they did at all. White bodily proprieties of ownership are not easily dislodged. The new 'improvisation' of this discussion is, admittedly, predominantly discursive. It awaits an opportunity for the testing and altering of heteronormatively shaped bodily proprieties that signal aversion to those with alternative sexualities.

Considering the formative traditions of many members, however, even cognitive flexibility for this new situation is no small thing. African Americans Pam and Betty, Ugandan Liana, and white North Americans Olive and Richard all acknowledged that they were brought up to consider homosexuality a grave sin. They were not unusual. Like those who left the church, many Good Samaritans were most likely taught such views. Given this traditioning, the theological logic articulated by several and assented to by the rest is impressive.

This improvisatory logic is clearly articulated at the retreat. It pulls from various communal images and is founded on the development of capacities through incorporative practices. The drawing from the images, however, is selective. The commitment to welcome is clear throughout the group's deliberations. There is a mix of people at the retreat: some, like the students, more committed to the justice-oriented images of welcome, and some—Betty and Olive and others—were great fans of Dan and his messages of acceptance. All shared appreciation that the community was to be inclusive and (even if they did not use this language) that it should 'not see color'.

With the logic of conviction, however, we see a particular trajectory emerge. The group agrees upon a conviction logic where Christians are to be made uncomfortable so that they can take on their prejudices against the 'Other'. While the logic of self-scrutiny and self-interrogation *may* develop into such a logic, it does not automatically do so. For some in the church, the discomfort had not proved a transition for change, but rather the 'panic of normative whiteness' that led to denial and flight.[13] In this discussion, however, 'being convicted' is fundamentally about change in relation to the 'Other'. It not only requires attention to individuals' biases toward the 'Other', but is a group interrogation of the ways the *community* has failed to properly and publicly recognize its prejudices toward various 'Others', from people defined as 'black', to 'homosexuals', to hypothetical outsiders such as polygamists. As a conviction discourse that requires change of social prejudices, this is also a discourse of significant flexibility. The challenge to her comfort level, as Betty would say, must happen repeatedly, for what is at stake is the encounter with *new* 'Others'. *This practice of welcome is personal work that is never complete.*

The logic of flexibility is also operative in this discussion. And while the conversation is not focused explicitly on God-dependence, its entire framing is what it means to be faithful to God, not simply about being inclusive. What the group called being '*faithfully* inclusive', has Jesus as a model, as Ronnie pointed out. But what that Christology authorized is an eminently flexible right relation to God. Nothing is named as a permanent condition of God's presence or approval. No positions, beliefs, or specific behaviors are put forward as qualifications

---

[13] Thanks to Maurice Wallace for this phrase.

for membership in the community. By implication, no positions, beliefs, or behaviors are claimed as qualifications for this faithful relationship to God. One simply has *to know how to read a new situation*, its conditions of welcome, and be open to change. Performing gospel here takes the shape of *situational competence for welcome.*

Take Betty. Raised in a conservative black Baptist tradition that taught her that homosexuality is a sin, she has acquired dispositions (likely related to being an outsider herself) that enable an extension of the logic of welcome to a new situation. Even though Betty intends to bring those she welcomes to another understanding, she and others agree that the only conditions on being included, the only criterion for being 'human', is being willing to change. The shape of Christian community is thus one of *accountability*, but hers is a fundamental claim about *flexibility* and need for change in the community as well.[14] The former invokes the need for change and transformation; it is not mere tolerance of diversity, a pluralism making no claims upon participants. The latter recognizes that equally constitutive of Christian community is openness to new forms of relationships, to new definitions of the neighbor.

The combination of discourses in this response to the crisis, then, suggests divergent functioning of the shared images that make it one place. Most apparent in the group's self-interpretation is that the discourse of conviction requires a new relation to the neighbor, and, importantly, that prejudices about that neighbor need to be investigated for this to properly occur. That new and welcoming relation to the neighbor is understood to be a sign of proper God-dependence. As a *newly defined* neighbor, this notion of faithfulness requires flexibility. It may require rejecting some of your tradition, as it did for Betty and a number of others. Although not articulated theoretically by the community, we might say that this flexibility is an openness to changing definitions of the religious tradition and its authorities. What appears to be the constant 'norm' (or sign of God's presence) is not authorization by Scripture, but a practice of welcoming all to a communal effort to continue to be accountable and to continue to be transformed.

---

[14] There were other Bible study discussions involving Beatrice, Pam, and Liana with similar discussions about the need to welcome homosexuals.

A very different set of trajectories from the shared images is suggested by the departing families and the logics they employed. One combined a discourse of conviction that remained stalled with self-scrutiny and interrogation with an appeal to God-dependence that simply authorized the participant's position. Such a logic is at least suggested by Wanda's departure, which was justified to Gerald in terms of the authority of Scripture.[15] The appeal by Kathy and Miguel and their family to the authority of Scripture used a similar logic, although with less reliance (at least in public conversation) upon discourse of self-scrutiny. The citation of biblical passages condemning homosexuality functioned as a conversation-stopper, performing the logic of 'authoritative religious judgment'. Typically used in conflict, this logic did not invite dialogue, mutual disclosure, or accountability. By citing a reading of Scripture that could not be contested, this trajectory of faith could be seen as an exercise in invoking God simply to authorize its position. For if Scripture is viewed as a self-sufficient warrant for a claim, that is, all the evidence needed, it is because the Bible's content is conceived as identical with what God wants, even a form of God's presence.[16]

These examples of the use of Good Samaritans' primary images show how different accounts of welcome and divergent impulses became centrifugal forces. Although all members of the church affirmed the goodness of its diversity—racial, ethnic, and ability-related—the meanings of welcome took different 'voyages' through the community. 'God loves all people', 'we're all the same', 'we don't see color here, just Christians', and so on ultimately routed differently via the refracting media of the place. For some the self-scrutiny discourse did not link up to the impulse to attend to difference and prejudice. Nor did the God-dependence discourse link up with the need for flexibility in response to newly discovered prejudices and barriers to community or to the unpredictability of life. As a result, until they were tested, the convergences

[15] This does not mean that Wanda never understood Scripture in relation to a pre-text of the shape of Christian life, as illustrated in the first biblical practices—a life that included risk, danger, and approbation of a multiracial community. It is the logic that she employed around her family's decision to leave that I invoke here.

[16] This is true insofar as what David Kelsey has called the 'ideational mode of presence' (or identification of God's presence with particular content) dominates a faith world. See David Kelsey, *Proving Doctrine: The Uses of Scripture in Modern Theology* (Harrisburg, PA: Trinity Press International, 1999), 14–31, 161–2.

around the self-imaging of Good Samaritan as a place where all are welcome had concealed the potential for very different, conflicting accounts.

What emerged as potentially different places takes particularly clear shape with regard to degrees of comfort with diversity. The circulation of meaning via refracting media suggests that differently habituated bodies contributed to the resonances of these images and to their different outcomes. The belief by many that the departures were connected to the race of the new minister hints at racialized resonances that were always operative in the place, resonances to which persons of color were more attuned. Although these never surfaced in confessions, racialized resonances are surely worth considering in terms of larger social structures, where supports for obliviousness and its injustices reside. Lest we suggest that the place was only defined by the faith discourses, we need to analyze its practices in relation to the relevant discourses and forces of the larger racial formation. For to recognize that any place is made of many overlapping social habituations is to realize as theorist Michael Curry puts it, that 'we are always in more than one place at once'.[17] Closer look at these other 'places' Good Samaritans were when 'in church' and the power relations that construct them will complete the chapter's look at the complex unity of the place.

BEING IN MANY PLACES AT ONCE: THE POLITICS OF PLACE

A host of places converge in Good Samaritan. It is a place of globalized capitalism with its deindustrialized regions, gentrified urban neighborhoods, and the community's immediate location as an outer urban mixed-zone. It is a place of gendered capitalism, which discounts the domestic work of many church members. It is a place of global displacement, as well.[18] The marking of African members as

[17] Reference to Andrew Pickering, author of the 'mangle of practice', in Michael R. Curry, ' "Hereness" and the Normativity of Place', in James D. Proctor and David M. Smith (eds.), *Geography and Ethics: Journeys in a Moral Terrain* (New York: Routledge, 1999), 96.

[18] Barbara Ehrenreich and Arlie Russell Hoschschild (eds.), *Global Woman: Nannies, Maids, and Sex Workers in the New Economy* (New York: Henry Holt, 2002).

both black and foreign had more force in the US than their advanced degrees and work credentials. To be at Good Samaritan is to be in the racialized nation of the US. It is also to be in the national place of segregation by abilities.

The results of being constructed by these many places are not just the differences of multicultural pluralism, the 'kind of difference that doesn't make a difference', as Stuart Hall puts it.[19] These are cultural representations and social structures that locate subjects differently in relationship to power and well-being. As glimpsed in our look at the community, the globalized, gendered, racialized, and 'normal-bodied' US and its forces do not go away with the friendly intersubjectivities of the Sunday service.

So how to think about these larger social places in relation to Good Samaritan's very local shared vision and sometimes-divergent logics? In lieu of treating every place that is relevant, my primary focus will be the emergent *formation of racial democracy*, which will model thinking about the differently abled as well.[20] Social scientists Michael Omi and Howard Winant define a racial formation as 'the sociohistorical process by which racial categories are created, inhabited, transformed, and destroyed'.[21] A racial or other social formation aids in conceptualizing how a marked difference shapes our lives in a particular historical period. Three things bear remarking.

First, the breadth of a social formation. A social formation is about more than legal structures. Take what I'll call an 'able-ness formation'. Attempts, such as the Americans With Disabilities Act (1990) (ADA), to outlaw discrimination against persons with disabilities are crucial to their well-being, as was civil rights legislation against racial discrimination. However, a racial or able-ness formation is not just politics;

[19] Stuart Hall, 'What Is This "Black" in Black Popular Culture?', in Michele Wallace and Gina Dent (eds.), *Black Popular Culture* (Seattle: Bay, 1992), 23.

[20] The civil rights movement provided landmark legislation for changing power structures for persons with disabilities. The Brown v. Board of Education decision provided grounds for getting children with disabilities access to public schools (Mills v. Board of Education 1972). This movement to reject whiteness as a qualification of full citizenship finds its legal parallel in the intent (if not the result) of the ADA to prohibit discrimination on the basis of disability. Thus an able-ness formation is also one of an emergent ability democracy.

[21] Michael Omi and Howard Winant, *Racial Formation in the United States: From the 1960s to the 1990s*, 2nd edn. (New York: Routledge, 1994), 55.

it is about all ' "levels" of lived experience simultaneously'.[22] Cultural representations—particularly of bodies—along with legislative and economic realities are fundamental for defining well-being. From New Testament views marking subjects with disabilities as sinners, ancient images of monstrosities and idiots to medicalized definitions (modernity), influential representations of persons with disabilities powerfully affect lives. Even now such persons continue to be represented as objects—from objects of violence and fear to objects of pity.[23] Anti-discrimination laws are thus only part of the needed transformation; new cultural representations are equally vital.

Second, the impact of formations occurs at the level of the everyday.[24] As seen in the racialized and normate bodily practices accompanying the explicit communications of church members, regular everyday practices are the primary point of entry for the oppressive force of these power-laden places. It is the routine and repetitive practices through which people come to understand what is expected and 'appropriate' in a particular context that constitute the opportunity not only to reproduce racist and able-ist social realities, but to contest them as well.[25] A formation becomes reality in what Philomena Essed calls 'everyday racism' or 'everyday able-ism'.[26]

The issue, then, is not whether Good Samaritans *meant* to be racist or able-ist or not. Even in a community formed around inclusiveness, subjects reproduce supports for social inequalities simply by unconsciously following inherited scripts, scripts that activate dominant group power by *repetition and confirmation* of its assumptions. Resisting the scripts likewise activates that group power, but reroutes and confounds it. So the important question is how, amidst this

[22] Michael Omi and Howard Winant, *Racial Formation in the United States: From the 1960s to the 1990s*, 2nd edn. (New York: Routledge, 1994), 1–23, 97–112, 96.

[23] James C. Wilson and Cynthia Lewiecki-Wilson, 'Disability, Rhetoric, and the Body', in James C. Wilson and Cynthia Lewiecki-Wilson (eds.), *Embodied Rhetorics: Disability in Language and Culture* (Carbondale, IL: Southern Illinois University Press, 2001), 1–26.

[24] See Omi and Winant, *Racial Formation*, 59–61. Philomena Essed, *Understanding Everyday Racism: An Interdisciplinary Theory* (Newbury Park, CA: Sage, 1991), 185–282.

[25] 'Structures and ideologies do not exist', argues Essed, 'outside the everyday practices through which they are created and confirmed.' Essed, *Everyday Racism*, 44.

[26] Everyday racism is defined as 'the situational activation of racial or ethnic dimensions in particular relations in a way that reinforces racial or ethnic inequality and contributes to new forms of racial and ethnic inequality'. Ibid. 51.

inevitable reproduction, Good Samaritan's inclusiveness practices create new possibilities.

To identify these possibilities, we turn to the third feature of the formation, what links everyday practices and these larger structures. For racism, that link is *racial projects*, which organize the meanings and effects of difference in particular ways.[27] Conservative 'nationalist projects' are about segregating races, for example, as are white supremacist biologistic racist accounts of difference.[28] Racial projects relevant to Good Samaritan are those that claim all persons are equal, those consonant with the US social formation of democracy. Where they differ among themselves is in the ways they define and treat difference.

The racial project of the early civil rights movement centered around the view that race was like ethnicity, a matter of shared culture and origins. Discrimination consisted of prejudice and discriminatory practices and would be solved by the end of institutional and legal discrimination. Such a project appealed to language of commonality, the goal of a color-blind society, and calls to treat everyone the same. Equal opportunity legislation was to be the solution, and the expected result would not only be integration, but assimilation into the melting pot that America had become—a 'race-free society'. A challenge to the biological definition of race, this ethnicity version of difference was an improvement over certain authorizations of racism. But the *legacy* of 'color-blindness' is another story.

Symbols take on new meaning in new contexts. Take the recent appropriation of color-blindness by the racial project of the new right and neoconservatives, argue Omi and Winant. The neoconservative project advocates race-free thinking in a way that ignores the continuing damage—the residuals—of historic racism. Treating race as a form of ethnicity makes race as insignificant as being Irish.[29] 'Not seeing color' trades on the value of 'equality' as treating everyone the same; however, it constitutes a virtual obliviousness to continuing forms of

---

[27] As an 'interpretation, representation, or explanation of racial dynamics', a racial project links and justifies a historically situated 'effort to reorganize and redistribute resources along particular racial lines'. Omi and Winant, *Racial Formation*, 55–6.

[28] Ibid. 58–9.

[29] Noel Ignatiev, *How the Irish Became White* (New York: Routledge, 1995).

oppression.[30] This racial project resists affirmative action along with so-called 'set-asides'; it makes cases for 'reverse discrimination'. Finally, it defines racism as a matter of *individual* rather than group concern; racism is understood as individual acts of malice, not of a racially organized social order.[31] The *effect* of color-blindness in this project, then, is quite at odds with its use in the civil rights movement.

In contrast with this neoliberal project, a third racial project combines claims for equality with recognition of the ongoing significance of racism as a social formation, significantly moving beyond the civil rights era attachment to color-blindness. This project understands that racism's effects still permeate the full range of social experience, and cannot be reduced to intentional acts *or* sheer bigotry. 'Race matters', as Cornel West would say; it is *not* analogous to being Irish. Assigning race (or racelessness) is a way of hierarchally defining and organizing bodies that is founded on an invisible privileging of those designated 'white'. Not the same as rac-*ism*, attention to race is essential for change. To ignore race in the guise of claiming public commitment to a race-free society is to engage in obliviousness that supports the dominance of whiteness. These 'liberal' racial projects and 'radical democratic' projects require egalitarian policies and politics, but, in contrast with the neoliberal project, only as combined with attention to racial difference.[32]

EVERYDAY PRACTICES: REPRODUCING OR CONTESTING OBLIVIOUSNESS

Of these different racial projects, the most obvious one supported by Good Samaritan's practices is that of civil rights equality with its dream of a world where, as Martin Luther King Jr would say, it's not the color of your skin, but the content of your character that

---

[30] Reliance upon 'formal-race', a use of race that disregards 'ability, disadvantage, or moral culpability', is a feature of the legal philosophy of 'Color-Blind Constitutionalism'. Neil Gotanda, 'A Critique of "Our Constitution is Color-Blind" ', in Kimberle Crenshaw, Neil Gotanda, Gary Pelle, and Kendall Thomas (eds.), *Critical Race Theory: The Key Writings that Formed the Movement* (New York: New Press, 1995), 257–75.

[31] Omi and Winant, *Racial Formation,* 121–36.

[32] Ibid. 58–9.

matters.[33] The dominant discourse of Christian welcome illustrates this. Oft-repeated claims about the community invoked a place where 'it doesn't matter what your skin color is', as Kathy put it, where 'God loves us all, black white, special needs...', as Mary said. Excepting the God-language, many of the distinguishing character- istics of the community's images for color-blindness clearly line up with those of the national formation of racial democracy. But welcome and the claim not to see color can articulate to very different national racial projects. What matters then is whether these practices invoke color-blindness to *avoid dealing* with resid- uals of historic racism or to effect something else. As with contem- porary national racial projects, the answer to that has to do with whether and how difference is attended to at Good Samaritan.

An early example in the church's life links to the conservative projects. When increasing numbers of black bodies disrupted some members' 'everyday' expectations of white propriety—expressed in the claim that the church was getting 'too black'—these self-proclaimed inclusive Christians exposed the unsaid culture of white dominance. 'God loves all his children, but let's not overdo it,' they seemed to say. This form of aversiveness to a perceived destabilizing of white domin- ance and obliviousness to the harms of racism is consonant with the most superficial racial equality projects in the US, such as the neoliberal or those that do not attend at all to the need for change. Difference, then, is allowed if it is minimal and discrete.

At first glance, all the practices of welcome that invoke color-blind- ness would seem to risk denial of the significance of race, and, by implication, the significance of disability as well. Insofar as they suggest that simply being Christians together or that God loves us all is enough to negate the impact of racism or able-ism, they resonate with the view that these problems have simply disappeared with legislation. We might, then, identify all the language of inclusion as signifying practices that reproduce patterns of 'not seeing' in the form of white (or normate) obliviousness. However, the combination of different senses of welcome

---

[33] 'I have a dream my four little children will one day live in a nation where they will not be judged by the color of their skin but by the content of their character. I have a dream today!' Martin Luther King, Jr., 'I Have a Dream', in *A Testament of Hope: The Essential Writings of Martin Luther King, Jr.*, ed. James Melvin Washington (San Francisco: Harper and Row, 1986), 219.

found in the logics of conviction and God-dependence suggests that Good Samaritan has negotiated at least some practices that cannot be reduced simply to such problematic reproductions. While incomplete, the logics of welcome have very different trajectories that link them to different social projects.

A first most superficial form of welcome connects to a project of openness to difference characteristic of tokenism. It consists of a kind of inclusionary vision and 'nonprejudice' that obtains for some whites, that is related to being in the majority and thus able to control the few who are 'Other'. While it appeared most explicitly in the early departures, hints of this posture returned with the conflict over homosexuality. While there was no avowed claim to leave because the new minister was black, the perception by African Americans that his race mattered in these departures is a significant indicator of the power of racialized social scripts.[34] The logic of welcome that dominated for the group that left focused around the nonlegalist accepting atmosphere of the church and links up with the most superficial version of color-blindness. 'Conviction' in this logic meant self-scrutiny; it was *not* tied to scrutiny of one's prejudgments of the 'Other'. 'God-dependence' was more connected to divine authorization of a position than to the flexibility to see social reality differently, including one's own social location.

In important respects the color-blindness that resonates with this logic of faith is that of racial projects that deny the significance of race. They deny the significance of race as *something that needs to be dealt with*, that is; thus they would tend to support a ' "color-blind" racial politics and "hands off" policy orientation'.[35] 'To not see color, just Christians' on this logic suggests an account of *Christian identity as a project of denial/projection by the advantaged*—denial of the inherited residuals of racism and projection of premature reconciliation by those most fearful of losing power.

A different logic emerged, however, that signals resistance to the dominant codes of everyday racism. Even as they sometimes spoke about not seeing color, these members' take on welcome took it in a

---

[34] All that I can describe is other peoples' perception of what they were doing and why. Kathy and Miguel commented after Gerald came that there were more black people in the church now than whites.

[35] This is akin to a neoliberal position. Omi and Winant, *Racial Formation*, 58.

very different direction. What was compelling about welcome to them was *who* was welcomed—the marginalized. This view played out in a logic of conviction that required dealing with one's 'uncomfortableness' and one's prejudices about the 'Other'. From the logic itself, then, color-blindness simply could not mean ignoring difference. Difference had to be dealt with, one way or another.

Even within this logic, of course, 'color-blindness' signifies differently according to how a subject is racialized. Admittedly its use by white Good Samaritans tended to underestimate the significance of race, especially at first. Many of the white members did not see racism as a system, but thought of it only as acts of meanness. African Americans, on the other hand, saw it as a system as well as quite personal. It was their interaction with each other in the church, Dan said, that helped the white people come to understand something of 'the realities of racism through African Americans' eyes'. Having much more to learn, so to speak, did not mean that these Good Samaritan whites did not begin the journey. Earlier examples of confession by Rita and Dora's public apology were small steps; others advanced further.

The dramatic accounts of conviction as change came from Betty. Positioned as a member of a group that had to internalize the fact that the dominant groups 'fear and loathe them', she dealt with her 'prejudices' in a unique and radical way—by getting some freedom from this self-hatred and being open to a profoundly altered sense of whiteness.[36] Pointing out that not seeing color means different things to different people, Pam also negotiated welcome complexly. Racism is alive and well, she insisted, so 'I do see color'. But '[m]ore than that, I see Jesus in you. And then I don't see color'. Not seeing color as an African American Christian, said someone, means 'rejecting white people's logic'. However, for these Good Samaritans it did not mean rejecting white people. To 'not see color, only Christians' on these terms suggests that *Christian identity is a commitment to change of self and the other.*

The ability to *confront* these biases and to learn something new about the stranger, Betty says, is a 'litmus for those who stay at Good Samaritan'. Altogether different from the projects that simply underwrite tokenism and wish to be race-free, this logic is congruent with

---

[36] This is a feature of aversive racism. Iris Marion Young, *Justice and the Politics of Difference* (Princeton: Princeton University Press, 1990), 148.

and supportive of larger racial projects that combine both egalitarian policies and politics with focus on more than formal race. It resonates with and advances what is key to these current best projects. As Omi and Winant put it, 'To oppose racism one must *notice race*.'[37] This logic requires noticing the complexities within the category of those designated as having race, not only as the biases Africans and African Americans had toward one another, but the (relative) white privileging of African and Caribbean persons of color over African Americans as well.

However, the logic exceeds even these combinations. Not only does it require more than tolerance and attention to race, the concerns of liberal projects, this Good Samaritan logic is inherently improvisational. As Betty followed the logic of conviction and God-dependence that compelled her own transformation, she not only worked on racism, she moved, as did the communal thinking, to the new outsider and expected that there would always be another. The God-dependence of the logic required just such an ongoing flexibility, a position quite different from simple interest-group politics.

Now what about projects for 'everyday able-ism'? In many ways less advanced than the democratic racial formation, something akin to a democratic and transformative formation to challenge the dominant definition of the 'normal' body with its 'Othering' implications for Daphne, Billy, or Esther in society is a hope for the future. In the current 'normate formation', difference is clearly marked. Many forms of segregation and exclusion still apply, both as physical barriers and as cultural objectifications of subjects, including Christian forms of healing ministry.[38] As a challenge to that formation, the church's 'everyday practices' for welcoming group home members were only a start. As unusual as its regular inclusion of 'special needs' participants is in US churches, Good Samaritan's practices stopped short of mainstreaming. Not only were the services best designed for these members held separately with only a few loyal 'normal'

---

[37] Omi and Winant, *Racial Formations*, 158.

[38] For a critique and alternative approaches to the central healing images in Scripture, see Kathy Black, *A Healing Homiletic: Preaching and Disability* (Nashville: Abingdon, 1996). Sharon Betcher, 'Monstrosities, Miracles and Mission: Religion and the Politics of Disablement', in Catherine Keller, Michael Nausner, and Mayra Rivera (eds.), *Postcolonial Theologies: Divinity and the Empire* (St Louis: Chalice, 2004), 79–99.

members involved, but the regular Sunday services did not adequately solicit their different modes of communication. Everyday practices of aversion were being replaced, but never completely or with the changed practices that came of deep interpersonal knowledge.

The disappointing effect of the ADA on the employment rate of the disabled is paradigmatic here.[39] Creating legal barriers to their exclusion does not alter the dominant sensibility about the worth and dignity of persons with disabilities. It does not erase the everyday scripts and expectations that lead people to react with aversion or pity. To fully address a 'normate formation' would require attention to the way identities are produced by cultural representations—particularly of bodies—and the supporting power structures that allocate status and resources. It would mean seriously questioning definitions of 'normal' such that, like the important recognition that race is a social construction not a biological essence, definitions of what is 'normal' are also seen as social constructions that contribute to the dis-abling of populations. It would question the 'medicalization of disability', where society relegates people 'to the social status of "invalidism"', creating what Swinton calls the subject position of the 'in-valid'.[40]

While the relevant history of changing formations is only now being written, it is fair to say that Good Samaritan is shaped by a 'body project' dominated by what Sharon Betcher calls the 'ideology of normalcy'.[41] Good Samaritan welcomed people from group homes, but unlike the interracial relations in the church that occur within and without church activities, most interactions with group home members occurred only in worship services. Indeed, the very distinct 'Otherness' of the group chosen to represent persons with disabilities—persons lacking language abilities, some lacking bodily control, and most housed in segregated group homes—highlights the *difference* between the 'normate' and the 'non-normal'. The wide range of disabilities that characterize all human beings at some

[39] In an interview on National Public Radio, Joseph P. Shapiro said that only 30% of the disabled are employed and that the ADA has seen no change in their employment rate. Tuesday, 26 July 2005. See Joseph P. Shapiro, *No Pity: People with Disabilities Forge a New Civil Rights Movement* (New York: Times Books, 1994).

[40] John Swinton, 'Building a Church for Strangers', *Journal of Religion, Disability and Health*, 4/4 (2001), 41.

[41] Betcher, 'Monstrosities, Miracles and Mission', 95.

time in their lives is not so visible, lessening the possibility that disability as a shared *continuum* might disrupt disability as a form of *Othering*. At this point Good Samaritan's practices compare to projects of inclusion that fail to deal with the serious imbalance of power. To 'not see difference, just Christians' in this case, again risks defining Christian identity as an amiable tolerance.[42]

Granting the limitations, however, the habituations of members into incorporative practices of communication with persons with disabilities are important beginnings for this shift of cultural formation. While oppressive formations affect us through everyday practices, it is in the *alteration* of everyday practices that resistance is initiated. Such beginnings are seen particularly in the parents who develop respectful alternatives not only to the rituals of degradation, but to the notion that behavior is simply disruption rather than communication, so that, as John Swinton says, 'developmental disabilities ... are not problems to be solved, but rather authentic ways of being human'.[43] There the possibility of friendship emerges rather than paternalism with its continued reproduction of the 'in-valid'.[44]

And it is friendship that a more advanced project might develop were it to follow out the logic of communal accountability and require something on the order of the L'Arche community. There to live in community with handicapped people assumes that '"[t]o live with" is different from "to do for". It doesn't simply mean eating at the same table and sleeping under the same roof. It means that we create relationships of gratuity, truth and interdependence; that we listen to the handicapped people; that we recognize and marvel at their gifts.'[45] In this context, there is something right about 'normalization' when it

---

[42] Because this is an inclusionary practice that brings persons into face-to-face communion, however superficially, this has elements of the tolerance Ghassan Hage calls 'strategies of condescension', but is not as oblivious. Ghassan Hage, 'Locating Multiculturalism's Other: A Critique of Practical Tolerance', *New Formations*, 24 (1994), 30.

[43] Swinton, 'Building a Church for Strangers', 25.

[44] A notion of friendship with persons with intellectual disabilities characterizes the L'Arche community. See Jean Vanier, *The Heart of L'Arche: A Spirituality for Every Day* (New York: Crossroad, 1995), 30–3. Also see Stanley Hauerwas, 'Timeful Friends: Living with the Handicapped', in John Swinton (ed.), *Critical Reflections on Stanley Hauerwas' Theology of Disability: Disabling Society, Enabling Theology* (Binghamton, NY: Haworth Pastoral, 2004), 11–26.

[45] Jean Vanier, *Community and Growth* (London: Darton, Longman, and Todd, 1979), 106, quoted in Swinton (ed.), *Critical Reflections*, 12.

means treating persons with disability such that they 'should be respected, loved, or gotten angry at in the same way as any other person'.[46]

Good Samaritan became a place, or places, to appear. These places were not complete; they were not experienced equally by all. But an acknowledgement and honoring of persons previously perceived as 'Others' happened in the community. African Americans appeared in humanizing ways for white people. Whites appeared more humanly for Africans and African Americans. And African Americans and Africans came to understand each other in new ways. Some members of the church began to 'hear from' and acknowledge persons with disabilities in new ways.

As for its relation to larger places, it must be said that Good Samaritan was not a self-consciously politicized place. Its members were not typically involved in political movements or activism; nor were they likely to take on the many tasks required to alter the inadequacies of the contemporary democratic racial formation and the normate formation. However, insofar as change requires altered everyday practices, as I have argued, Good Samaritan was clearly a place of emergent transformation. To have a 'place to appear' where one is acknowledged and honored for one's humanity requires face-to-face relationship. Because bodily habituations and their inherited proprieties with accompanying fears and aversions are involved, convictions and verbal commitments will not suffice. These relationships must disturb and challenge inherited scripts and expectations around race and dis-ability if they are to disrupt the obliviousness and many other harms that attach to 'not seeing'.

In this sense, Good Samaritan was at least two places that overlapped for a number of years. One was more characterized by the joy of acceptance and a nonjudgmental Christianity. The other resonated in many ways with that place of forgiveness and a sense of welcoming family. That overlapping place highlighted the *who* of welcome—'outsiders'—and

---

[46] Professor of Special Education Jeff McNair resists arguments that they have to 'somehow justify their existence through their presence' or because we will learn something from them. Jeff McNair, 'Response: The Limits of Our Practices', in Swinton (ed.), *Critical Reflections*, 68–9.

did so in a way that complemented the Christianity of acceptance and forgiveness. This 'outsider Christianity' only actually became a different 'place' when its commitment to diversity combined with openness to change came in conflict with views about authority and dis-ease with too much difference.

When interpreted in light of the larger places Good Samaritan inhabited, its practices look both conformist *and* resistant. In one sense, it was a 'color-blind' place that wanted difference without attention to power issues and residual racism and able-ism. As such Good Samaritans reiterated the larger national projects that trade on 'equality' and nondiscrimination. 'We are all the same' as a refusal to attend to race has its religious analogue when Christian identity provides the opportunity for denial of complicity and projection of premature reconciliation. As a 'color-blind' place that welcomed the 'Other' in a way that demanded self-criticism and continued openness to a new challenge, however, Good Samaritans' practices refused that first script. To develop Betty's comments a bit, this place required a paradox: faithful Christians must 'see color' in its form in the sense of a continuing racism and able-ism, and they must 'not see color' as a commitment to change with the 'Other'. With a litmus test requiring only the willingness to work on yourself, this logic imagined resistance that far exceeds current liberal democratic projects.

8

A Theological Reading of Place

> The divine, previously considered coextensive with infinite
> space and its most privileged inhabitant, is now *spaced-out
> into places*, the very places we inhabit in daily life.
>
> Casey, *Fate of Place*

Two main topics have driven this exercise in practical theology. First
and foremost, the concern has been to explore the practices of a
particular Christian community with regard to how they helped
create a place for all to appear. Framing those practices with postmodern place theory brought into view the way bodies and desire,
fear and pleasure complicate the dynamics of welcome. But regardless of how respectful of the bodied and affective, the practical
theological task is not complete with thick description alone, however expanded. The second topic of concern is the implications of
this display for theological reflection itself. What can be said about
the theological character of this reading of place—what has it to do
with honoring the worldliness of an incarnate God? To address this
second topic, I turn briefly to the challenge that honoring worldliness
presents for some traditional ways of thinking about theology.

FAITH-PLACE AS CHALLENGE

This portrait of 'everyday faith' is an example of the subject matter of
practical theology, that is, the life of faith when considered as contemporary situation—'the way various items, powers, and events in the

environment gather to evoke responses from participants'.[1] While it is no surprise that situational faith is complex, *theologically* speaking it does seem to pose a challenge. The 'various items, powers, and events' that constituted the situation of Good Samaritan appear a sort of hodgepodge. They made meaning by way of nonbiblical and nontheological terms and the resonances of multiple refracting media. Practices with no explicit religious discourse were important; nonsymbolic practices dependent upon bodily communications were essential to the participation of a number of Good Samaritans.[2] Bob's associative thinking about heaven in the 'special needs' service was not peculiar to him.[3] Resonating connections were crucial to everyone's understanding of Christian faith.

One response to such a hodgepodge might be the judgment that these Christians are simply confused—badly informed at best, inadvertently heretical at worst. Several contemporary theologies convinced of the centrality of practice are still adamant that doctrine, rightly understood, must ultimately govern.[4] (On such a view Cathy, Tim, and friends would have 'misunderstood' the Eucharist when they preferred 'passing the peace' because of its affective pleasures.[5]) A related judgment might

---

[1] As explained in Ch. 1 this follows Edward Farley's account of practical theology, which fills in the frame of the 'situational' character of lived faith. Edward Farley, 'Interpreting Situations', in *Practicing Gospel: Unconventional Thoughts on the Church's Ministry* (Louisville, KY: Westminster John Knox, 2003), 38, 36.

[2] See Ellin Siegel and Amy Wetherby, 'Enhancing Nonsymbolic Communication', in Martha E. Snell and Fredda Brown (eds.), *Instruction of Students with Severe Disabilities*, 5th edn. (Upper Saddle River, NJ: Prentice-Hall, 2000), 409–51.

[3] In the service Bob spoke in images of heaven and God and angels, saying, 'and laying on your back, the clouds above roll by'.

[4] Theologian of practice Miroslav Volf says, it is Christian beliefs that 'ultimately ground Christian practices'. And while the systematic relation between beliefs may be loose, he continues, 'fit they must'. Your understanding of theological anthropology must fit with your doctrine of the Trinity, must fit with your doctrine of the Lord's Supper, and so on. 'Theology for a Way of Life', in Miroslav Volf and Dorothy C. Bass (eds.), *Practicing Theology: Beliefs and Practices in Christian Life* (Grand Rapids, MI: Eerdmans, 2002), 261. Arguing for ecclesiological ethnography because theological readings must respect situations, Nicholas Healy still authorizes his interpretation with Trinitarian doctrine. Nicholas M. Healy, *Church, World and the Christian Life: Practical-Prophetic Ecclesiology* (Cambridge: Cambridge University Press, 2000), 21, 38, 5.

[5] Miroslav Volf worries about 'misunderstanding' of the Lord's Supper and seems to only have 'normal' people in view. The implied view that orthodoxy is necessary and that the orthodox can somehow 'cover' for those without highly developed cognitive abilities is problematic. See his 'Theology for a Way of Life', 254–5.

be that the church has become 'accommodated to the world'. Its use of 'color-blindness', for example, was an adaptation of popularized legal terminology and made meaning through the larger social formation of democracy. In any case, the challenge of the place would be to get ministers to teach historic doctrine more successfully to their congregations and to be more systematic in their own thinking, maintaining clearer boundaries between church and world.

However, I contend that the theological challenge of Good Samaritan as place is not to compel more control by doctrine, but to *respect the way situations occur* and to do so with particular attention to lived or everyday theologizing. Insofar as they represent the 'practical theology' of these believers—participants' faith responses to an evoked situation—Good Samaritans' practices appear irregular, but for the reasons most everyday theology is irregular. As Tanner says, Christians are always making meaning in the fashion of the bricoleur—'a creativity expressed through the modification and extension of materials already on the ground'.[6] Furthermore, despite being neither systematic, purely ideational, nor clearly bounded, the gathering of these 'items, events, and powers', so to speak, *was productive* of places to appear. Given the character of place, its inevitable combination of incorporative and inscribed communications, its horizonal boundaries, overlappings and containment of conflict, and contradiction along with convergences, this messiness is neither surprising nor necessarily detrimental to faith.

'Academic practical' theological reflection that would intervene, then—as in, normatively assess a situation for purposes transcending that situation—must take seriously its similarity with ordinary faith. Theological reflection arises in an organic way out of Christian life in order to address real life problems.[7] The earlier image says it well, namely, creative thinking originates at the scene of a wound. And such creative thinking is formed by a *combination* of convictions— theological and faith-driven at the same time as cultural, political,

[6] Theological creativity is 'the creativity of a postmodern "bricoleur"—the creativity, that is, of someone who works with an always potentially disordered heap of already existing materials, pulling them apart and putting them back together again, tinkering with their shapes, twisting them this way and that. It is a creativity expressed through the modification and extension of materials already on the ground.' Kathryn Tanner, *Theories of Culture: A New Agenda for Theology*, Guides to Theological Inquiry (Minneapolis: Fortress, 1997), 66.

[7] Ibid. 71.

and autobiographical.[8] Any number of possible stipulations of relevance or dispositions in the communal repertoire allows a developing situation—a 'wound'—to appear significant. This situational matrix for creative response means that there is always an 'outside'— some other perception and its signifiers—involved in creating what it means to be faithful at any particular time. It means that what is 'inside' is complex. Convictions are 'not all held at the same level or operative at the same time'.[9] Sometimes traditions about Jesus matter most, sometimes questions of church membership do, sometimes it is a mix of things.

Theological reflection is not a linear form of reflection that starts with a correct doctrine (or a 'worldly' insight) and then proceeds to analyze a situation; rather it is a situational, ongoing, never-finished dialectical process where past and present ever converge in new ways. We might say that my initiating sense of Good Samaritan had to do with reading wounds of racism and able-ism as antithetical to Christian community. That, combined with a rather inchoate sense that bodies mattered, generated the need for categories like incorporative practices. Such 'pre-doctrinal' discernment has resonances with traditional theological topics such as theological anthropology; but the sense that racialized and normate bodily interactions demand attention for faithful life together is not reducible to any classic doctrine of human being.[10] It is only as categories foreign to a traditional theological repertoire are appropriated that the generative role of *new* situations can occur, sometimes provoking the need to rethink what has counted as tradition.[11]

---

[8] Even an academic project that wishes to create system and coherence is generated both by a disposition of faith and by relevant current definitions of logic, something external to 'pure theology'. Take, for example, Thomas Aquinas's use of Aristotelian categories.

[9] Convictions (or beliefs), as Fish puts it, are 'nested', which is to say they do not all hold the same importance or matter equally at the same time. Stanley Fish, 'Change', *South Atlantic Quarterly*, 86/4 (Fall, 1987), 429.

[10] With the advent of liberation-type theologies, theological anthropology has necessarily begun to factor in race and ability. See e.g. Dwight N. Hopkins, *Being Human: Race, Culture, and Religion* (Minneapolis: Fortress, 2005).

[11] So multiple are the kinds of thinking in the nonlinear process that is theological reflection that David Kelsey invokes a mobile, an aesthetic image. Kelsey, *Proving Doctrine: The Uses of Scripture in Modern Theology* (Harrisburg, PA: Trinity Press International, 1999), 137. For an example of a liberation theological definition, see Thomas H. Groome, *Sharing Faith: A Comprehensive Approach to Religious Education and Pastoral Ministry: The Way of Shared Praxis* (New York: Harper, San Francisco, 1991).

The point here is to recognize the *primacy of the situation* for theological reflection, specifically the primacy of the situation as a *matrix* (not a 'norm') for the generation of judgments.[12] Far from a rejection of tradition, this account simply acknowledges what liberationists and historicists have long maintained, that is, theology's inevitable entanglement with other signifiers. As such, the normative function of theological discourse cannot be a matter of whether faith's discourse is *accommodated* or not to worldly media of communication. *Pace* Barth, it inevitably is.[13] Reflection will always make meaning with contemporary worldly discourse. Because the shape of any situation will always resignify whatever discourse is appropriated—'secular' and religious alike—whatever being faithful might mean, it cannot entail repetition of the past, even as it requires critique of the present as well. Instead, like the understanding of a *habitus*, theologizing requires the competence to read a situation and to improvise a creative response.

The task remaining, then, is to do what everyday practical theologies are not disposed to do with complexity, that is, to reflect upon the explicitly theological character of my evaluative account with attention to theological themes and loci that best aid in understanding this place as well as its implications for others.

PLACE AND THEOLOGICAL ANTHROPOLOGY: MARKED, BODILY MEDIATED FEAR AND DESIRE

In important respects this narration of obliviousness and its redress is already a theological reading of the place, and not only because theological anthropology emerges as an issue. While not fully explicit, mine is a narrative ordered by identification of harms and signs of

---

[12] Edward Farley, *Theologia: The Fragmentation & Unity of Theological Education* (Philadelphia: Fortress, 1983), 165. Reading of a situation does not become the sole, thus absolute, authorization of a judgment, which is how a 'norm' functions. See Kelsey, *Proving Doctrine*, 160.

[13] My position is also at odds with the method of 'critical correlation', which suggests that there is clearer demarcation between the discourse of faith and discourse of the world (or 'human experience') than I do.

their 'redemption' in a Christian community. As such it maps out a terrain of *needed and actualized transformation* with the potential for connections with more formal reflections of faith. The task remaining is to make those connections—to ask how the diminishing of fearful obliviousness and protective vigilance through enhancement of places to appear can conceivably be a narrative about the presence of God. I turn now to the implications of this wound for more explicit categories of theological reflection.

Discourse about God is generated in a variety of ways. It can occur as a response to metaphysical questions about the world or about the structure of human being. Talk of God also takes form as thanksgiving and praise. More formally put, this latter form of discourse can occur as a knowledge or wisdom—traditionally called *theologia*—that accompanies a transformed life.[14] This is to say that convictions about God occur as responses to human dilemmas, to suffering, fear, and injustice, but, importantly, to these situations *as they are redemptively altered*— where amelioration of human dilemmas and suffering takes place. While none of these examples is mutually exclusive, it is this last sense of discourse about God, or at least the potential for such a sense, that has ordered this display of Good Samaritan UMC.

The potential for such a reading, as I said, is found in my reading of the wounds of racism and able-ism, namely, obliviousness, aversion, and hypervigilance, as human harms altered by the emergence of places to appear. Displaying such alterations as redemption is, however, not just a tracking of any sort of change. Since my concern is with a *theological* reading of human being as created to be in relationship to God, that change needs to be read as transformation of human *sinfulness*, the broken relation to God. Not yet read explicitly as sin, my categorical display of obliviousness, aversion, and protective vigilance is suggestive of such an interpretation, as the emergence of 'places to appear' is suggestive of redemption of such sin. The more fully theological reading of Good Samaritan that follows, then, will be a tracing out *not just of what members say they*

[14] Farley points to this central way that God becomes a reality for Christian faith when he says that God 'comes forth as God' (as opposed to coming forth as an idol or false substitution for God) in the situation of redemptively altered existence. Farley, *Divine Empathy: A Theology of God* (Minneapolis: Fortress, 1996), 19, 52–61.

believe about God, but of *transformation in the lived practices of the place.*[15] What that assumes, moreover, is that reference to the divine in this interpretation of Good Samaritan can be indirect, occurring not as a proffered account of God but as *testimony to transformations* that are attributable to God.[16]

With witness to such transformations also comes the question of new insights raised by the situation. And the most immediately relevant theme here is the traditional locus of theological anthropology. Because what mattered in Good Samaritans' life together was racialized the analysis has been directed to the role of hitherto ignored features of human being. With their focus on the affective, from the visceral and aversive to the pleasurable, the various categories of practice used to display vehicles of harm now invite (re)thinking of theological anthropology, a (re)thinking that will begin with *creaturely desire.* To provide an entrée to an explicit account of the God-sustained character of the community's life, I now turn to just such an elaboration of desire and accompanying theo-logic for my reading of Good Samaritans' practices

For theological anthropology, desire has long been a fundamental index of the theonomous or God-dependent character of finite human being. Desire for God defines the purpose of human life. God is that ultimate good that fulfills the deepest human need. A deeply embedded tradition, this view of the human *telos* as passion for the eternal is articulated by theologians from Augustine and Paul Tillich to feminists Marcella Althaus-Reid and Wendy Farley. Importantly, such a teleology of desire suggests a way to think about sin that (logically) mandates a redemptive relationship with God, the eternal, as its 'antidote'. It is an antidote characterized by the joy and pleasure that attends relation to the true source of human well-being. In distinction from notions that sin is error, on this view sin is the disordering of God-directed desire—'passion

---

[15] Here I follow Farley's distinctions. See *Divine Empathy,* 9–19, 52. Nothing guarantees that a claim to redemptive alteration cannot be an expression of false consciousness. I am simply articulating the context of meaning that follows from this logic.

[16] This is to say that my articulation itself might best be construed as testimony. This is hinted at by James Nieman when he speaks of a church's theology functioning as critical discourse for witness. Nieman, 'Attending Locally: Theologies in Congregations', *International Journal of Practical Theology,* 6/2 (Fall, 2002), 201. The question then is how/whether this is saying anything more than it is an emic or insider perspective.

gone wrong'.[17] It cannot be ameliorated by knowledge, that is, the correct worldview, but requires a relationship to that alone that can properly fulfill desire, the true God.

The constitutive role of desire in human life connects to another defining theme of theological anthropology—the relation to the neighbor.[18] Our social relations are not just secondary or optional in Christian traditions; the relation to the neighbor is a central litmus for the God-relation. A central biblical theme in both testaments, such a view is definitional to liberation theologies, which claim that proper God-relation requires identification with the oppressed. Not confined to liberationists, desire for God's *world* as well as for God is fundamental to theonomous existence. The issue is not God *or* world. As one theologian puts it, a theocentric view intends 'to relate to all things in ways appropriate to their belonging to God'.[19] While loved differently than God—as *finite* rather than eternal— communion with others and pleasure in the things of the world constitute proper honoring of God's good creation.

Read with this 'theo-logic', then, much of Good Samaritan's practice can be interpreted as signifying the pursuit of created, finite goods, displaying desire for God's world as well as for God. Desire for survival, for well-being, pleasure, joy, and communion with others— all these define what it means to be a creature of God. Most explicitly seen in the aesthetic and bodily joy experienced in the community's worship and the pleasures of activities and relationships, worldly desires were all a faithful honoring of the creation as finitely good. The importance of relations to the neighbor was exemplified in the community's attempts to welcome 'those who are not like us'. Read theologically, these practices attempted to reconcile groups divided by sins of racism and able-ism. With the move to such categories as sin, however, analysis becomes more complex.

[17] For an overview of biblical notions of sin and evil, see Paul Ricoeur, *The Symbolism of Evil*, trans. Emerson Buchanan (Boston: Beacon, 1967).

[18] For comparisons of early Fathers on this subject with regard to sin, see J. Patout Burns (trans. and ed.), *Theological Anthropology*, Sources of Early Christian Thought (Philadelphia: Fortress, 1981).

[19] Julian N. Hartt, quoted and elaborated helpfully in James M. Gustafson, *Ethics from a Theocentric Perspective*, i. *Theology and Ethics* (Chicago: University of Chicago Press, 1981), 158.

According to a theocentric view of human being, broken social relations are signs of deformed desire. Yet such a reading presents the immediate challenge of identifying broken relations in the community. There is little sign of overt malice or oppression in the church; Good Samaritan is notable, after all, for its unusual inclusiveness. To interpret the community through the lens of sin, I propose that it is the more ambiguously harmful practices that require attention. From the explicit aversion of the early members who left the church to modes of obliviousness among those who remained, the complexity of social segregation needs elaboration. For this we need a language of sin attentive to the paradox of finitude and freedom.

The freedom of a finite creature is a contradiction of sorts. Such a creature is free to act on desires and to imagine in unlimited ways. However, as finite and limited, such desire has anxiety as its negative side. Not inherently sinful, anxiety is the precondition of human creativity, as Reinhold Niebuhr points out.[20] An anxious response to the world is a natural result of the wish to survive, thus perception of threat and resulting fear can be a valuable warning of the need for self-protection. A fearful response that takes the 'Other' as potential threat, however, has possibilities besides self-protection. Some perceptions of threat move from visceral fear of the unknown and its imagined harms to aversiveness and vilification of that which is 'Other'. Since aversiveness itself can vary from mere unease to revulsion, two points bear mention. These reactions and the symbols that come to justify them are potential precursors to forms of violence. However, there is a continuum, not a radical disjuncture between finitely good desire and its appropriate fear/anxiety and the desire that moves into vilification and harm of the neighbor. Just this dynamic of finitude and freedom, displayed as finite desire and ever-fractured by fear and anxiety, has been interpreted by critical modernist theologians not as sin, but as its *precondition*.[21]

---

[20] Reinhold Niebuhr, *The Nature and Destiny of Man*, i. *Human Nature* (New York: Charles Scribner's Sons, 1964), 183.

[21] Søren Kierkegaard, *The Concept of Anxiety*, trans. R. Thomte and A. B. Anderson (Princeton: Princeton University Press, 1980). Important in the development of this concept were Heidegger, Karl Rahner, Paul Tillich, Reinhold Niebuhr, and Edward Farley. For the sake of clarity and brevity, I will draw mostly on Niebuhr's account with correctives as needed. Niebuhr, *Nature and Destiny of Man*, 179–86.

Developed by modern theologians attempting to make sense of traditions of original sin, this precondition results from the insecurities of finitude, which unavoidably invite sin.[22] The inevitability of death and of frustrated human desire, the mix of pain and disappointment with pleasures—all tempt the creature to escape the anxieties of finitude. These conditions of temptation, as Reinhold Niebuhr calls them, make sin inevitable but not necessary.[23] What might be acceptance of this unavoidable insecurity becomes instead a desperate attempt to escape it. And from a theocentric reading of human being, such escape is inevitably a securing with something that is not God. While escape can occur as sensuality or sloth, its primary form as 'idolatry' indicates its failed resolution of desire. The only true fulfillment of desire is the dependence upon that which is truly God, a dependence that, however sustaining, is never a rescue from the threat of being finite. And the cost of such failure is ongoing broken relation to the neighbor, who is perceived as all manner of threat.

The concept of sin's precondition is useful for interpreting Good Samaritan, particularly with regard to its story of obliviousness. However, to connect church members' postures of fear/anxiety and aversion with these theological categories requires their expansion. Sinful response to Good Samaritan's environment is more complicated than the theme of pride, which virtually dominates traditional accounts of idolatry. This is especially true if we consider the ways bodily incorporating practices complicate threat.[24] The double-consciousness and fearful vigilance of African Americans around whites, for example, make sense as participation in the threat of existence, but not as prideful responses that absolutize (or secure with) the self. Something else is at

[22] This account affords a critical reinterpretation of the Fall to avoid a literal reading, interpreting bondage as the result of a structural possibility in finite, temporal human existence.

[23] See Niebuhr, *Nature and Destiny of Man*, 179–86.

[24] Appealing to Augustine and Luther, Niebuhr calls pride the most basic form of sin in biblical and Christian tradition. He takes the biblical view to be that 'mortality, insecurity and dependence are not of themselves evil but become the occasion of evil when man seeks in his pride to hide his mortality, to overcome his insecurity by his own power and to establish his independence'. Ibid., 174, 186. Pride has already been decentered by feminists. Valerie Saiving, 'The Human Situation: A Feminine View', in Carol P. Christ and Judith Plaskow (eds.), *Womanspirit Rising: A Feminist Reader in Religion* (New York: Harper & Row, 1979), 25–42. Judith Plaskow, *Sex, Sin and Grace: Women's Experience and the Theologies of Reinhold Niebuhr and Paul Tillich* (Lanham, MD: University Press of America, 1980).

work than 'man's self-glorification' in the self-loathing of marginalized groups invited by society, at least in the testimonies of Good Samaritans. The intersection of gendered and racialized habituations shaping Betty and Letty, for example, echoes the denigrating social images of black women's bodies identified by womanist theologians.[25] Operative in the everyday, these and other deforming images must be taken into account in any theological reading of anxiety as precondition for sin.

Not only does the identification of sinful response primarily with pride or will-to-power fail to do justice to the depravations of this contemporary situation, but the modernist paradigm for finitude and anxiety/threat requires adjustment as well.[26] Niebuhr's definition of the structure of threat as 'involvement in finiteness and his transcendence over it' describes anxiety for a subject defined as neutral, not marked by difference.[27] It may make sense for the dominant subject unburdened by the 'limitations' signaled by 'race' or dis-ability. For subjects marked as having race or dis-ability, however, the precondition for sin is not a generic vulnerability to the hypothetical limits of being human. The 'temptation' that precedes their sinful brokenness is always already signified on their marked bodies, which themselves bear the accumulated social meanings of both threat and invisibility. What theology needs is to recognize *social mediators* of threat, social mediators that are always bodied and always marked.

With these important alterations, the modernist concept of fear and threat as ever-present preconditions of sinful deformation does provide an important lens, allowing us to locate the mix of desire, fear, and threat in the social typifications that attend enculturated bodies at Good Samaritan. Individual experience of desire and fear is thus shaped by the larger places that converge in Good Samaritan. Betty's sense of her 'nappy hair' as ugly and of whites' hypersexualization of black women's bodies both came from the racialized and gendered cultural stereotypes residual in the social formation. Along with the political and economic forces that locate them differently in relation to status and power, Good

[25] Cheryl Townsend Gilkes, '*If It Wasn't for the Women. . . .*' *Black Women's Experience and Womanist Culture in Church and Community* (Maryknoll, NY: Orbis, 2001), 181–95.

[26] Niebuhr acknowledges the inequality of guilt and that pride is connected to social power; however, my claim is that to truly factor in the markers of social power requires a different account of vulnerability. Niebuhr, *Nature and Destiny of Man*, 208–27.

[27] Ibid. 175, 106–203.

Samaritans are shaped by these reigning typifications of groups, both dominant and marginalized. White members' freedom not to notice their racialization comes from typifications as well. Whiteness as a social image is not neutral. The list goes on: cultural traditions that vilify blackness; those that mark gender; the 'colorism' that granted the lighter skinned higher status than the darker skinned; exoticizing culture that played Africans off against African Americans for the approval of the dominant race; white members' fearful response to a perceived domination by black bodies; the lingering presence of rituals of degradation in the discomfort felt by persons, both black and white, with members of the group homes—all of these reactions were shaped by social typifications, not invented by individual actors.

On such terms, sin as broken relation to God cannot be reduced to individual agency. The residuals of historic exclusions represented in these typifications create a 'naturalized' universe that does not easily disappear. This is not to deny that sin is a relational reality performed by individuals. Effects of these typifications—fear, the delusions of fear, and the resultant 'not-seeing' of repression and denial—do reside in the unconscious of individual agents. And while they can take form in explicit acts of malice and violence, their more widespread public display occurs in the 'practical consciousness' of everyday habits. Realities of obliviousness and its buried aversions are communicated to others in largely unconscious ways. Rather than oppressive acts originating with members, then, the typifications at Good Samaritan were displays of the larger social 'places' that shaped it. Overreaching and exceeding an agent's intentionality, they were not always necessarily what s/he meant to communicate.

Thus typifications that vilify difference are not actual broken relations between individuals (Good Samaritans)—although they become that. They display the broken socialities of larger institutions and historical legacies. As such, these converging enculturations signify both as sinful social inheritance, and also as *preconditions* of sin in Niebuhr's sense of temptation.[28] Attention to the enculturated

---

[28] Niebuhr saw the disjuncture to be between the finite self's bodied, located character and its capacity for self-transcendence. He did recognize a social inheritance of sin that transcended individual agency but not as this incorporative everyday practice. See his *Moral Man and Immoral Society: A Study in Ethics and Politics* (New York: Scribner, 1960).

bodily practice as constitutive of this finite self shows that the disjuncture is not simply between one's finite and partial location and one's escalating fears about possible threats, as Niebuhr would have it.[29] The character of threat for the world of Good Samaritan has a multilayered character that includes not only the possible disjuncture between desires and the reality of one's location, but the inheritances of larger historical typifications of the 'Other'.[30] Racialized, gendered, and other typifications constitute a display, then, of *social anxiety* gone bad.

These particular habituations into patterns of obliviousness and vilification cannot be avoided. Having emerged from social oppressions, legal and economic, they have an 'afterlife' in incorporative everyday practices. Internalized by members, such meanings were activated by face-to-face bodily encounters. The difficult-to-define boundary between living with fear and succumbing to sinful avoidances of finitude is, then, not a boundary but a continuum. The multiple habituations remind us that there are not simply oppressors and oppressed; indeed, there are no subject positions that escape the everyday 'isms'. As they shaped the deserting members who were explicit about their aversion with the claim 'too black', these inheritances affected the people who remained as well.

But just as all were complicit, there were different ways of occupying these social realities. For example, the convergence of whiteness and gender has created subject positions for white women in the US that invited both self-denigration and obliviousness to racial privilege. As pride and will-to-power are not adequate descriptions for the ways differently habituated subjects respond sinfully to threatened existence, neither are dominant Christian traditions adequate to enable the participation of differently abled persons. Indeed, recognition of social inheritances as the bearer of 'conditions of sin' is not adequate to account for how group home members might be sinners—a topic

---

[29] Niebuhr, *Nature and Destiny of Man*, 182.

[30] This 'Othering', as philosopher Susan Wendell says, groups people 'as the objects of our experience instead of . . . subjects of experience with whom we might identify', allowing them to become 'symbolic' of something we reject and fear. Susan Wendell, *The Rejected Body: Feminist Philosophical Reflections on Disability* (New York: Routledge, 1996), 60.

too complex for this project.[31] It does invite exploration of the ways these subjects have been dis-abled by traditional Christian categories. Biblical images of redemption as healing and wholeness are likewise problematic, for they implicitly associate disability with sin or punishment for sin.[32] For many of these differently abled members the capacity for relation to God cannot be defined by reasoning abilities or language, both long-standing terms for the *imago Dei*. If anything, honoring these members of Good Samaritan suggests a need to rehabilitate the long-suspect category of the body for the image of God, namely, to be in relation to God is to be a *bodily responder*.[33] Insofar as Christian tradition undermines this, it is a bearer of conditions of sin.

Finally, the anxiety of finitude must be seen in its tragic dimension. Not primarily about a front-page horror story, the tragic character of finitude refers to the inevitable accompaniment of desire of any sort by frustration. Whether due to sheer limit or to conflicting aims, failed desire is unavoidable at both interpersonal and institutional levels.[34] Categories of anxiety and threat entail the inevitability of human suffering. Creativity itself is inseparable from suffering. Just as the good ends of individuals conflict, the good aims of institutions create new harms and override the ends of individuals. White women's desire to be treated as fully human, to be protected from domestic violence

[31] I risk employing sin here in the way criticized by Wendy Farley, i.e., that it 'can limit our perception of how we are bound to harmful ways of life'. I hope not, however, if we attend to the way threat is social diminishings. Wendy Farley, *The Wounding and Healing of Desire: Weaving Heaven and Earth* (Louisville, KY: Westminster/John Knox, 2005), 24.

[32] See Kathy Black, *A Healing Homiletic: Preaching and Disability* (Nashville: Abingdon, 1996). For another important critique, see Sharon V. Betcher, 'Monstrosities, Miracles and Mission: Religion and the Politics of Disablement', in Catherine Keller, Michael Nausner, and Mayra Rivera (eds.), *Postcolonial Theologies: Divinity and the Empire* (St Louis: Chalice, 2004), 79–99.

[33] Their communication happened without verbal/linguistic capacities, without a communicable reflective 'mental representation of the desired goal'. Consequently, nonsymbolic communication with its parallel forms of 'intentionality'—responses that indicate a desired object, or frustration or satisfaction of a desire—must be factored into our account of finitely good human being, of what it means to be *imago Dei*. Siegel and Wetherby, 'Enhancing Nonsymbolic Communication', 415.

[34] The human 'condition is not tragic simply because suffering is an aspect of it but because sufferings of various sorts are necessary conditions of creativity, affection, the experience of beauty, etc'. (As Robin Lovin helped me see, I depart somewhat from Niebuhr here.) *Good and Evil: Interpreting a Human Condition* (Minneapolis: Fortress/Augsburg, 1990), 29, 253–4.

and marital rape, for example, has played itself out in inspirational struggles for gender justice in the US. Efforts to gain agency in a patriarchal society, however, have almost inevitably sponsored race-blind gender legislation, as the intersectionality of oppressions reveals. That, combined with the male-defined legislation against racial discrimination, rendered invisible the distinct realities of being a black woman.[35]

At Good Samaritan the tragic comes into view at a number of points. While it is important to honor the able-ness of group home members, many have limitations that can intensify the inevitable tragic character of finitude. Tim's cerebral palsy intensifies his physical suffering. But creativity itself brings suffering, with a tragic mismatch between capacities for the 'Other' and the ends of inclusive welcome. Attempts of a person with Down syndrome to reach out are repulsed by many so shaped by 'Othering' social systems that they take it as frightening behavior. Good Samaritans' notion of generous ministry as 'people not like us' signified an act of 'welcome' that confined the category of 'special needs' to those *so unlike* other members, that, without real structural alterations, little identification or mainstreaming could occur.

Kathy and Miguel, Wanda and her family broke with the segregated practices of most Christians by choosing to be in an interracial church. They gave differences over homosexuality as their reasons for leaving the church. Perception of their leaving, however, was inevitably determined by these racialized inheritances. This is not to make them blameless, but to recognize the multiple layers of desire that inevitably come into conflict. The tragic is the reminder that the family's own (fearful?) response to something could have been aversiveness to the blackness of Gerald. It could have been a response connected to a self-loathing inherited from their conservative religious backgrounds. It was expressed as desire to be faithful to a God whose authority was understood in a biblicist way. Regardless of what it was, their desires inevitably contributed to their playing into a racist script. To put the tragic character of social sin more starkly, the 'paradox of being good and also being racist is central to being white'.[36]

[35] Kimberle Crenshaw, 'Demarginalizing the Intersection of Race and Sex: A Black Feminist Critique of Antidiscrimination Doctrine, Feminist Theory and Antiracist Politics', *University of Chicago Legal Forum* (1989), 139–67.
[36] Nibs Stroupe and Inez Fleming, *While We Run This Race: Confronting the Power of Racism in a Southern Church* (Maryknoll, NY: Orbis, 1995), 97 ff.

THE GRACE OF THE PLACE

Just as these deformations cannot be reduced to intentional acts of malice or misinformed prejudice, they are not redeemed simply by good intentions or right thinking. The conviction that 'we don't see color' did not and does not cause racial reconciliation; nor does sincere belief that Jesus is Lord, or that God is three-in-one. Residuals of historic exclusions gain new life in inherited incorporative practices, and they shape even the nicest and most enthusiastic would-be agents of change. For real transformation a deep change of consciousness is required, a change of consciousness not simply in the form of new ideas, but in newly developing habituations as well—in the bones. And transformation will be ever incomplete.

Be that as it may, read through a theo-logic of desire what I trace at Good Samaritan is not simply (incomplete) social transformation; it is divine grace. The divine, as Casey puts it, is not 'coextensive with infinite space', it is '*spaced-out into places*, the very places we inhabit in daily life'.[37] Signs of divine grace thus appeared in the everyday, which we remember is the necessary point of entry for changing larger social formations. Everyday, face-to-face alterations of relationality at Good Samaritan were the site of this redemptive change. Places to appear emerged in multiple ways there, from the acknowledgement of group home members performed in worship to the confessions of deeper understanding between Africans and African Americans and between black and white. Betty's freedom to trust a white man, her capacity to criticize her own prejudices and be open to change in spite of the gendered and racialized hostilities of most of her life is a testimony to this ultimate reality. Other testimonies about the changing of consciousness—the black man's empathy for the working-class white woman, Africans' for African Americans, and so on and so on—are traces of this God-founded redemptive relation as well.

The fullest and most powerful *articulation* of the contours of grace in these everyday places is found in the clarification of mission spurred by the church crisis. Including the goodness of creatures,

---

[37] Edward Casey, *The Fate of Place: A Philosophical History* (Berkeley and Los Angeles: University of California Press, 1998), 341.

the recognition of sin, and the move toward redemptive relations, this consensus regarding faithful inclusiveness is a creative articulation of the flexible character of graced community. To create a place to appear is to welcome absolutely anyone. It is to refuse conditions of membership that have long made the church an exclusive community even as it expects transformation. From racial difference to sexual orientation, qualifications for full participation have historically all too often vilified certain differences. In contrast this version of Good Samaritans' ecclesial vision had only the willingness to be changed as its condition of membership. And according to this logic, that willingness would need to go far beyond mere toleration. Because difference did matter. Whatever overlooking difference might acceptably mean it could not entail the failure to deal with its historic residuals of harm.[38] It could not mean leaving privileges of race and ability in place and uninspected. As a consequence the sense of difference as the finite goodness of creaturely variety was often honored as members made delightful new discoveries about one another.

The flexibility in this vision was based upon a gradually developing habituated skill that received articulation in the group's 'ecclesiology'. Its improvisational character was more advanced as an incorporative practice than as a facility with the languages of official Christian tradition. However, it can still be read as a testimony to the God of redemption. For its security is found in something other than a stable fixed sociality. Its identity implicitly resides in something besides social identities or markers of status. The vision of welcoming the eunuch was expanded to such an extent that at the very least its promise would be sustainable only by a redeeming God. That Good Samaritan dispersed to become other places is a bit of a tragedy, but may be also a hopeful dissemination of the community's wisdoms.

Admittedly, Good Samaritan was only a beginning place for the development of places to appear—white privilege was never explicitly acknowledged, the group home members were never fully incorporated. However, it did initiate a form of ecclesial practice desperately needed by contemporary communities. Good Samaritan drew marked and

---

[38] I am not saying they dealt with all these issues of difference, simply that their understanding of faithful inclusiveness required it.

unmarked bodies together in face-to-face relationships—relationships that began to break the power of 'Othering' that made certain groups 'objects' and made them subjects with whom members could begin to identify.[39] It positioned subordinated and dominating groups of people in places that invoked reconciling relations while they developed the sometimes-painful new habits that might someday make those claims really true. It acted on the wager that such a place might begin to create alternative mutualities, or at least could offer the chance to invent new bodily memories to go with its new images of the 'Other'.

To take seriously the importance of incorporative practices, then, is to agree with and extend the advice of a minister of an interracial church. We must recognize the thinness of claims of welcome and inclusivity, the ineffectiveness of just preaching Christ's love for *all* people. Not so much a call to make your practice fit your claims, this is rather a call to recognize the incorporative character of tradition. White people, as Revd. Nibs Stroupe says, must 'remain in the presence of black people or other people of darker color'. They must resist flight and the attraction of homogeneity.[40] Likewise, people designated as 'normal' must put themselves in the ongoing presence of those misleadingly labeled 'abnormal'. For it is ongoing face-to-face relationships that create a place where the sinful inheritances of vilified 'Otherness' begin to be dislodged.[41] Ongoing relationships, that is, that are defined by language and commitment that both honor difference as well as refuse to let it matter in the old ways. It is these relationships that may very well strengthen the capacity to *live with* rather than escape the tragic complexities of finitude. As Pam put it, one must certainly see race and, I would add, constructions of the normal that 'Other' persons with disabilities. At the same time, one must *not see* race—or these markers of difference—by 'seeing Jesus' in the other.

[39] Wendell, *Rejected Body*, 60. This is especially important for the group home participants. However limited, they did become subjects for many members.

[40] This is the most important demonstration of a fierce dedication to equality by whites, says Nibs Stroupe. 'To accept white segregation is to return to the addiction of the system of race.' Stroupe and Fleming, *While We Run This Race*, 133, 134.

[41] The L'Arche community certainly illustrates this. See Jean Vanier, *The Challenge of L'Arche* (Minneapolis: Winston, 1981).

PRACTICAL THEOLOGY AND THE PLACE

This look at Good Samaritan does not pretend to carry out all the tasks of practical theology. As an exercise in academic theology shaped by the interests and pressures of its social location in the professional managerial class, this account needs more critical attention to my place.[42] Despite my good intentions, the multiple structures that habituate me—especially enculturations of whiteness and the normate—have still rendered me oblivious to realities at the church.[43] Were I to complete this account of practical theology as a full-blown *habitus*, it would require not only competence for a situation and relevant improvisatory skills, but also acknowledgement of the theologian's (my) incorporative practices and how they have shaped the reading.

A second unfinished task concerns the implications of this reading of Good Samaritan for the situation of the church, not simply its implications for academic theology as presented here. Practical theology involves 'guidelines and specific plans' for the particular situation, what Browning calls the full task of 'strategic practical theology'.[44] Finally the implications of this reading for the other tasks of theology, particularly the role of other knowledges in theological judgments, are only hinted at. (What contribution, for example, might psychology make to the hermeneutic notion of 'refracting

[42] See my discussion of my kind of work as that of the professional managerial class in *Changing the Subject: Women's Discourses and Feminist Theology* (Minneapolis: Fortress, 1994), 319–23, 386–93. Some version of Toni Morrison's analysis of the function of Africanist images in American literature could be usefully employed with regard to my account. Morrison, *Playing in the Dark: Whiteness and the Literary Imagination* (New York: Vintage, 1993), 51–9.

[43] I used participant observation rather than participatory action research (PAR), defined by inclusion of participants as the co-constructors of a project. With roots in the critical pedagogy of Paulo Freire, PAR involves groups and communities in analysis of and change in their own settings. See http://en.wikipedia.org/wiki/Participatory_Action_Research.

[44] For the first, see the tasks defined by James N. Poling and Donald E. Miller, *Foundations for a Practical Theology of Ministry* (Nashville: Abingdon, 1985), 69, 92–7. For 'strategic practical theology', see Don Browning, *A Fundamental Practical Theology: Descriptive and Strategic Proposals* (Minneapolis: Fortress, 1991), ch. 3.

media'?[45]) My implicit claim that other knowledges are crucial needs taking up in a fuller, more critical form.

What *has* been accomplished in this project of practical theology is a proposal for how to construe the subject matter of contemporary situation and to construe it theologically. As such my project is similar to but not reducible to what several theologians call practical theology's descriptive task.[46] I have argued that the very construction of the situation has significant implications for the broader theological task. I now turn to concluding observations about that.

Some of the most obvious implications come from the use of place theory, which has attended to what has been overlooked in centuries of associating bodies and desire with carnality and sin, that is, the fuller constructive ways that bodies matter. I took the importance of the bodily continuum of experience in understanding Good Samaritan to mean that the most relevant theological loci were those of theological anthropology—the nature of a creature whose proper end is relationship to God, the *imago Dei*. When bodies are simply ignored, or treated as media of carnal desire, forms of communication are missed that are crucial to honoring the image of God in all creatures, and the media of our affective responses are overlooked. To correct theology's obliviousness to persons with disabilities and to the complexities of racialization, elements of theological anthropology require revision.

To be in relation to God is to be a bodily responder; construction of the image of God must reflect that reality. Sin and redemption take on more complex forms—from the marked nature of theological discourse to the tragic and complex social nature of both obliviousness and appearing. Since bodily practices are as significant in conveying redemptive relations as sinful ones, they merit treatment in an account of normative tradition.[47] Being formed in the faith is always

---

[45] The 'path' of discourse—'strewn with previous claims that slow up, distort, refract the intention of the word'—begs for psychological analysis. Holquist, in *The Dialogic Imagination: Four Essays by M. M. Bakhtin*, ed. Michael Holquist, trans. Caryl Emerson and Michael Holquist (Austin: University of Texas Press, 1981), 432.

[46] Browning's account of this task recognizes the value-laden character of description, even identifying its religious dimension. See *Fundamental Practical Theology*, 47–9; Poling and Miller, *Foundations*, 70–7.

[47] While praxis, the liberative dialectic of reflection and action in social context, is congenial to what I intend here, I will continue with the language of practices to make the points about the role of bodies in communication and habituation.

already habituation into incorporative practices as much as it is into ways of believing. Traditioning is always constituted by bodily proprieties, which in contemporary culture are marked by race, gender, class, and attitudes around normal bodies. Traditioning about loving Jesus is always *simultaneous with* habituation into being a southern white boy or a young African American girl. Being 'faithful to Jesus' is about bodily proprieties as much as it is about biblical literacy. The skill to read a situation theologically and faithfully demands more than the ability to argue.

Implicit in this reading of place is also the theological topic of ecclesiology. The face-to-face character of place and the fact that face-to-face bodily contiguity activates communication means that culturally marked bodies have no small significance in creating the Body of Christ. Attention to the location of those bodies suggests that new conditions on participation in Christian community may have come into existence in the US. While requirements for membership are no longer circumcision or works-righteousness, others have taken shape, at least unofficially, through the unconscious legacies of racial and ability segregations. Despite claims of universal welcome, the majority of churches in a society saturated with residuals of racism and able-ism formations are homogenous with regard to race and ability. While not on the order of Luther's Ninety-Five Theses as challenge to the larger church, Good Samaritan's practices disrupted much of what is naturalized in homogeneity—the identification of sacred space with reverential quiet; the comfort of seeing yourself in your fellow worshipper; of 'owning the space', if you are white; of having an escape from double vigilance, if you are not. To take this challenge seriously for its own construal of 'church', ecclesiology must recognize the literally marked character of the Body of Christ.[48]

A faithful response to situation as presented in this account is not an exercise in systematic theology, but its parameters have implications for the systematic task. Simply put, a system does not determine how to interpret a situation such as Good Samaritan. Rather, already defined by theologically inflected inclinations, the situation generates selective appropriation from and sometimes rejection of systematic

---

[48] Since the Body of Christ is always marked—it is racialized, gendered, marked by valuations of ability—the continued 'difference blindness' of all but the liberationist (marked) theologies appears problematic.

traditions.[49] My evaluation of the faithfulness of the community through reconfigured traditions of theological anthropology has selectively appropriated tradition and argued for its alteration in light of the situation. While not quite the same as the ad hoc adjusting of everyday theology, the latter has its academic theological analogue in what Stanley Fish calls the nested character of communal convictions.[50] Some convictions are more deeply embedded than others and less likely to change in radical ways. The choice here of theological anthropology articulated as a theonomous logic of practices rather than the Trinity or a doctrine of atonement was based on what emerged with the fuller display of bodied, desiring, and marked multiply conditioned human practice.[51] It was a judgment that certain themes, such as desire-defined God-dependence, are more deeply embedded than others. It contributed to stipulations of relevance that made realities such as obliviousness and visceral reactions to the 'Other' of primary importance.

By linking discourse to affectivity, practices to bodily communication as well as proclamation, interpretation, and cooperation, place theory suggests the import of this wound for all theological reflection in an even broader sense. Attention to marginalizing differences is not simply a concern of this place, Good Samaritan; it is essential to theology. Attention to the wound around socially defined forms of difference suggests more than the obvious point that Christians need to care about racism and able-ism. The social effects of the appeal to color-blindness by the neoliberal project suggest that dominant ways of being Christian are likely to be ineffective and supportive of the status quo. By ineffective 'dominant ways of being Christian', I do not mean exclusivist, racist discourse of the segregation era or speech

---

[49] I suspect that the honoring of nonsymbolic communicators could require an even more severe critique of the cognitive nature of faith than I have provided.

[50] Fish, 'Change', 429.

[51] Attention to the media of divine reality, to what has often been termed 'human experience', is not, as Barth would have it, a reduction of theology to anthropology. Rather it is a contemporary version of the various ways theology is a thematization of human piety or relation to God. From the earliest concern with what faith looks like, to Calvin's insistence of the inseparable nature of knowledge of God and knowledge of ourselves (*Institutes*, i. i. l,15), to Schleiermacher's post-Kantian display of the God-redeemed structures of corporate life, the theological task of ever-complicating attention to the shape of human life does not signal its accommodation or deformation.

explicitly banning persons with disabilities, but rather reliance upon central themes of the faith: loving the neighbor, claims that all are children of God, and that God is radically gracious and present in God's son, Jesus Christ. Even themes of sin, the call to repentance and change—all of these discourses can be easily assimilated into the larger racial and normate projects that support the status quo.

Such assimilation is clearly seen in the larger projects of the social formation. There, 'not seeing' color, like 'not seeing' disability, are practices that easily reproduce the obliviousness to human suffering and deprivation that continues in the US. By appeal to 'equal treatment', attention to race, for example, is construed in the public domain by some as unfairly granted 'special rights' to minorities, a virtual 'injustice' that discriminates against dominant populations. But the Christian version of this 'not seeing' race is hardly better. Not only can it lend easy support to those larger projects, but it supports a misleadingly *benevolent form* of avoidance and denial—*amiable tolerance*, as I called it. Cose's quote is worth repeating: not seeing color is like 'that [behavior] exhibited by certain people on encountering someone with a visible physical handicap; they pretend not to notice that the handicap exists and hope, thereby, to minimize discomfort'. Yet the very wish to avoid tension and minimize conflict, he says, is quite costly.[52] As the last chapter suggested, this Christian version of blindness to difference can produce *Christian identity as denial and projection by the advantaged.* Such generically inclusive behaviors are not simply kindly Christian displays of love for humanity; rather they reproduce daily racism and able-ism.

Color- and ability-blindness, as well as gender-blindness, take shape in the academic theological world as the refusal to recognize that the worldliness of all theological discourse includes its marked character.[53] One source of this is the universalizing impulse of Christianity; Christianity wishes to proclaim a God of creation, who loves all creatures. However, failure to recognize the marked/located way

[52] Ellis Cose, *Color-Blind: Seeing Beyond Race in a Race-Obsessed World* (New York: Harper Collins, 1998), 189–90.

[53] Liberation, black, feminist, and womanist theologies have long been making the claim that theological discourse is marked by images valorizing the world of the dominant population. More recently queer theologies and theology around issues of disability have joined the chorus as well.

that the certifying discourse of theology names and acts is precisely *not* to care for all creatures.[54] Theology done thusly risks duplicating the phony universal concern of neoliberal political projects that ignore the residuals of racism in the name of treating everyone the same. Recognition is required, then, that theological discourse, like any other, is marked, not neutral, and as such inevitably reproduces the shape of the world *as it is experienced by dominant populations.* Without this, topics such as 'race' and 'ability' will continue to be treated as 'issues' that are only relative to specific contexts rather than markers of all discourse, whether explicit or not.[55]

Finally the complexity of place has forced the analysis away from common markers such as institutions, fixed beliefs, or unchanging practices as the indicator for normative ecclesial 'boundaries'. Insofar as there is a boundary between what is faithfully Christian and what is not, I have defined it as an always-moving phenomenon— those ambiguous places undergoing redemptive alteration. In that sense, my portrayal of Good Samaritan as place can be seen as a form of testimony to that which indicates the reality of God. While differently nuanced, it is a portrayal in the lineage of modern Reformed traditions that were also concerned with displays of redemptive existence rather than claims to (direct or speculative) knowledge of God. Just as the church has always disagreed about the particulars of such displays, my own judgments are also subject to dispute. The lines between seeing and not-seeing, fearing and rejecting are not always easy to draw. To acknowledge this worldly way grace happens, however, should not mean a refusal to claim it. In all its fragility and ambiguity, redemptive existence did occur as places of appearing for Betty and Liana, for Daphne and Tim, and for many others of this faith community. It occurred in the worldly church that was Good Samaritan.

[54] For an account of academic theology as 'certifying discourse', see my *Changing the Subject*, 303–4.

[55] Thus there are courses in church history and 'black church history', or theology and 'feminist theology', etc., implying that the courses without qualifiers are about everybody.

Index